Late Modernity in Crisis

Late Modernity in Crisis

Why We Need a Theory of Society

Andreas Reckwitz
Hartmut Rosa

Translated by Valentine A. Pakis

polity

Originally published in German as *Spätmoderne in der Krise. Was leistet die Gesellschaftstheorie?*
© Suhrkamp Verlag Berlin 2020. All rights reserved by and controlled through Suhrkamp Verlag
Berlin.

This English edition © Polity Press, 2023

The translation of this book was supported by funding from the Gottfried Wilhelm Leibniz Prize of
the German Research Foundation.

Polity Press
65 Bridge Street
Cambridge CB2 1UR, UK

Polity Press
111 River Street
Hoboken, NJ 07030, USA

ISBN-13: 978-1-5095-5629-8 – hardback
ISBN-13: 978-1-5095-5630-4 – paperback

A catalogue record for this book is available from the British Library.

Library of Congress Control Number: 2022948144

Typeset in 10.5 on 12 pt Times New Roman MT
by Fakenham Prepress Solutions, Fakenham, Norfolk NR21 8NL
Printed and bound in Great Britain by CPI Group (UK) Ltd, Croydon

The publisher has used its best endeavors to ensure that the URLs for external websites referred
to in this book are correct and active at the time of going to press. However, the publisher has no
responsibility for the websites and can make no guarantee that a site will remain live or that the
content is or will remain appropriate.

Every effort has been made to trace all copyright holders, but if any have been overlooked the
publisher will be pleased to include any necessary credits in any subsequent reprint or edition.

For further information on Polity, visit our website:
politybooks.com

Contents

Acknowledgments

We would like to thank a number of people who contributed to the creation of this book. In particular, Sigrid Engelhardt, Bettina Hollstein, Jörg Oberthür, and Peter Schulz (on Hartmut Rosa's side), and Vincent August, Nicolas Hauck, and Laurin Schwarz (on Andreas Reckwitz's side), delved into our respective texts and helped to improve them in important ways. Eva Gilmer, our editor at the Suhrkamp Verlag, also accompanied this book project with her typical competence and dedication. Our special thanks are due as well to Martin Bauer for engaging us in an exceptionally stimulating and focused conversation.

Introduction

We first met in early 1997, at a doctoral seminar held by the German Academic Scholarship Foundation in a monastery in Münsterland. One of us (Hartmut Rosa) was finishing his dissertation on Charles Taylor, while the other (Andreas Reckwitz) was just beginning his doctoral research on cultural theories. At the seminar, there were lively discussions about the cultural turn and the importance of social constructivism to the social sciences and humanities. It was the 1990s. In Germany, the wall between East and West had fallen (a great deal of dogmatism had fallen away along with it), and such questions were typical of the time. This seminar also marked the beginning of a conversation between us – a conversation about academic, professional, and personal matters – that has not stopped since.

After we had received professorships in the mid-2000s and pursued various avenues in our books and research projects – on the topics of acceleration, resonance, and controllability for one of us, and on the topics of the subject, creativity, and singularization for the other – our life trajectories often went their separate ways, but they continued to cross as well. An example of this is the 2016 Congress of the German Sociological Association, which took place in Bamberg. There, one of us (Hartmut Rosa) gave a presentation about his book on "resonance," while the other (Andreas Reckwitz) served as the respondent to this paper. It was after this conference that we first devised the idea of writing a book together, in order to juxtapose and create a conversation between our quite different – yet in many ways related – theoretical perspectives on modern society and on what sociology can and should do.

Our idea remained latent for a long time. Inspired by recently enflamed and lively debates within and beyond the discipline of sociology concerning the question of how sociology should be practiced, what it can and cannot accomplish, what need there is for a theory of society, and what society might expect from such a theory, we ultimately decided to take on the task. The final impetus behind this decision came from the insight that we share a common motivation that would make such a book meaningful and perhaps even seem necessary: the motivation of emphasizing that the task of formulating a theory of society (and thus also a theory of modernity) should be the central objective of sociology. This conviction has characterized the work of both of us since the 2000s.

Such an understanding of the discipline is far from obvious when one examines the present landscape of the social sciences in Germany and abroad – indeed, it faces resistance from many fronts. There is, instead, a curious discrepancy within this intellectual sphere. On the one hand, there is a clear and growing public interest in comprehensive theories of contemporary society (and of human society and history as a whole); among sociologists, on the other hand, there is a conspicuous lack of desire (and perhaps courage) to produce such theories of society. In other words, while the "demand" for a theory of society has been growing, the corresponding "supply" – expected from the international discipline of sociology – seems to be diminishing.

Regardless of what the field of sociology has been willing to supply, public interest in such a theory – in comprehensive analyses and interpretations of contemporary society, but also in the long-term transformation of human society from its beginning and into the future – has, if anything, been intensifying during the second decade of the twenty-first century. This is true not only in Germany and in other so-called "Western" societies (in Europe and North America especially), but also beyond: in China, India, Brazil, and in the Arabic-speaking world as well. This is perhaps surprising. After all, as long ago as 1979, Jean-François Lyotard famously argued in his book *The Postmodern Condition* that we had reached the end of the "grand narratives" of modernity and modernization.[1] According to Lyotard, the grand theories about social development that had characterized classical modernity had lost credibility, and what was needed instead were "minor narratives" and specific analyses – limited in time, space, and subject matter. Lyotard's critique of the legacy imposed by the philosophy of history and its (from today's perspective) naïve and one-sided stories of progress was certainly justifiable, but his prognosis that overarching theoretical interpretations were superfluous was ultimately false. As we have learned in the meantime, such large-scale interpretations are precisely what we need.

In the two decades between 1985 and 2005, social scientists could have complained with good reason about the public's waning interest in social analyses, but at least since 2008 there has been a noticeable revitalization of public interest in the big picture. "What sort of society are we really living in?" "In what direction is society headed?" These are the sorts of questions that are (once again) being asked. The public discussion is no longer satisfied with small-scale empirical analyses of special issues, and it is certainly no longer content with "minor narratives." What has crystalized instead is a sense of curiosity and a rather urgent desire for comprehensive analyses of the social condition. Over the past few years, and each in our own way, both of us have experienced this at first hand. Our own attempts at producing a theory of society have each received surprisingly widespread attention, not only within but also outside of the academic sphere: in the media, in politics, in business, in the worlds of art and culture, in ecclesiastical and social organizations, and not least among university students. Moreover, we have received numerous reactions from people highly interested in society and politics, from sympathetic and critical private readers alike, whose thirst for knowledge and impressive powers of observation make any member of the academic establishment who sneers at the alleged simple-mindedness of so-called "laypeople" seem conceited.

This increased interest in theory and in the "big picture" – in a theory that goes beyond the heterogeneous threads of everyday experience and presents a scientifically supported, meaningful whole – has identifiable causes. The most important of these is certainly the fact that, over the last ten years, the accumulation of social crises has jolted Western societies into reflecting critically about themselves. The global financial and economic crisis of 2008 raised awareness about the structural features of post-industrial capitalism and its social consequences, not least among them the intensification of social inequality. Insight into the threatening consequences of climate change has attracted massive attention to ecological questions about the history of the relationship between humankind and the natural environment, and about what characterizes the Anthropocene epoch. That the geology of the earth itself can be altered by human activity has, for many people, led to a profound sense of ontological uncertainty. Finally, the international rise of right-wing populism has sparked a broad discussion about its structural causes and about the winners and losers in modernization. In general, whereas the 1990s seemed to have brought the world to the "end of history" – to the threshold of a *posthistoire* in which there were apparently no alternatives to the Western model of stable free-market democracies – and to have ushered forth a promising new era of globalization, digitalization, and the knowledge society, the horizon of progress seems to have shrunk rather rapidly since then. On the geopolitical level, in fact, the "Western model" is in retreat. All these moments of crisis are linked to new social and political movements, ranging from Attac and Fridays for Future to the French *gilets jaunes*, Black Lives Matter, and indigenous movements. The self-reflection that all these crises have induced, however, remains at least implicitly reliant on a theory of society, or on other large-scale models of social development: How can the phenomena under discussion be classified, how can they be explained, and what consequences should be expected from them? What alternatives are conceivable, and which of these would be desirable?

The second reason for this intensified public interest in comprehensive syntheses is obviously related to the fact that the public itself has changed. There are many indications that this change is a reaction to the explosion of information and opinion outlets brought about by digitalization over the last decade. In the world of digital media, information about social issues and critical commentary on these issues follow each other endlessly, to an extent that is now beyond our capacity to absorb. An unmanageable amount of heterogeneous and fragmented bits and pieces of information and opinion is churned out in an endless stream: political events, social statistics, human-interest journalism, interviews, scandals, personal commentaries. At the same time, the Internet is an affective medium that can effortlessly link information to states of emotion – not least to negative emotions such as indignation or hate – or, conversely, provides the information – the necessary "fuel" – for every new outrage. In light of this mixture of ever new, atomized information and short-lived emotions, however, the need to comprehend the overarching contexts of social and historical developments becomes all the more urgent. Sufficiently large numbers of citizens are weary of mere snippets of information and wish to understand broader social contexts in an academically grounded, empirically informed, and theoretically sophisticated manner. This process of social self-understanding thus requires holistic, integrated formats of analysis and explanation; these formats are expected, desired, and demanded by the intellectual milieu. However, if sociology, despite its potential and competency in this very field, refuses to supply these desiderata, it shouldn't be surprised when other "providers" step in to fill the gap.

There has been no shortage of such interpretations, and they have been well received internationally. Prominent in the field of history, for instance, are the books by Yuval Harari, who has written no less than a total history of the human species from prehistoric times to the present and has drawn political conclusions on the basis of this panorama.[2] Noteworthy, too, are proponents of Big History such as David Christian, who has attempted to integrate natural history and cultural history.[3] The field of economics has recently produced several incisive and comprehensive syntheses of social developments, and these works have found an international audience. This is true, for instance, of Thomas Piketty's books about the transformation of the economy, the state, and the distribution of wealth; of Branko Milanović's work on global inequality; and of Shoshana Zuboff's work on the consequences of digitalization.[4] In addition, there have been successful works of more general nonfiction – albeit firmly supported by scholarly research – that provide synthetic overviews and have been discussed intensively by the public. Such books include Pankaj Mishra's *Age of Anger*, which explains today's global culture of resentment, and Maja Göpel's *Unsere Welt neu denken*, in which the author reflects on the political consequences of climate change.[5]

And sociology? Here we encounter the aforementioned discrepancy. As desirable as interdisciplinarity may be, and with all due respect to the explanatory powers of other disciplines, the whole point of sociology is to work on the "big picture" of a theory of society and to provide a comprehensive theory of modernity. Since its beginnings as a scientific discipline, the project of sociology has been to reconstruct the structural features and structural dynamics of modernity – or even of societal models in general – and thus to investigate the context of economic, technological, cultural, political, and social change. The disciplinary project of sociology therefore also, in a sense, consists in analyzing the crises of any given present; it is a crisis science. The theoretical and empirical foundation of sociology, which is constantly being renewed and enriched by other disciplines, is indeed lavishly endowed. We are convinced that sociology has the empirical, conceptual, and theoretical means to function as a systematic science *of* society in its totality.

Although sociology seems to be in a very good position to produce a theory of society, the discipline is nowadays oddly reluctant to fulfill this task. This is true in particular at the international level, where English-language sociology continues to be dominant. At sociology departments in the United States and Great Britain, the willingness to produce a theory of society and to formulate theories of modernity or late modernity has, in our opinion, noticeably declined over the past two decades. This is rather remarkable, because things used to be otherwise. As recently as the 1990s, social scientists from the Anglophone sphere published an abundance of influential and much-discussed contributions to the theory of society, and these studies resonated deeply in the international discussion. One only need think of Zygmunt Bauman's *Modernity and Ambivalence*, David Harvey's *The Condition of Postmodernity*, Scott Lash and John Urry's *Economies of Signs and Space*, Anthony Giddens's *The Consequences of Modernity*, or Manuel Castells's magnificent trilogy *The Information Age*.[6]

What explains this unwillingness among sociologists to formulate a theory of society? The first and most important reason is certainly the push toward more and more empirical specialization in the social sciences. This trend has been reinforced by the expectations of a competitive scientific world in terms of quantifiable research findings, publications in peer-reviewed journals, and the acquisition of third-party funding. The radical differentiation of sociology into a bunch of hyphenated subfields, each with its own qualitative and quantitative data and studies, has undoubtedly led to more productivity, but it has also meant that there is now less room for work on broader theoretical syntheses within the institutionalized field of sociology. Any ambition to work across these hyphenated subfields, to subject their findings to theoretical analysis, and to unify them has thus been restricted on an institutional level. Moreover, within a system oriented toward rewarding empirical research – a system governed by the "new public management" of universities – it has become increasingly unattractive to write books (which are still the preferred format for theory). According to this system, a whole book often "counts" no more (if not less) than a single article published in a top-tier journal, which is now the gold standard of empirical research. An ambitious project such as that proposed by Niklas Luhmann in the late 1960s at Bielefeld – "Topic: the theory of society; Duration: 30 years; Costs: none" – would seem highly anomalous in today's academic environment.

A second cause of the rather weak status of the theory of society within contemporary sociology lies in the effects of the aforementioned postmodern critique of science that has been widespread, especially in the Anglophone sphere, since the 2000s. In its current iteration, this critique can be summarized as follows: In light of the interpretive and selective nature of science, and in light of the heterogeneity and plurality of discursively produced realities, doesn't every holistic theoretical claim, every effort to comprehend "the whole" seem futile – or, even worse, necessarily one-sided and biased? Is it even possible to write about modernity or late modernity as *singular* concepts? This way of thinking has considerably discouraged and restricted theoretical work, even though, upon closer inspection, it is unconvincing. In the end, all scientific research – from a single case study of certain statistical correlations to an entire theory of society – is selective, regardless of whether it deals with "minor" or "major" phenomena. While it is undoubtedly true that scientific self-reflection is a good thing – this is one of the important conclusions of the postmodern critique of science – it would be unproductive to abstain from working on comprehensive theories for this reason alone. Nowadays, the fact that any effort to present an overview of society's formations as a whole immediately provokes considerable – and apparently a priori – opposition from so many different camps, each of which is quick to point out the theorist's inevitable "gaps" and "blind spots," seems to deter many social scientists from engaging in theory at all. In Anglo-Saxon sociology, the confluence of empirical specialization (modeled after the natural sciences), postmodern fragmentation, and the "new public management" of universities has brought us to this point. With respect to theory, the implications are clear: it is under pressure and in danger of disappearing entirely.

Because today's historical and cultural situation has generated so much demand for social theory, at least some sociologists – given the aforementioned fragmentation of their discipline – ought to stand up and take on the challenge. Because the Anglo-Saxon social sciences still set the pace on the international level, the impediments discussed above have affected the entire European continent, the German-speaking world included. It is no coincidence, however, that this book has been written by two German sociologists, for it is also true, in general, that social theory tends to be pursued more vigorously here than in the United States or Great Britain, for example. There are reasons for this as well. In Germany, from a historical perspective alone, there has long been a stronger connection between sociology and social philosophy (particularly in the theories of the Frankfurt School). Because of this, the question of social context has remained an important issue in German sociology. In addition, there is also the tradition here of understanding sociology in terms of lifestyle patterns and their historical transformations. This tradition goes back to Max Weber and Georg Simmel, and it encourages sociologists to view "the whole" from the perspective of cultural theory. Beyond this, one can also point to the approach of systems theory, which is still viable, and to the theory of modernity associated with it (as developed by Niklas Luhmann). Finally, there is the fact that the German-speaking world is more welcoming to public intellectualism than the Anglophone world. Here, public intellectuals – sociologists among them – are respected and given a voice, not only in the media but also in the broader realms of politics, culture, and even business, which helps to explain why it is somewhat easier here to develop systematic theories of (late) modernity than is the case in the international mainstream.[7]

Were this not the case, this book would probably not exist in its present form.

All national differences aside, it remains the case that, within modern sociology as a whole, social theory does not occupy a secure position. Instead, such a position has to be fought for. The present book seeks to respond to this situation by asking "What is achieved by a theory of society?" In doing so, it seeks to explore the *conceptual means* with which a theory of society can operate in order to accomplish what is expected of it. It is no surprise that, despite the many commonalities between us, we ultimately reach very different conclusions in our respective answers to this question. In order to examine the possibilities, difficulties, and limits of working on a theory of society from our different perspectives in a systematic way – and in a way that facilitates comparison between our views – we have each composed our opening text so as to present our approaches in a step-by-step manner: First, we present our views on what is meant by "theory" and how social theory (*Sozialtheorie*) and the theory of society (*Gesellschaftstheorie*) differ from one another. Next, we develop our specific perspectives on modernity in general and on late modernity in particular. Finally, we each discuss the implications of the relationship between a theory of society and its object, and why this relationship should be of a critical nature. It is our common belief that the theory of society should ultimately serve to diagnose the crises of the present. We each consider late modernity to be in a state of crisis, and we are convinced that determining the manifestations, causes, and consequences of this crisis is the central goal that a modern theory of society can and should achieve. We have endeavored to do so in this book.

The condensed presentations of our two perspectives form the bulk of the text, but they are also the starting point for the final section of the book, which contains an intensive conversation about our approaches. This conversation, which took place in March of 2021 at the Suhrkamp Verlag in Berlin, was moderated by Martin Bauer, to whom we owe considerable thanks for taking on this task (which was far from simple) and for presiding over the event with such aplomb. Even though theoretical work remains dependent on the medium of writing, orality is still the best medium for speaking not *about* one another, but *to* one another in a constructive inter-action. Even theory cannot do without face-to-face encounters if it is to be debated and remain resonant. For it is only in this form that it is set in motion and brought to life, that it loses its abstract rigidity and begins to take on color and create sparks.

Andreas Reckwitz and Hartmut Rosa

Part I
Andreas Reckwitz
The Theory of Society as a Tool

1
Doing Theory

Theory is itself a practice or, to be more precise, it is an ensemble of practices. One would have to conduct a detailed sociology of the social sciences to gain a full picture of all the practices that are used in what we call "doing theory." Practices of reflecting on and trying out concepts, collecting and juxtaposing empirical material, excerpting, assembling card indexes and databanks, discussing ideas, visualizing arguments, and, not least, writing and composing texts – whether by hand or with a computer – are all important in this regard. Relevant too when doing theory is the struggle between orthodoxies and heterodoxies that takes place in the field of social science. The personal experiences of theoreticians, moreover, influence their questions and basic intuitions, while current political debates, historical sensibilities, and contemporary cultural problems are also reflected in theoretical work. Theory inevitably develops within a social context. The word *theoria* – literally the "observation" of reality from a distance – suggests that this activity takes place from a neutral standpoint, or that it is the expression or result of "pure thinking." In fact, however, theory is a thoroughly practical and interpretive affair – in a sense, it is a cultural technique for producing a generalized understanding of the world. The productive practices of theory, for their part, are tied to variable practices of reception: to working through theories as part of one's academic socialization, reading for the sake of furthering one's education, reading freely out of a desire to understand the world or effect political change, or reading with the aim of bringing about a subjective transformation, after which "one is no longer the person one used to be."

From antiquity, it was philosophy that first provided an institutional home to the practice of theory in Europe. With the gradual differentiation of the modern sciences, however, interest in theory has moved into specialized academic disciplines, the social sciences included. Because the latter, like all modern disciplines, regard themselves as sciences of reality that derive their propositions from real-life experiences, this raises the question of the precise place of theory in relation to empiricism. In order to understand the specific value of theory for sociology, however, that which is subsumed in Germany under the category of "sociological theory" must be distinguished from what is called "social theory" in the English-speaking world. Within social theory, in turn, there is a central distinction between social theory and the theory of society.[1] Essentially, sociology as a science of reality focuses primarily – in terms of everyday research – on what Robert K. Merton called "middle-range theories," that is, on sociological theories. Within the framework of sociology's internal division of labor, these theories pertain to specialized questions and individual social phenomena, and they rely on a variety of qualitative and quantitative methods. In general, it can be said that such theories demand the immediate empirical validation of their descriptions and explanations; at the same time, and as the name implies, the range or scope of their statements is limited.

By comparison with the numerous middle-range sociological theories, social theory operates on a more abstract level. Here we are dealing with theory in the stricter sense, and this is true of both of its branches. Both social theory and the theory of society provide the general and fundamental vocabulary for answering two elementary questions. Social theory asks: "What is the social?" and "From which perspectives can it be analyzed?" The theory of society asks: "What are the structural features of society and particularly of modern societies?" and "What are the concepts with which these societies can be investigated?" To answer its questions, social theory has developed basic concepts such as action and communication, norms and roles, power and institutions, the order of knowledge, practice and discourse. Max Weber's *Basic Concepts in Sociology* and Émile Durkheim's *The Rules of Sociological Method* are classic works that seek to establish the vocabulary of social theory; more recent books of this sort include Niklas Luhmann's *Social Systems*, Anthony Giddens's *The Constitution of Society*, and Bruno Latour's *Reassembling the Social*. The theory of society, in contrast, formulates basic assumptions about overall societal structures, phenomena, and mechanisms as they have unfolded in the course of history. It is interested above all in the structures of modernity, which it examines via theories of capitalism, functional differentiation, individualization, or aestheticization (for example). Karl Marx's *Capital* and Georg Simmel's *The Philosophy of Money* are two classic examples of books that present such approaches to the theory of society, while more recent examples include

Pierre Bourdieu's *Distinction* and Manuel Castells's *The Rise of the Network Society*.

The twin contexts of the question of sociality, on the one hand, and the nature of modern society, on the other, were constitutive of the emergence of sociology in the nineteenth century. They guided the authors of the founding generation – Marx, Weber, Simmel, Durkheim – who are still influential today. Despite the gradual fragmentation of the discipline, these problems also remain significant to sociology in the twenty-first century – and, from my perspective, they *should* remain foundational, given that they provide the framework that holds together sociology's numerous and multifarious empirical analyses. Without social theory, sociology would lose itself in the extreme specialization of its undoubtedly necessary detailed studies. The tools of social theory and the theory of society maintain a reference point to the totality of the social or to society in its entirety – a reference to the whole, to the big picture traditionally cultivated by philosophy. At the same time, social theory and the theory of society provide the cultural and political public sphere with comprehensive and incisive interpretations that lead society toward self-enlightenment.

In this chapter, I intend to explain more precisely what social theory and the theory of society mean, what distinguishes them from one another, and to whom they are directed. In doing so, I will emphasize my understanding of theory as a tool. In my second chapter, I will outline the particular version of social theory that I use as a toolkit for analyzing society: the theory of social practices. The third chapter will work through the three dimensions of modernity that are central according to my perspective on the theory of society: the dialectic between opening and closing contingency; the rivalry between a social logic of the general and a social logic of the particular, and between rationalization and culturalization of the social; and, finally, a paradoxical temporal structure characterized by a regime of novelty, a dynamic of loss, and a hybridization of time. In light of these categories, I will explain, in my fourth chapter, a model of historical transformation and how it pertains to modernity: from bourgeois modernity through industrial or organized modernity up to late modernity. Here, the causes of the specific crises of present-day late modernity will also be made clear. In the fifth chapter, I will elaborate the ways in which, in my view, theory should pursue a critical orientation, without becoming "critical theory" in the narrower sense. The project in question could be called "critical analytics." Finally, in a coda, I pose the question of how one can best work with theories, and I argue in favor of engaging with them in an experimental manner.

1.1 Social Theory

First, it is important to clarify that both social theory and the theory of society combine two functions, each of which addresses different audiences. On the one hand, they are oriented toward empirical research in the social sciences, which they process and to which they provide impulses; on the other hand, they circulate as comprehensive theories within the intellectual sphere and are thus addressed to the sciences as a whole and to the non-academic public.

I would like to demonstrate this first of all in the case of social theory. The latter poses elementary questions about the form of the social – that is, it asks about the concepts with which the social can be understood. Here, "the social" designates a collective level – a level beyond individuals, their individual action, and their particular interests. This assumption is the basic outlook of the sociological way of thinking. But what, exactly, are the elementary features of the social world? Sociology has never been able to agree on a single theory of the social; instead, it has developed a plurality of different perspectives on sociality. This is understandable, because a pluralistic (scientific) culture, which modernity has tended to produce, offers space for the development of various vocabularies for theorizing the social. In their understandings of the social, these theoretical languages can be culturalist or materialist, holistic or individualistic, structuralist or process-oriented, and they can revolve around various guiding concepts (action, interaction, communication, practices, structure, etc.).

In this way, social theories develop basic conceptual frameworks, and these essentially have the status of a heuristic that guides the empirical analyses of sociology. They also provide a basic conceptual orientation for the empirical research practices of other disciplines in the social sciences and humanities, for instance history and cultural anthropology. Like so-called "sensitizing concepts," social theories point the way toward the phenomena and connections that empirical research ought to investigate – toward practices, communication, power dynamics, discourses, artifact structures, *dispositifs*, social systems, and so on. In the sense of a heuristic, they assume the role of a search-and-discover technique for empiricism. Without any social-theoretical perspective of this sort, empirical analysis would remain blind or would be based on unsophisticated assumptions about everyday life.[2] This also means, however, that a good social theory will have to meet certain standards of quality: it must provide the tools with which empirical researchers can analyze a variety of different phenomena from a rich perspective.

In addition to its heuristic function for empirical research, however, social theory also has its own autonomous significance – namely, that of social ontology. On this level, it acquires, as it were, its own "reflective value," which is independent of empirical research; it is the locus for reflecting about the social world in a fundamental way. Social theory thus provides the human sciences with an elementary vocabulary for understanding the human world as a sociocultural world by formulating a social ontology of action, culture, language, affectivity, materiality, structures, and processes. With respect to this task, it is engaged in an intensive exchange with philosophy, which, for its part, has also promised since its beginnings to develop a social ontology of the human world. Moreover, there are also close connections between the social theory of sociology and the social-theoretical considerations of other disciplines, such as the cultural theories formulated in the fields of cultural anthropology and media studies. In general, social theory – as a site for contemplating the sociocultural world – is thus an interdisciplinary undertaking of the human sciences, and it is only seldom constrained by disciplinary boundaries.[3]

As an ontology of the sociocultural world, social theory earns its independent reflective value not only from the inner sanctum of academia but also from the broader, non-academic public sphere. Secularized modernity, in which religion and theology have lost their monopoly on interpretation, is confronted with the challenge – chronically underdetermined and controversial as it is – of enlightening the *conditio humana*. Although philosophy has traditionally risen to this task, social theorists from John Dewey to Bruno Latour, from Helmuth Plessner to Jürgen Habermas, have also made fundamental contributions to this endeavor of self-enlightenment. In this regard, social theory competes especially with the natural-scientific approaches of the life sciences – evolutionary biology, evolutionary psychology, neurophysiology, etc. – to offer non-academic readers a basic vocabulary with which to understand themselves.

1.2 The Theory of Society as a Core Task of Sociology

In the social sciences, however, "theory" means not only social theory; it also means the theory of society. What distinguishes the two? The short answer to this is: the universality or historicity of their object. Admittedly, social theory often (though not always) conceptually reaches the macro-dimension of the social, the level of institutions, classes, orders of knowledge, or society as a whole. It can thus make claims about society, though in doing so it largely remains within a universalistic conceptual framework. Social theory is concerned with sociality and the nature of society *in itself*. That is, it is concerned with the structure of human practice unbound by time and space. The theory of society, in contrast, is concerned with *specific* societies and how they exist at specific times and in specific places. In short, it makes general statements about *particular* societies. At the heart of the sociological theory of society stands *modernity*, that type of societal configuration whose roots go back to the beginning of the European modern era. Over the course of industrialization, democratization, secularization, individual-ization, and the rise of science, modernity has been developing in Europe and North America since the eighteenth century, and it has since had formative effects – peacefully or violently – in different varieties and hybrid mixtures across the globe.[4]

In order to determine the nature of this modern, (at first) Western society, the theory of society can, so to speak, look far beyond it, in terms of both time and space. The modern society of the Western sort can thus be compared to those forms of society that existed before the early-modern and modern eras (nomadic and agrarian societies, as well as feudal kingdoms), and to those that existed and continue to exist beyond the European and North American context. The theory of society thus offers the possibility of developing a general theory of societal change and of global interrelations from the earliest human societies to the present, and it also offers the possibility of making systematic comparisons between different types of societies.[5]

Despite this interest in the long-term transformation of society, the modern Western society remains at the heart of the sociological theory of society in Europe and North America. In other words, the central task of the theory of society is to formulate a theory of this modernity.[6] The reason for this is obvious. Although the theory of society has its share of historical ambition, it is guided first and foremost by its interest in the *present*. It aims to understand the structures and dynamics of present-day society. This *theoretical* goal of elucidating "our" society provides the background for the *practical* efforts that sociology engages in directly or indirectly. These practical efforts can strive to alter the political configu-ration of societal institutions or even to change the ways in which individuals evaluate their own forms of life. Both efforts necessarily take place in the present, or with an eye toward the future. From a sociological perspective, of course, present-day society is just one society. It is the society characterized by modernity; it is *modern* society, as it developed from feudal, traditional, and religiously oriented "pre-modernity." It is only to modernity understood in this way that the aforementioned nexus of theory and practice is applicable. Only modern society presumes that its institutions and forms of life are not immutable but are, rather, susceptible to being formed or configured by political and sociocultural factors. Without this political or personal interest in shaping society – a basic motivation that presupposes the *possibility* of change – the theory of modernity cannot be understood.

If, however, the theory of society is essentially a theory of modernity, then this presents a few historical complications. Whereas authors such as Weber, Durkheim, Tönnies, and Simmel – who were active around the year 1900, when the final vestiges of traditional society were disappearing – were still able to regard their own present as *the* modernity, what we call modern society has since transformed considerably. By now, as of the year 2021, modernity itself has at least 250 years behind it, and thus it is by no means exclusively the epoch of our present day. Upon closer inspection, it becomes obvious that the structural features of society in the year 1800 were different from those in the year 1900, whose own features were no longer identical to those around the year 1950, which in turn differ from those of our current society. This does not mean that, within the history of modernity, there are not also continuities and unifying features that have recurred over the centuries. In light of modernity's great ability to transform itself, however, it is hardly surprising that several of its basic structures have changed profoundly. In any case, the fact that modernity itself has a history poses challenges for the theory of society in the twenty-first century.

Particularly since the mid-1970s, it has become clear that the "new" present – which was at first referred to as "postmodernity" or "high modernity" but by now largely goes by the name of "late modernity" (an umbrella term with some flaws of its own) – has, over the course of globalization, post-industrialization, digitalization, and liberalization, brought about new structures that fundamentally differ from those of the previous two versions of "classical modernity," that is, from the structures of bourgeois and industrial modernity. This has also influenced how one goes about "doing theory." Only those who believe that modernity is timeless and unchanging – that we have arrived at a sort of *posthistoire* – assume that today's society can be understood with reference to the same abstract features (capitalism, functional differentiation) that had defined early stages of modernity. Paradoxically, it is precisely this insight into the fundamental *historicity* of modernity – not only its origins but also its broad course of development – that lends intellectual consistency to the realization that the *present* version of modernity is itself highly specific and singular. In this light, the theory of society has developed, beyond a general theory of modernity, a more specific contemporary "offshoot": the theory of late-modern society or, in short, the *theory of late modernity*. In its more pointed and publicly accessible manifestations, this theory can appear as though it belongs to the genre of so-called "diagnoses of the times," but as a version of the theory of society, it is decidedly more than such a diagnosis.[7] Of course, the theory of late modernity must operate in close contact with the theory of modernity as a whole, be it in a historically comparative manner or with an eye toward identifying continuities. Without any comparisons to what has come before, it is impossible to appreciate what is new.

From my perspective, working on a theory of society as a theory of modernity in general, and on a theory of late modernity in particular, is not an ancillary or specialized problem of sociology. It should ultimately be its core task. The multitude of empirical studies provides set pieces that can and must be processed within the framework of the theory of society. The challenge of analyzing the structures of contemporary society in their particularity – precisely because this society is new, unusual, and even surprising, and because the appropriate terms for understanding it are lacking – is a challenge that characterized the primal scene, so to speak, that gave rise to the social sciences in the nineteenth century. The open question with which sociology has wrestled from the beginning is this: What is modern about modernity? This is the problem that motivated all the early studies: Marx's analysis of the dynamics of capitalism, Weber's examination of formal rationalization, Durkheim's study of the ongoing social division of labor, and Simmel's investigation of individualism were all essentially propelled by an epistemological interest in coming to terms with the novelty and uniqueness of the structures of modernity, which were at first difficult to understand. This primal scene has recurred again and again throughout the history of sociology; from it, the discipline derives its lasting fascination with the novelty of modernity.[8] The theories of late modernity and postmodernity that have been appearing on the intellectual stage since the last quarter of the twentieth century – Daniel Bell's *Cultural Contradictions of Capitalism*, Luc Boltanski and Ève Chapiello's *The New Spirit of Capitalism*, Ulrich Beck's *Risk Society*, or Antonio Negri and Michael Hardt's *Empire* (to name just a few works) – are motivated by the exact same theoretical goal: the goal of making the historical otherness of contemporary society comprehensible in its basic structures and dynamics.

This situation also helps us to answer the question of how to think about the relationship between social theory and the theory of society. Although, in terms of basic concepts, nothing is more elementary to the discipline than social theory, the end game of the entire undertaking known as sociology is nevertheless to understand modern society. Now, it goes without saying that, without social theory and the fundamental conceptual insights that it brings to our understanding of the social, of culture, power (etc.), there could be no empirical analysis and no theory of modernity. The social-theoretical vocabulary provides the conceptual background that allows certain phenomena and certain connections to become visible in the theory of society in the first place. A specific social-theoretical vocabulary – think of the role of world images in Max Weber's work or that of the sacred in Durkheim's, or consider the role of communicative action in Habermas's philosophy and the idea of communication as observation that is so crucial to Luhmann's theories – sensitizes researchers to see particular social contexts (while also, implicitly, sensitizing them *not* to see others). The theory of society thus needs the preparatory insights of social theory in order to do its work. Conversely, however, it is also true that a social theory without a theory of society would be like swimming on dry land. Social theory is not an end in itself; it is not a self-sufficient undertaking. Ultimately, it paves the way for the theory of society. That said, a particular theory of society cannot simply be derived from a social-theoretical vocabulary. The theory of society cannot be a mere product of social theory, and this is because the connections that the theory of society focuses on never emerge purely from a general vocabulary of the social, but rather – and more importantly – from efforts to ascertain a particular historical or contemporary reality.[9]

1.3 Functions of the Theory of Society

As in the case of social theory, it is possible to identify some basic features of the theory of society. The latter has a two-sided relationship with empirical analysis. On the one hand, it is built on the basis of empirical research and experience, and its intrinsic value depends on observations and studies of the concrete phenomena of change as these pertain to economic structures, political systems, family relations, or cultural currents. A good theory of society must take into account the available knowledge about all the main facets of society – economics, politics, culture, and so on. The theory of society thus brings together studies and observations from various dimensions of society – studies and observations that would otherwise be compartmentalized in various branches of empirical research – and then relates them to one another in an effort to create a *synthesis* that brings to light the connections that exist among different phenomena and individual structures. It sees the forest, not just the trees. Ideally, and in order to present a full picture of modernity, such a theory should be able to make pronouncements about the structures and transformations of the following major elements of society: first, the economy; second, the state and politics; third, the social structure (the configuration of social groups); fourth, culture (systems of ideas and orders of knowledge); and fifth, technology. Finally, one should expect this theory to address, sixth, the relationship between society and individuals – that is, the way in which the society in question subjectivizes individuals and thus also the way in which the individuals in this society typically conduct their lives.

On the other hand, it is not just the case that the theory of society is constructed on the basis of empirical research. Once such a theory has become established, it will itself guide empirical research by making basic concepts and explanatory hypotheses available and by providing a broader macro-sociological context for detailed empirical investigations. To give just one example: Karl Marx's theory of capitalism was only able to be written and gain plausibility because its author had kept a very close eye on the radical economic changes taking place at the time. After its publication, this theory was then, in turn, able to motivate, and serve as a framework for, a great deal of empirical research. In general, the theory of society demonstrates its fecundity by absorbing and insightfully processing existing empirical observations and studies, on the one hand, and, on the other, by theoretically elucidating new observations and encouraging future research. It can thus be claimed that a good theory of society paves the way for an *empirical research program* and provides an agenda for future research. In this respect, it is itself a heuristic tool. The fact that the theory of society is influenced by empirical research and yet influences it in turn has ramifications not only for its relationship with the empiricism of sociology but also for its relationship with other disciplines. As already mentioned, the act of formulating a theory of society is always an interdisciplinary undertaking, and it requires input from the field of history and from other historical subjects (from literary history and art history, for instance). Fields such as political science and economics, social and cultural anthropology, cultural studies, and social psychology all play a part in this as well. In the end, however, the key role in the formation of the theory of society is played by sociology, for the simple reason that it takes into account all the dimensions and sub-dimensions that constitute society as a whole.

What is decisive is that, beyond its synthesizing function, the theory of society offers *theoretical surplus value*. It develops its own concepts for the overarching structural features of the societal context in question, and these make it possible, in turn, to analyze phenomena on an individual basis. In other words, it works out the overall structural dynamics of society so that processes and transformations can be broken down analytically and explained. Among the concepts developed to describe such sweeping structural features, classic examples include capitalism, rationalization, secularization, functional differentiation, individualization, discipline, risk politics, and symbolic class conflict. A consistent concern of the theory of society is to identify the causes that are responsible for the reproduction of the structures of society in a particular historical phase (or even in all historical phases) and to identify reasons to explain the transformation of these structures.

The theoretical surplus value of the theory of society means that it brings a conceptual *excess* to the table that goes beyond what is known from empirical studies. Therein lies its originality and its creativity, at least in the best cases. Typically, the theory of society has the quality of a – synchronic – comprehensive *tableau* of interconnections, as well as that of a – diachronic – grand *narrative* of process logics. It makes use of narrative patterns (of rise, decline, perpetual conflict, ever new disappointment, etc.), and it develops terminologies and metaphors to convey the nature of certain contexts (society as an organism, system, or antagonism; actors as deceived deceivers; the iron cage of bondage; the cunning of reason; the rulers and the ruled, etc.). As a *tableau of society*, the theory of society is therefore always also a *narrative of society*.[10]

Because the theory of society is not a middle-range theory, it can be empirically supported, but it can never be empirically proven or disproven in a strict sense. What W. V. O. Quine described in his post-empiricist theory of science as the "underdetermination of theory by evidence" applies perfectly to the theory of society in its high degree of abstraction. Theory does not merely illustrate facts; it goes beyond them in its interpretation and in its own theoretical complexity. In principle, one and the same "fact" – like an ambiguous image in the experiments of perceptual psychology – can be used in meaningful ways to support different theories.[11] The theory of society thus provides a complex and systematic *manner of interpretation* for understanding the chaotic abundance of societal facts in their entirety. As a heuristic of this sort, it gives order to the social world according to a defined and selective perspective that is undoubtedly influenced by the specific problems that theorists perceive in their respective time (problems that, in turn, inevitably change). *Totality* is the vanishing point, the horizon of the theory of society, but this totality can never be fully achieved, of course, and certainly not in a neutral manner. Rather, theory always functions in the mode of conceptually increasing *refinement* by recognizing overarching patterns in a multitude of empirical phenomena and by necessarily emphasizing certain elements and connections at the expense of others. It is always a *particular* theory of the *general*: a single vocabulary that claims to comprehend the whole of society (or the totality of the social).

It follows that empirical reality will always be too diverse and varied for any theory of society (or social theory, for that matter) to illustrate and elucidate all of these multifarious elements with its refined horizon of interpretation. In this sense, "theory" must be understood in a post-empiricist manner. Jorge Luis Borges made this point succinctly in his one-paragraph story "On Exactitude in Science." In order to represent all the spatial details of the earth, we would need a map with a scale of 1:1, which would of course cover the entire earth – an impossible undertaking that pushes the human desire for orientation to absurd limits.[12] In the end, one would see everything and nothing at the same time, given that the comprehensiveness of such a map would render it useless. Things are quite similar with the theory of society: in order to make contexts and connections visible, it has to be selective. It overlooks certain things, blurs some others out; one could say that its conceptual framework has inherent "blind spots." Theory thus reduces the complexity of empirical reality, but through its analysis of connections and dynamics it also builds complexity, whereby it gains its theoretical surplus value. In this respect, theoretical reality is always richer and more complex than bare empirical facts could ever be. Like science as a whole, theory is a social practice engaged in a "way of world-making" (in Nelson Goodman's terms).[13] The world (or, better: *a* world) is scientifically and theoretically created in a particular way.

In addition to its function as a framework and instigator of empirical research, another significant aspect of the theory of society is the role it plays in stimulating intellectual discussion outside of the scientific sphere. If, since its beginnings, the primary objective of sociology has been to enlighten modern society about itself, then the theory of society is responsible for performing a special task within this arrangement. It has a reflective value for the human sciences as a whole, but also for society beyond the walls of academia. Consider again the primal scene of sociology's emergence as a discipline: in a sense, modernity and sociology originated together. For only in modern society was it first possible – and does it remain possible – for society to understand itself *as* society. The interest of the non-academic public, in which the theory of society resonates, is certainly always focused on individual and specific social phenomena and trends, but it is ultimately guided by the question of how society as a whole is structured, and how it changes as a whole as well. The theory of society is therefore also an interpretive tool for the broader public. Both the cultural and the political public spheres are interested addressees of its theory. The cultural public sphere consists of private readers who expect theory to offer interpretive approaches to assist them in reflecting about their own lives within society at large. The political public sphere consists of citizens of a political community and the corresponding mediators of information (civil society, the media itself) who expect theory to provide impulses that might contribute to their understanding of social crises and guide their decisions to take political action.

1.4 Theory as a Tool

Central to my understanding of theory, as I have already suggested, is the metaphor of the *tool*. Regardless of whether we are dealing with social theory or the theory of society, theories at this level of abstraction are interpretive toolkits; they provide tools for empirical research, for the human sciences, and for the non-academic public. Such an understanding of theory as a tool, however, is not self-evident. It is my opinion, nevertheless, that all available social theories and theories of society can be treated as tools in this sense. This does not mean, however, that they have necessarily regarded *themselves* as tools, or even that they are primarily understood as such by the scientific community. It therefore might be useful here to discuss an ideal-typical distinction between two meta-theoretical understandings of theory: *theory as a system* and *theory as a tool*.

The understanding of social theory and the theory of society as a theoretical system has its origins in philosophy and continues to exert considerable influence in the social sciences. This is the classical understanding of theory. Theory as a system means: a deductively operating conceptual system with unambiguous definitions, premises, and conceptual conclusions has been established, and this system claims to have the widest possible scope of applicability. This means: the theoretical system forms a unified whole and is self-contained. Once it has been developed, it can be applied indefinitely. Although it might be possible to supplement it and refine it here and there, its fundamental elements cannot be changed without causing it to collapse as a whole. The idea of theory as a system also suggests that a given theory must be accepted *in toto*: One either accepts the theory completely and learns to think and speak in it, or one leaves it behind entirely – a partial reception was not intended by its founder. In the history of the theory of society, two theories in particular stand out for having been designed as systems of this sort: the theory of capitalism by Marx and Engels, and the theory of differentiation by Parsons and Luhmann.

A fundamental alternative to "theory-as-system" is opened up by understanding theory as a tool. This latter understanding has also existed since the beginnings of social theory and the theory of society. Neither Max Weber nor Georg Simmel formulated a theoretical system; instead, they made contributions to the theory of society by making use of a variety of conceptual tools. The same can be said of more recent influential thinkers such as Michel Foucault or Bruno Latour and also of most theorists of late modernity, from Anthony Giddens and Donna Haraway to Luc Boltanski. It may not be a novel thing to do, in other words, but understanding theory as a tool has clearly proven to be, in our late-modern scientific culture, an especially productive approach.[14]

The understanding of theory as a tool has considerable implications for how theory is done and how it is dealt with. What are the features of "theory-as-tool"? First, and fundamentally, what one expects from it is *not* a self-contained conceptual system that can be applied as a whole to everything, but rather heuristic fecundity in concrete analytical situations. The point is to provide an epistemic tool for future empirical analyses in a new and surprising way by means of conceptual refinement. The public, too, turns to theory for an intellectual tool with which to see individual social phenomena in a new context, a context that brings problems to light on a different cultural, individual, or political level.

The quality of a theory of society as a tool manifests itself first and foremost in its ability to inspire both within and beyond academia. It is measured not simply by what it *knows* but also, and more importantly, by what it is *capable of.* In this respect, the practice of theory always has the character of an *experiment* in which concepts and theoretical connections are tested and refined in dialogue with the objects in question. To work in this way is to allow oneself to be surprised by the materials of the world – which have the character of "epistemic things" (in Hans-Jörg Rheinberger's terms) – and also by the consequences of one's own conceptual design.[15] In these experimental contexts, one can tinker around with different conceptual tools and draw upon various empirical materials, so that the theory, for its part, remains "in flux." This is not a matter of reaffirming the familiar system of thought, but rather about discovering the utility value of certain tools. In the latter, one hopes to find analytical flexibility and nimbleness. Tools are good when they can be useful in a wide array of situations, and when they help to generate interesting insights in entirely new contexts. In addition, although "theory-as-tool" is highly amenable to empirical research, it is typically more acutely aware of its textuality – that is, of its property as a linguistic vocabulary – than it is conscious of itself as a specific manner of interpretation. For this reason, it usually engages quite actively with the interpretive characteristics of the theory of society discussed above: narratives, tableaus, and conceptual ambivalences. Far from attempting to eliminate the latter, it aims instead to "play" with them in a constructive manner. Whereas theory as a system will find itself in a dilemma when pushed to its analytical limits, this is not a problem at all for theory as a tool. It is in the nature of a tool that one cannot do everything with it; certain tools are only useful for certain things, different jobs require different tools, and so on. Rather than weaken theory, this fact strengthens it.

To understand theory as a tool means that it is not presumed to be a deductive and hierarchical conceptual system; instead, theory adopts the form of a conceptual *network*, to which theorists and users alike can constantly add additional nodes. From the perspective of the theorist, this means that the goal is not to develop, once and for all, a conceptual system on the basis of rigid premises, so that it can simply be applied later on. Rather, a conceptual network can constantly evolve in multiple and unpredictable ways. As this happens, formerly dominant nodes and relations can recede into the background while new conceptual nodes and relations emerge. One can embrace certain aspects of the old while turning away from others.[16] In this way, theory thus takes on the form of a *bricolage* of concepts to be tinkered with.

With such an understanding of theory, theorists are not committed to continuity but are free to try out new tools on new topics that have captured their interest. A clear example of this is the approach taken by Michel Foucault, who repeatedly developed new conceptual tools – genealogy, *dispositif*, discipline, governmentality, technologies of the self – which, though rather loosely related to one another, gave rise to an increasingly more complex form of analytics. Yet the network-like nature of theory also means that the act of "doing theory" can be decentered away from the position of any given brilliant author-subject. In other words, a theoretical tool created by person *A* can be picked up by person *B* and developed in a different direction, only then to be applied by person *C* in a different context or in a different form. Theory is in fact worked on by a social network, which does not leave it unchanged. This collaborative approach is also, of course, a hallmark of empirical research, a fact that, to some extent, blurs the traditional dualistic line between theory and empiricism.

A good example of such a network-esque development of theory is the field of practice theories, which has been growing steadily since the turn of the millennium and which has been worked on collaboratively by numerous scientists around the world.[17] To this extent, the term *network* applies not only to the *intellectual* form of the theory but also to the *social* form in which people work on it. Whereas the model of "theory-as-system" lives with the implicit contrast between a charismatic (theory) leader and his proponents (his "school"), the model of theory as a tool reimagines the act of "doing theory" as a social form in the style of collaborations and projects.

The network-like nature of "theory-as-tool" also means that theories of this sort lend themselves to being combined with other theories – they are not closed off from the world, but can instead be hybridized. Whereas "theories-as-systems" survive by building up a strong internal identity, by differentiating themselves clearly from the outside, and thus seem to rival other similarly constructed theories, "theories-as-tools" can be connected to one another without any problem at all. Networks, in other words, can be linked together. This fits in neatly with the pragmatic spirit of the tool. A single author can try out unusual combinations in his or her theoretical work by bringing together, say, the concept of capitalism with that of postmodernity, or by drawing a connection between the sacred and performativity, but these combinations might just as well be made and disseminated within the broader intellectual sphere without this one author's intervention. With this combinational technique, concepts from different theoretical contexts can be reinterpreted, they can be appropriated by others, and their point of reference can be broadened or narrowed. In this sense, theory entails a practice of recontextualization.[18]

2

Practice Theory as Social Theory

We have seen that theories of society necessarily need social-theoretical vocabularies. There is, however, a broad range of social theories. At our disposal are, among others, the individualistic theory of action, social phenomenology, structuralism, systems theory, and structural functionalism, to name just a few examples from a broad and varied field. Treated as analytical tools, they all have their methodological advantages and disadvantages. The vocabulary that I have chosen to adopt is that of practice theory, which is also known as the theory of social practices or praxeology. As a socio-ontological perspective and as a social-theoretical heuristic for empirical analyses – not only in sociology but in all the social and cultural sciences – the theory of social practices, in my opinion, enables a view of the social world that is as comprehensive as it is focused, and it opens up highly fruitful research perspectives. Praxeological social theory thus provides the background for my contributions to a theory of modernity. I would therefore like to invite you to participate in an experiment: the experiment of seeing the world praxeologically.

Practice theory has certain theoretical features that distinguish it from other current social theories in a fundamental way. Before I go into these, however, I should note that the appeal of practice theory to me also lies in the fact that it is unequivocally a social-theoretical *tool* and not a theoretical system. This has the aforementioned advantages of all "tool theories," among them the unproblematic possibility of tinkering with its guiding concepts, combining it with other theories, and bringing it into conversation with new objects and concepts in surprising ways. This fluidity is also the reason why there is no such thing as *the* theory of social practices in the singular. Praxeology does not have a founding author or a canonical text. As suggested above, it is, rather, an interdisciplinary and collective theoretical movement, or a social network of theories that began to come together in the 1970s in various places and has been growing since the 2000s with the help of a broad range of international collaborations.

For anyone interested in sophisticated monographs on practice theory, Pierre Bourdieu's *Outline of a Theory of Practice* and Anthony Giddens's *The Constitution of Society* belong on top of the reading list. Indispensable, too, are Theodore Schatzki's books *Social Practices* and *The Site of the Social*, which approach the theory from a socio-philosophical perspective. More broadly, it can be said that Harold Garfinkel's ethnomethodology, Judith Butler's theory of performativity, Henri Lefèbvre's theory of space, and certain works by Michel Foucault – those devoted to governmentality and to technologies of the self, for instance – can also be regarded as significant nodal points in this network. The works of Bruno Latour and his actor–network theory may have a different point of departure (one that is decidedly materialistic), but they can likewise be situated within the context of the praxeological network of theories.[1]

2.1 Features of Practice Theory

Despite all the differences between individual praxeological approaches, a few common features of a theory of social practices constitute its basic social-theoretical vocabulary. Its starting point is that the social world is composed of ensembles of practices that are constantly reproduced and yet are always in a state of change. What is meant by practices are activities, recurrent in time and across space, which are undertaken both by human actors in their corporeality and by inorganic or organic entities – that is, by artifacts. These practices, which are in a constant state of becoming, presuppose orders of knowledge – and cultural orders that dictate what can be thought and said – that are processed discursively, incorporated by human actors, and enable these actors to organize reality in a meaningful way. From a praxeological perspective, the smallest unit of the social is thus not individual action, interaction, or communication, and neither is it the norm or the rule (all of which are traditional sociological concepts); rather, it is the practice as a repeated, spatially dispersed, and knowledge-dependent activity of bodies and things. Performatively, the social is continually produced in this "nexus of sayings and doings" (as Schatzki put it). Practice theory has earned a special place among social theories because it situates itself outside of three common dualisms: the dualism between action theory (individualism) and the theory of order (collectivism), the dualism between materialism and culturalism, and the dualism between situation-oriented micro-theory and structure-oriented macro-theory.

The opposition between the "two sociologies" of individualism and collectivism – that is, between a social theory that adopts the subjective perspective of actors, and another that proceeds from the supra-subjective order of a collective (from a system and its norms, for instance) – pervades the entire history of social theory.[2] The figures of *Homo economicus* and *Homo sociologus* exemplify these two theoretical extremes. In contrast to this, the praxeological point of departure is neither individualistic nor collectivistic in its orientation; rather, it assumes that subjects and sociality origi-nated together, so to speak. As repetitive and spatially distributed activities, practices designate a genuine and emergent level of the social that cannot be reduced to the characteristics of individuals or their actions. A social practice is never "possessed" by an individual; its immanent structure is independent of the particular qualities of individuals. Unlike the individualistic concept of action, which refers to the intentional act of the individual actor, the concept denotes a supra-individual and therefore social phenomenon. It denotes a *cultural technique*, in the broadest sense of the term,[3] that is repeatedly appropriated and perpetuated by a wide variety of individuals. Such practices include a practice of writing a diary or crafting, a practice of arguing or brainstorming, a practice of lab work or digital meetings, a practice of ballroom dancing, a practice of financial transactions, a practice of legal proceedings, a practice of thinking or being silent, and so on.

The concept of practices, however, always takes into account the corporeality and mentality of human actors, who, as socialized subjects, are a necessary part of any practice. From a praxeological perspective, subjects are not outside of the social, and the social does not hover, in a sense, above the minds and bodies of individuals. Rather, the social functions as practice via individual subjects and presupposes their physical and intellectual activity, as well as their subjective understanding of action and the world. In order to be able to participate in a practice, subjects must be "subjectivized" accordingly – that is, they must have already acquired corresponding competencies, forms of knowledge, and patterns of interpretation (what Pierre Bourdieu called a "habitus"). In such a way, they become actors who carry out practices – and they are able to reaccentuate these practices at the same time.

Practice theory also distances itself from the second traditional dualism mentioned above, that between culturalism and materi-alism. It neither sides with the culturalist camp by treating ideas and symbolic orders as the foundation of the social, nor exclusively focuses materialistically on the ways in which nature and the world of things are processed. In this respect, practice theory is an intellectual hybrid. It is a theory of culture, but at the same time it is also a materialist theory; it makes productive use, in other words, of the apparent paradox of a *cultural-theoretical materialism* (or, formulated the other way around, a *materialist theory of culture*). Both materiality and culture are conceived in praxeological terms from the outset: neither materiality nor a system of ideas is assumed to *precede* practice. Rather, materiality is thought to exist only in its practical materialization (in the practical act of "doing matter"), and culture is thought to exist only in the practical act of "doing culture."

This intertwinement of the cultural and the material is consistent with the structure of practice theory. On the one hand, practices are treated as thoroughly material phenomena that are materialized in two forms: in human *bodies* and in non-human *artifacts*. In contrast to the obsession with the mind and the neglect of the body that characterizes much of social theory in the long tradition of the Cartesian and Kantian philosophy of consciousness, practice theory emphasizes the physicality of practices, which are activities manifested, as it were, through the medium of the human body (a world-changing, energetic, affective, and neuronal organism). At the same time, and unlike in the traditional focus of social theory on intersubjectivity or interpersonal relationships, practice theory also assumes that social practices always involve non-human (organic or inorganic) entities, which are connected to human beings via these practices and co-determine which practices are possible in the first place, so that entire socio-ecological configurations are formed. This enables practice theory to account for the dynamics involving such things as tools, machines, buildings, media technologies, books, algorithms, screen images, sound sequences, animals, plants, forests, and climate conditions. As necessary "participants" in practices, these "artifacts" – a term that illustrates both the objectivity of material entities and their relations to human beings – operate in their own ways *within* the social.

That said, practice theory fundamentally has a cultural-theoretical perspective on the social world. Social practices are not only material practices; they are cultural practices as well. They are not simply patterns of behavior, but necessarily contain orders of knowledge that give them their form in the first place. Orders of knowledge – that is, classification systems that represent the world in a meaningful way and, by creating distinctions (codes), enable actors to interpret the world in a meaningful way – are exactly what culture is in the general sense.[4] These orders of knowledge provide more or less comprehensive systems of interpretation, as well as practical and methodical knowledge that makes it possible to engage in practices. They are applied when carrying out a practice and they provide the interpretive background knowledge (the "know-how") for doing so. Within a social context, orders of knowledge thus acquire an intelligibility of their own – an ability to be understood by others – and a basic level of self-reflexivity over the course of being competently applied by individuals. In light of the implicit character of knowledge, however, this self-reflexivity should not be confused with intellectual self-reflection. To give an example: The practices that constitute modern education – such as teaching, learning, student interaction, lesson planning, the formation of peer-groups, etc. – can be understood as activities involving bodies and things. At the same time, they are based on complex and often implicit notions of what constitutes education – that is, these practices are based on codified knowledge and practical knowledge, on an understanding of the relationship between teachers and pupils; on concepts of performance, competition, hierarchy, and resistance; and on knowing how to control one's body, concentrate mentally, and communicate in an elaborate way. Unlike many other cultural theories, practice theory decenters the social role of language and communication. Orders of knowledge are often implicit (they are not always explicitly expressed), and practices of linguistic communication represent only *one* among many other sorts of practices that are relevant to the social.

The third dualism that practice theory undermines concerns the traditional opposition between micro-theory, which takes specific situations as its starting point, and macro-theory, which attempts to identify overarching structures. Fundamentally, this boils down to the temporality and spatiality of practice. On the one hand, social practices can be interpreted on a micro-sociological level: they always have to be executed anew in a specific situation – that is, at a particular time and place. In a sense, each situation represents a new beginning and every context is different and infinitely complex, and this is what gives rise to the eventfulness, situatedness, and unpredictability of practice. Accordingly, it is impossible to posit the existence of a single, overarching structure that exists outside of time and space and determines, precisely, which activities can be enacted in the here and now. In positive terms, there is in practice theory a constitutive openness to the surprises and deviances that any given micro-situation might have to offer.

At the same time, situational activities do not exist without conditions; they always have preconditions that go beyond a given situation and exist outside of the time and place of the situation at hand. For this reason, praxeology has a decidedly macro-perspective on the social. Social practices are social to begin with because they spread through space – they *diffuse* into it – and because they are *repeated* in time, so that they are potentially *reproduced* in time and space. Social practices acquire the nature of a routine, so that they typically "bind time and space" (as Giddens put it). In doing so, individual practices become intertwined with entire complexes of practices – just think of global capitalism. In these large-scale and deep-reaching networks of practices, many different activities depend on one another, influence each other reciprocally or unilaterally, and coordinate with one another across temporal and spatial boundaries. In socialized bodies, in things, and in traditional orders of knowledge, there is a force of inertia that favors the long-term establishment of such complexes of practices.

From a praxeological perspective, the "micro" and the "macro" are therefore no longer to be pitted against one another. So-called "micro-phenomena" are always linked, spatially and temporally, to certain macro-phenomena, while these so-called macro-phenomena exist only as they are manifested in individual micro-situations.[5] Instead of seeing things in terms of "two levels" – situation and structure, micro and macro – praxeology thus proceeds from what Latour called a "flat ontology" of the social, which, as the name implies, exists on one level alone. Understood in praxeological terms, the social is inclined, on the one hand, toward "deterritorialization" (to borrow a term from Deleuze and Guattari), which means that it tends to dissolve existing borders and create new networks as surprising events and situations arise. On the other hand, however, it is also inclined toward reterritorialization – that is, it tends to establish orders in the form of regulated complexes of practices across temporal and spatial boundaries.[6]

2.2 Four Social Phenomena from a Praxeological Perspective

From a praxeological perspective, the social thus consists of practices and of entire networks of practices; at the same time, these are practice–body–artifact complexes and practice–knowledge complexes. Practices reproduce themselves and they are always creating new networks. Within the framework of a praxeological social theory, all social phenomena, which are already familiar from other social theories, take on a specific meaning. I would like to take a closer look at four of these – discourses, affects, subjects, and institutions / forms of life – and examine them through a praxe-ological "lens," so to speak.

The question of how *discourses* fit into the praxeological framework may sound difficult, but it is in fact easy to answer.[7] Discourses are a sort of practice; indeed, they are discursive practices that operate neither above nor below other practices. In this respect, practice theory differs from radical discourse theory, for which the social is basically discourse, and it also differs from materialism, for which discourses represent a mere super-construct of culture. From a praxeological viewpoint, discourses are *practices of representation*: within them, phenomena of the world are repre-sented, interpreted, and thematized in a particular way, so that what arises within them – and sometimes goes beyond them, if they are persuasive enough – is an interpretive order of the effable. Discursive practices also always require specific materialities – that is, they depend on media in the broadest sense (texts, images, sounds, etc.). Praxeologically, they are especially interesting because they take certain orders of knowledge, which are silently present as *implicit* knowledge in other ("non-discursive") practices, and they make these orders of knowledge textually or visibly *explicit*. Within discourses, knowledge and cultural representations are turned into a theme of their own. There is no reason to believe in a strict dualism between practice and discourse. In modern societies especially, non-discursive and discursive practices often join together and give rise to entire *practice–discourse formations*.[8]

Affects, too, acquire a specific value within praxeology's theoretical framework.[9] Individual practices and entire networks of practices are typically characterized by a specific sort of affectivity, by an emotional-affective mood. They are *practice–affect complexes*, and they should be studied as such. In this case, practice theory thus steers clear of the rationalistic neglect of affect that is so common in much of social theory. Within the framework of practice, subjects are affected in a typical way by other subjects, by artifacts, etc. These sensations of affect are, for their part, a material phenomenon, in that they involve the objective "affective intensities" of bodies (as Massumi put it), and they are also a cultural phenomenon, in that their emergence and effects depend on specific emotion-related manners of interpretation – for instance, on interpretations of what is threatening or lamentable, and how to deal with such things. What is decisive is that, from a praxeological perspective, affects and emotions are not treated as psychologistic characteristics of individuals (as part of their private mental state, as it were); instead, they are understood in the sense of "doing affect" – that is, as a component of practices *themselves* (in the context of which they can be analyzed in social and cultural terms). A practice–affect complex can contain specific affective orientations – joy, desire, interest, sadness, rage, fear, shame, envy, and so on – and individual practices can differ considerably in their affective intensity. Romantic love thus forms a specific practice–affect complex, while market competition forms another. Moreover, a single practice–affect complex can give rise to conflicting affective orientations. The educational system, for instance, can arouse feelings of curiosity and enthusiasm just as easily as it can provoke one to fear failure and angrily resist authority. In its affectivity, a practice thus contains its own forms of motivation, a structure that may seem attractive and desirable or off-putting and unappealing.

Practice theory also adopts a specific perspective toward *subjects*.[10] Practice theory does not treat subjects as autonomous actors, but rather as bodies (together with the "minds" enclosed within them) that find themselves in an ongoing process of subjectivation. One is not born a subject but rather becomes one by appropriating the orders of knowledge and competencies of practices. Subjects are formed, in other words, by the continuous activity of people "becoming subjects." In the process of subjectivation, the subject submits to certain criteria of "normal," appropriate, and competent subjecthood and, by submitting to these things and appropriating them, can become an ostensibly autonomous and reflective being who pursues interests with his or her own "subjective perspective." For different (complexes of) practices, this results in typical subject forms with corresponding abilities and relations to the world. The subject form is thus not exhausted by the set of roles that he or she plays, but rather proves to be a cluster of competencies, interpretive knowledge, and emotions, which (complexes of) practices require and in which these practices reproduce themselves. Furthermore, the subject form becomes an object of cultural representation via discursive practices, which therefore, at least in part, take on the form of subject discourses. Because many different manners of subjectivation can intersect in one person (woman, professor, white, wine lover, physicist, etc.), this creates a high degree of unpredictability, the effects of which are never revealed outside of, but always within, practice itself – or, to be more precise: within the process-based nature of practices. For this reason, practice–discourse–artifact complexes form specific subject cultures and subject orders.

Societies, from a praxeological point of view, denote the network of *all* interconnected (complexes of) practices. Within such a society – today, the global society – it is obviously not the case that *all* practices are networked with one another in the *same* manner, with the same intensity. Rather, there will be specific (sometimes closer, sometimes looser) interconnections between particular (complexes of) practices in a society.[11] Entirely different social entities – those entities, from bureaucracy to subcultures, which have been the traditional objects of investigation in the social sciences – can thus be described praxeologically in a new way, namely as ensembles of specific social practices. Here it is necessary to distinguish between two general aggregate forms within society: *forms of life* and *institutions*.[12] Both are equally relevant from a praxeological point of view, and both are active – beyond traditional dualisms à la system and lifeworld, community and society, social integration and system integration – on a single level: the level of social practices. They are thus not made of two different types of material, but they do differ in that they *arrange* or *order* practices in two different ways.

On the one hand, a society can be understood and studied as a compilation of forms of life. A form of life is the coordinated ensemble of all the practices that constitute the sociocultural life of a number of individuals – that is, all the activities of a human body-and-mind from birth to death. In a modern society, such a form of life typically includes practices of work, personal relationships (family, friends, etc.), dealing with media, consumption, the body (exercise, sexuality), politics, space (living, traveling), and practices of the self (biographical reflection), all of which are interrelated via orders of knowledge. In a (modern) society, it is characteristic for there to be not just one single form of life for everyone but a variety of forms that can be classified in terms of milieus, classes, and subject cultures (the middle-class form of life, the proletarian form of life, etc.).

On the other hand, a society can be viewed and analyzed as a collection of institutions. The differentiation of institutions does not take place alongside that of forms of life but rather intersects the latter diagonally. Institutions are coordinated ensembles of practices whose coherence results from specialization of one sort or another. These can be individual organizations, but they can also be entire social fields – such as economics or politics – which are characteristic of the functional differentiation of modernity. Institutions are thus not thought about in traditionally norm-theoretical terms, but are rather defined by what they actually *do*. In the sphere of the modern economy, for instance, practices of market exchange, mechanical production, planning, and risk analysis are all interrelated. In the political sphere, practices of legislation, debate, administrative activity, and public relations are similarly enmeshed with one another. All of this, in turn, requires not only specific bodies and artifacts but also specific orders of knowledge. What is important is that individual practices cannot be assigned exclusively to one form of life or exclusively to one institutional structure. Rather, they always participate in *both* aggregate forms of society.[13]

In general, a praxeological perspective on forms of life and institutions does not presume that they are necessarily homogeneous, monolithic, or closed off from outside influences. Instead, the idea that they are formed by more or less loosely connected practices (along with related discourses and manners of subjectivation) is much more open to the immanent heterogeneity of the social than is the case in traditional concepts such as the system or the lifeworld. It is also the case, however, that this heterogeneity simultaneously includes processes and phases of homogenization and standardization, such as those that occur during the implementation of strict systems of norms or unambiguous subject positions. Forms of life and institutional structures are thus always mired in the field of tension between heterogenization and homogenization, and this tug-of-war is something that needs to be investigated in detail, both praxeologically and historically. On the one hand, they operate on the margins by marking boundaries and pointing out the differences between the inside and the outside. On the other hand, however, they are intertwined in multiple ways with the practices of *other* forms of life and *other* institutions, be it through unintended consequences, through attempts to gain control or influence, through matters of mutual dependence, or through their coincidental reliance on certain non-specialized practices and orders of knowledge.

Thus, from the perspective of practice theory, forms of life and institutions are generally not regarded as stable and atemporal structures but rather, in light of their processual nature and historicity, as active processes of "doing (forms of) life" and of "doing institutions." These processes are reproduced in society and also involve ever novel, experimental, and surprising acts, which arise from their respective contexts and instigate social change. With respect to both forms of life and institutional orders, practices (and complexes of practices) differ in terms of the degree of their *social power*, which is another important social-theoretical concept that can be interpreted in praxeological terms. A form of life or an institution can be powerful on account of its broad scope, its high rate of reproduction, its homogeneity, and the clarity with which it is demarcated, but it can also be powerful if it radiates outward and influences many other practices. In modern societies, these effects of power can go as far as creating hegemony – that is, a form of dominance that makes it seem as though there are no alternatives, in all of society, to certain practices and orders of knowledge, which are treated as the only desirable model available.

2.3 Practice Theory as a Tool

Like all social theories, practice theory serves a dual function. On the one hand, it offers a methodological heuristic for empirical analysis in the social and cultural sciences, thereby also providing the necessary background for the theory of society. On the other hand, it has the autonomous reflexive value of a social ontology, which, independent of empiricism, draws its own particular picture of the social. As a research heuristic, practice theory pertains to the entire breadth of all social phenomena that interest the social and cultural sciences: from climate change to changes in the working world, from ancient burial rites to middle-class reading culture and revolutionary struggles, from social media to sports. In short, every single micro- or macro-phenomenon can be investigated from a praxeological point of view. The guiding heuristic maxim of praxeology is: Treat every phenomenon as a nexus of "doings"![14] This involves questions such as the following: Which bodies and which things participate in this nexus? Which orders of knowledge are expressed in it? Which modes of subjectivation and which affect structures does it contain? It should not be forgotten that traditional objects of social-scientific research – such as organizations, subcultures, the state, capitalism, or globalization – can also be studied as nexuses of "doings."

It can be especially informative to examine under-researched phenomena such as singularities and losses – to name two topics that I have worked on myself – through a praxeological lens. Such an approach can make apparently trivial entities come to life as specific and highly complex processes of "doing." For singularities, this means that they are brought to light as being socially fabricated; they result from acts of "doing singularity," which are carried out in certain practices of observing, evaluating, producing, or receiving the singular. For losses, similarly, this means that they can be viewed as having resulted from an act of "doing loss" and not as practice-independent, "objective" societal entities. To lend them sociological contours, one must therefore ask: In which specific practices are losses experienced and processed? How are they remembered and forgotten? How are they discursively produced and articulated politically?

To conclude this portrait of the theory of social practices, I should stress that, despite the multitude of phenomena that can be studied with its aid, and despite its close relations to empirical research, it provides its own independent social ontology – a specific "world image" of the social. What this consists of can be made clear by comparing it to the images presented by other social ontologies.

They view the social as an agglomeration of the acts of innumerable individuals who, with their own interests and preferences, enter into contracts with one another; or as a system of norms, values, and roles; or as a deep cultural grammar that operates through every act; or as a consequence of economic production and the transformation of nature; or as the totality of communicative acts or language-based interactions. In contrast, the praxeological world image of the social is based on the idea of wide-reaching networks of activities. These activities involve bodies, things, knowledge, and the processes associated with them, and they intensify, reproduce, disappear, and are replaced by new activities. It is a world of doing and making and being made; it is a world of repetition and experimental renewal in time, and one of diffusion and contraction in space. It is also a world of mutual affect, a world in which bodies and things of all sorts affect one another. The worlds that are produced here are always cultural and material worlds in a state of becoming. This is also true of the world that modernity has brought about, and it is this world that I would now like to describe more precisely with the help of praxeological tools.

3

The Practice of Modernity

The core assumption of the sociological theory of modernity is that a profound transformation of nearly all complexes of social practices – and thus of society as a whole – began in the Western hemisphere in the eighteenth century and continues to the present day. But what, exactly, is new about modernity? To what extent do the last 250 years – or even the last 500 years, if the early-modern era is included – of European and North American social development represent something structurally different from the 150,000 years before then, during which *Homo sapiens* developed its social world? What worlds have been created by the practice of modernity?

In relatively concrete terms, the transformation from traditional to modern society can be attributed to individual historical processes: the Industrial Revolution and the rise of industrial capitalism, political revolutions and the processes of democratization, technological revolutions and the rise of science, the Enlightenment and secularization, the shifts toward globalization and imperialism, urbanization, and the emergence of nation states. In classic works on the theory of society, however, the definitions of modernity are more abstract: modernity as capitalist society (Marx), as a process of rationalization and of the "activism of world domination" (Weber), as a process defined by the social division of labor (Durkheim) or by functional differentiation (Parsons), as the development of qualitative and quantitative individualism (Simmel).

The achievements of these classic authors and the utility of their methodological instruments are undisputed. They remain valuable resources to this day. In my effort to define modernity, however, I would like to begin on a different footing and emphasize three elementary mechanisms that pertain to structural dynamics.[1] By this point, it would hardly be surprising to state that I understand the theory of society in the sense of "theory-as-tool" as opposed to "theory-as-system," as discussed above. My aim is not to formulate another theory of modernization on the basis of certain premises and abstract definitions, but rather to develop analytical concepts to facilitate, in Jean-François Lyotard's terms, the "re-writing of modernity."[2] In light of my understanding of the theory of society as a tool, moreover, it should also be no surprise that I came to these concepts through my own work on individual aspects of modernity, particularly in my books *Das hybride Subjekt*, *The Invention of Creativity*, and *The Society of Singularities*. Despite their relatively narrow concerns, the concepts that I employed in these books can also be used in a more generalized way to analyze modernity as a whole, as I hope to demonstrate below. To this end, my first step will be to outline the basic mechanisms in question. This outline will then be used as the basis for describing the general progression of modernity's transformation, and for developing an informed understanding of late modernity.

These are the three basic mechanisms of modern societies that form the toolkit for my analysis of modern society in general:

(1) The networks of practices that form modern society are characterized by an essentially never-ending dialectical process of opening and closing the contingency of the social.
(2) The practice of modernity is characterized by a conflict between a social logic of the general and a social logic of the particular. At the same time, it exists in the field of tension between formal rationalization and evaluative–affective culturalization.
(3) The practice of modernity is characterized by a radical temporal regime of novelty, the downside of which is a social dynamic of loss and temporal hybridization.

What these three interrelated basic features share in common is that they are not simply structural principles; instead, they each designate a field of tension. In light of these three fields of tension, we can understand the dynamics and potential conflicts of modernity and examine them in detail. My proposed type of analysis differs fundamentally from that used in traditional sociological theories of modernization. Whereas, there, modernity is made to seem like a linear process of development in which certain structural features become more prominent, the perspective that I espouse here considers modernity, at its core, to be an ongoing event defined by conflicts and contradictions. This perspective opens up the possibility of "re-writing" modernity. The three basic mechanisms can be applied in the same way that I understand the theory of society as a whole. On the one hand, they are the result of a refined synthesis, which is the result of working through empirical knowledge about modernity. On the other hand, they can serve as a theoretical heuristic for individual empirical analyses in the social and cultural sciences, thus forming the basis of an empirical research program. As for their relevance to public debate, these three basic mechanisms do not become "digestible," so to speak, until they are applied to the history of modernity, and particularly to the crises of late modernity.

3.1 Opening and Closing Contingency: A Dialectic without a Telos

A fundamental aspect of modern society, from the beginning and in all its subdivisions, has been its twofold orientation toward contingency: an awareness of the contingency of past or present institutional orders and forms of life, *and* the normative goal – pursued by any genuinely modern social world – of ensuring the long-term possibility of contingency itself. This is in fact what is new about modernity. That individual practices are contingent – that they can be improved or should be replaced – seems to have been inherent to the life of *Homo sapiens* and its forms of socialization from the beginning. What is specifically modern, however, is the idea that entire social orders are up for discussion, that they can be criticized as a whole and replaced by new and presumably better arrangements. On account of this orientation toward contingency, modern societies are no longer "cold societies." They are "hot societies."[3]

The rise of modernity thus goes hand in hand with an elementary *awareness of contingency*. On a basic level, this means that the social world of modernity – its forms of life and institutions – no longer proceeds from the assumption that it is self-evident, natural, eternal, or lacking alternatives. Rather, the assumption is that everything that exists in society could also be different. This applies to norms and values, people and things, but also to affects, time and space, institutional orders such as the law and the economy, and ultimately to society as a whole. The modern "contingency culture" (as Blumenberg called it) is associated with the basic idea that the social world can be shaped, changed, and controlled. In this context, to be contingent is to be open to the possibility of transformation (even revolution); it means being ready for a horizon of possibility to open up and be filled with ever new acts of "doing." Moreover, to be *open* to contingency is to expose the contingency of something that seems to be socially given and to confront it with other possibilities.[4]

In modernity, therefore, the social cannot *not* be contingent. Theoretically (if not always practically), everything is up for debate. Even in the early-modern era, this orientation toward the contingency of entire forms of life and institutional orders manifested itself quite concretely in various areas, for instance in the Reformation and the critique of religion, in political revolutions, in the early-modern natural sciences, and in the dissolution of feudal structures by markets. Being open to contingency and being willing to reshape the social world are thus not empty principles. Rather, it is typically the case that a greater openness to contingency arises whenever the existing institutions and/or forms of life are perceived to be *flawed* or *worthy of critique*. One of the central characteristics of modernity is that the status quo is always seen as being, at the very least, in need of improvement (often, it seems to be in need of a complete overhaul). The assumption that things need to be improved and the imperative to change them are guided by yet another typically modern idea: the idea of progress. Accordingly, there is an expectation that efforts to reconfigure the conditions of society will in fact bring about a continuous or sudden improvement in its structures.

Throughout the history of modernity, expectations for progress have indeed been fulfilled in many areas – from efficiency to emancipation, from prosperity to solidarity. Fundamentally, however, it can be said that the goal of transforming society in the name of progress is ultimately to create a genuinely modern social order, which, *for its part*, will make contingency a permanent feature of the society in question. This is the second level of the aforementioned twofold orientation toward contingency: society should be open to contingency in order to ensure that everything remains contingent. In modern discourses, this abstract goal of preserving contingency is often made more concrete with the semantics of "freedom" or autonomy. Conceptually, however, the opposite of freedom is oppression, and the contingency culture of modernity is ultimately based on this opposition.[5] Modernity's openness to the contingency of the social therefore has a goal, and this goal is to break up an oppressive status quo which is perceived to be flawed and worthy of critique, and to replace it with a status quo that permanently allows for new possibilities. The act of "doing contingency" thus always entails a specific act of "undoing order" – a dissolution of the present order. Every major contingency-enhancing episode in the history of modernity has been based on this pattern, as is clear from the Reformation (against the perceived oppression of Catholic or Orthodox Christianity), Romantic art (against the oppression of classicism), the French Revolution (against the oppression of absolutist rule), the spread of market structures (against the oppression of feudalism), and the Enlightenment (against the oppression of religion and prejudice) – to name just a few prominent examples. Conversely, Protestantism, Romanticism, parliamentary democracy, the market economy, and the Enlightenment – again, to cite just a few examples – all claimed to establish a new order guided by the idea of contingency – that is, an order that ensures the possibility of new opportunities ("freedom").

Therefore, we have not reached and never will reach the end of history. Instead, modern society's orientation toward contingency results in an endless dialectical process that remains ongoing in the twenty-first century. It is a process that oscillates between being open and being closed to contingency; it is a constant process of doing and undoing order, and it characterizes modern institutional structures and forms of life through and through. This process is continuously spurred on by a perceived lack of contingency ("too little freedom, too much oppression"), because society's openness to contingency never lasts forever. At a certain point, a closed attitude toward contingency will always set in, but this will come to an end when old practices are replaced by new ones. The perception that contingency is lacking thus arises from the discrepancy between the actual closing of contingency and the recurring desire for more contingency, between the establishment of order and the critique of this order. In modernity, the closure of contingency, in which new and (allegedly) better and more progressive institutional orders and forms of life emerge and become established on a long-term basis, regularly operates with the mechanisms of cultural *universalization*. The new order – middle-class society, socialism, neoliberalism, the culture of self-actualization or that of sustainability, for instance – should represent a generally valid order that seems to lack any viable alternatives (it seems universal, in other words) and thus conceals its own contingent nature. New orders therefore have the character of hegemonies; they form social and cultural contexts of domination. The process of *making contingency invisible by means of universalization* is thus just as typical of modernity as its openness to contingency.[6]

Of course, the closure of contingency brought about by a new social order is always just a temporary condition. Sooner or later, it will seem – at least from the perspective of some participants – as though it, too, is limiting contingency, and it will therefore be deemed flawed and worthy of critique. Its repressive downside (hegemony) will come into focus and attract attention. In modernity, a firmly embedded feature of the social is its sensitivity to contingency, and it is this sensitivity that motivates critiques of the dominant order. Thus, attempts to open up temporarily closed states of contingency happen again and again: ostensibly undogmatic Protestantism turns out to be morally repressive, parliamentary democracy is less devoted to the "people" than it claims, the liberal bourgeoisie turns out to be philistine, the market economy turns out to be an egotistical system of competition, the Enlightenment shows its (one-sided) rationalistic and Eurocentric face, socialism ends up restricting freedom and being inefficient, the alternative culture proves to be hyper-moralistic, and so on. Modernity is repeatedly driven by such *critical movements* and *innovative efforts*, which put the (perceived) lack of opportunities on the agenda and bring new options into play, be it new practices, new patterns of interpretation, new artifacts, new norms, new affects, or new subject forms. As a result, the temporary closure of contingency is opened up anew, and the game of being open or closed to contingency enters its next round.

From this process arises the structural dynamics of modernity: at all times, it is influenced in one way or another by the conflict of being open or closed to contingency. I have demonstrated this in detail as it pertains to subject cultures and their transformations from the eighteenth century to late modernity,[7] but the same mechanism can also be observed beyond this context. In short, modernity has unfolded in a *mode of ongoing revision*, in an endless dialectical loop consisting of stabilization, destabilization, and the re-establishment of order. This is the mode of a historical *dialectic without a telos*. It has, contrary to what Hegel suggested in his dialectical philosophy of history, no goal and it does not actualize what is "reasonable."[8] The concept of dialectics thus needs to be decoupled from historical-philosophical ideas about teleological development and the eventual resolution of all contradictions. It should be applied instead to the "dialectical" oscillation between open and closed attitudes toward contingency and thus to the ongoing dynamic between critique and the formation of structures.

The dynamic between opening and closing contingency can be observed on the meso-level of the social, for instance in the transformation of individual forms of life or institutions. On the macro-level, it structures the transformation of Western modernity as a whole, from bourgeois modernity to organized industrial modernity up to late modernity. In this light, there is no such thing as one single stable modernity; what constitutes modernity is subject to the self-transformations that take place in the mode of a dialectic without a telos. At the beginning of every phase or version of modern society, there is an attempt to open up contingency by critiquing the status quo, which is denounced for being insufficiently modern. This is followed by the (often hard-fought) establishment of new structures, until a new hegemony is formed by closing off contingency and universalizing itself. This hegemony then provokes new critique, and so on, ad infinitum. In other words, the idea that modernity will at some point reach its final form is, from this perspective, a contradiction in itself. There can be no *posthistoire* – no "end of history" – within the framework of modernity's contingency culture.[9]

3.2 The Radicalization of Worldmaking

The dialectic of opening and closing contingency is an abstract mechanism that raises the question of its concrete orientation. If, in principle, modern society treats all orders of the social world as contingent, how does it organize these orders? Modernity's tendencies in this respect have been discussed at length. Niklas Luhmann, for instance, has pointed to the formation of a modern logic of functionally differentiated fields (politics, the economy, family, etc.), and Bruno Latour has written about the plurality of modern "modes of existence" (technology, fiction, habits, etc.). Luc Boltanski and Laurent Thévenot have discussed the variety of modern "orders of justification" (the civic polity, the industrial polity, the inspiration polity, etc.).[10] It can certainly be informative (and persuasive) to break down the plurality of social worlds that characterize modern society.[11] However, I would like to emphasize two fundamental fields of tensions that pertain to modern "world-making" and intersect this plurality: two pairs of radically opposed practices of contingency management (or, I should say, two opposed complexes of practices) that characterize modern society as a whole. The first opposition is between a social logic of the general ("doing generality") and a social logic of the particular ("doing singularity"); the second opposition is between the rationalization of the social ("doing rationality") and the culturalization and valorization of the social ("doing value"). These two oppositional pairs are very often (but not always) coupled with one another: "doing generality" is often intertwined with "doing rationality," while "doing singularity" often goes hand in hand with "doing value." These oppositions provide an analytical framework for my theory of modernity.[12]

Modern society is a society of extremes. Unlike traditional societies, it radically rearranges the social world in contrary ways. One of these ways or orientations is "doing generality." In modern networks of practices, efforts are constantly being made to form objects, subjects, spatial and temporal entities, and collectives in such a way that they conform to generally valid (or even universal, if possible) rules and standards. This radical rearrangement of the social according to a social logic of generality usually involves the equally radical (and just as typical) modern process of formal rationalization, that is, the process of orienting practices toward norms of purposeful or social rationality.

From the beginning of modernity, however, there have been other (equally radical) forms of rearranging the social that are in opposition to "doing generality" and "doing rationality." In an anti-generalizing practice, objects, subjects, spatial and temporal entities, and collectives can be shaped in such a way that they are transformed into something particular, unique, and singular. In this case, they do not at all seem to be generalizable, interchangeable, and comparable, but are instead experienced and developed with their own "individual" (in the broadest sense of the word) inherent complexity. This social logic of the particular, with its processes of singularization ("doing singularity"), is often closely connected with what can be understood as an oppositional process to rationalization: the process of culturalizing the social, in which the elements of the social world are not ascribed any instrumental use or function, but rather an independent value of their own. The result of this "doing value," as the term implies, is a valorization of the social. Unlike the sphere of formal rationality, that of culture in the strict sense is a sphere in which values circulate. Rationalization and culturalization have contrasting affect structures. Whereas the former, which is based on objectivity, reduces affects, the latter intensifies them.

In general, modern society can only be understood as a *dual structure* defined by *tensions*: between processes of rationalization *and* processes of culturalization, between systems of functionality *and* spheres driven by values, between the dynamics of objectivity *and* those that intensify affect. Moreover, it can only be understood in light of the conflict between "doing generality" and "doing singularity." Sociology's widespread and familiar narrative of rationalization, which has often been invoked to explain the development of modern society and which can take the guise of a narrative of capitalization, technologization, or differentiation, is thus clearly in need of a correction. For equally important are the formational dimensions of culturalization and singularization, and thus the conflicted nature of the ways in which modernity has been created. Modernity is more than a rationalization machine; it is also a venue in which the social is radically culturalized – aestheticized, narrativized, ethicized, ludified, etc. It forms a space in which affects are intensified, and intrinsic value is ascribed or denied. At the same time, modernity is also a venue for processes of radical singularization – that is, for processes oriented toward producing unique entities. This second logic has accompanied modernity from the beginning, though over the course of its historical transformation there have been different and sometimes surprising ratios between the general and the particular, as well as between rationality and culture. These different mixtures and proportions are in fact a defining feature of any given version of modernity.

Without a doubt, "doing generality" is the primary social logic of modernity, but before I take a closer look at how it operates, I would first like to explain what I mean by "social logic." Social logic is what, in a fundamental way, "formats" social practice in a particular manner. It influences all entities or elements of the social that can become an object of "doings." To be more precise, any given social logic is directed toward five entities of the social: first toward objects or things, second toward subjects, third toward spatial entities, fourth toward temporal entities, and fifth toward collectives. In addition, social logic involves four different sorts of formatting practices, or practices of worldmaking: first, practices of evaluation; second, practices of observation or interpretation; third, practices of production; and fourth, practices of appropriation and reception. All the aforementioned elements of the social are formed in these types of practices.

It perhaps goes without saying that "doing generality" also affects all five aforementioned elements of the social, transforms them, and rearranges them by means of the four aforementioned types of practices. In the social logic of the general, objects and things are turned into standardized industrial goods, and subjects are transformed into players of formal roles and are attributed general and equal rights; spatial entities are transformed into uniform apartment buildings and industrial cities; temporal formats become standardized bureaucratic apparatuses; and modern collectives, under this logic, take on the qualities of formal–rational organizations. In the mode of "doing generality," all four of the aforementioned practices work toward "generalizing" the world. The latter is *observed* with generalizing intentions – traditionally, for instance, in the natural sciences and in the way that technology is related to the world. It is *evaluated* with normative and general standards – with respect to fulfilling the expectations of formal roles in the working world or in the eyes of the law, for example. The world is *produced* with the goal of standardization – the prototypical "creations" in this regard are industrially produced goods, but disciplined pupils in standardized school systems count as well. Finally, the world is *appropriated* as an ensemble of generalities, as is clear from the unemotional ways in which people deal with their roles in life or engage with technical objects.

In modernity, the social logic of the general is usually – if not always, as we will see below – connected with the process of formally rationalizing the social, as traditionally described by Max Weber.[13] Of course, rationalization itself must be understood as an ongoing act of making the individual elements of the social rational (as a permanent act of "doing rationality"). In the mode of rationalization, this is not regarded as an end in itself but rather as the means to an end. The goal of rationalization is optimization, so as to ensure that rationalization will take place on a technical level (in the production of goods, for example), on the cognitive level (in the sciences, for instance), and on the normative level (as in the formalization of the law and its ability to protect individual rights). On all of these levels – on that of the state, the economy, science, the lifeworld, etc. – regimes of rationality are established.

Fundamentally, it can be said that rationalization and the logic of the general are a response to the problem of scarcity and to the problem of establishing order in society. How can the social be formed so as to optimize the accumulation of resources? And how can it be formed so as to broaden the scope of possible actions while ensuring that these actions are coordinated with as little friction as possible? As a practice of modernity, "doing generality" seeks to deal with its inherent contingency by increasing efficiency and securing social order. For those alive during the early stages of modernity around the year 1800, it often came as a shock – or was felt as an emancipatory experience – to realize the great extent to which the practice of modernity strove to make all elements of the social either *identical* or *comparable*, aimed to subject them to the same standards, and endeavored to subject them to a rational and transparent structure. In the longer term, in fact, modern society turned out to be a veritable generalization machine: with increasing industrialization, juridification, urbanization, democratization, and bureaucratization. Throughout the entire history of modernity, "doing generality" and "doing rationality" have been present and always influential in new ways.[14]

That said, the processes of formal rationalization and "doing generality" are by no means as all-encompassing as they might seem at first glance. In fact, they are slowed or interrupted now and again by critical efforts, which give rise to alternatives. This, too, is true of the entire history of modernity. The social logic of the general has been challenged especially a rivaling manner of creating the social world: by the logic of the particular. The latter is often associated with the culturalization of the social (with "doing value"). By neglecting the conflict between these two social logics, one comes away with a partial understanding of modernity. This occurs quite often in theories that understand modernization as a seamless process of rationalization and thus operate with a rationalistic bias.

In order to leave behind this half-formed model of modernity, it is necessary to recognize the central conflict between the social logic of the general and the social logic of the particular, and it is necessary to recognize the conflict between rationalization and culturalization. Briefly, it can be stated that an *ongoing conflict between rationalism and Romanticism* has been at play throughout modernity.[15] For, in fact, the cultural movement of Romanticism around the year 1800 can be interpreted as the first radical expression of "doing singularity" and "doing value." Viewed historically, moreover, Romanticism's radical logic of singularity was clearly a *response* to the radicality of the logic of generalization.

The processes of singularization, however, go beyond this special historical context and are more abstractly constructed. In general, whereas the norm of "doing generality" is an efficiently organized, optimized, legally emancipated, and rational world, the ideal of "doing singularity" refers to a world of particularities – that is, to entities that are not to be understood as exemplifications of general rules but, rather, defy these very rules on account of their inherent complexity. Singularities seem valuable and positive (in an affective respect). There are not only gradual differences between them but also absolute differences. This is not a matter of rationality, predictability, efficiency, and optimality, but rather one of personal and collective identity, intrinsic value, lived experience, and intense affectivity.

"Doing singularity," too, involves a *social* logic in the sense described above. It, too, is engaged in the social *fabrication* of objects and subjects, spatial and temporal entities, and collectives by means of the practices of evaluation, observation, appropriation, and production. In this case, however, it is not oriented toward the general, but rather toward the particular. In the social logic of the particular, furthermore, the elements of the social are also radically rearranged. Thus, from a praxeological perspective, singularities do not objectively exist any more than "general" entities do; rather, they become singular within the framework of a particular manner of fabricating social practices. This applies to all five elements of the social. Under the logic of the singular, things and objects are not perceived to be interchangeable (whether works of art, religious doctrines, or brands); subjects become visible in their unique individuality, which can be evaluated positively and even come to be coveted (think of loved ones, stars, or charismatic leaders); spaces are appreciated for their uniqueness (cities, landscapes, extraordinary buildings, for instance); via singularization, temporal entities become occasions, events, and special moments; and even collectives can be singularized by means of some of their features and then become (small or large) communities with a unique identity of their own. This rearrangement of the social into a world of singularities takes place in the nexus of the four types of practices named above. The practice of evaluation, for instance, distinguishes what is original from what is typical (whether in art criticism or on Instagram), or it can distinguish an authentic politician from an inauthentic one. Through practices of observation, people develop the ability to differentiate the complexity and special features of, say, a city or a natural landscape. The intentional production of singularities can also take place, for instance in the form of consciously creating and staging singular places, events, things, or subjects. Finally, singularities correspond to a form of appropriation that differs from the practical sort, an example of which could be an emotional and intensive lived experience.

I have already pointed out that the spread of the social logic of the particular is typically accompanied by a process of culturalization and the intensification of affects. In the strong sense of the term, *culture* denotes the opposite of (formal) *rationality*.[16] In the course of what can be called culturalization, the five entities of the social are not treated as means to an end but rather as inherently valuable elements – as something that seems *valuable* in and of itself. This is how "doing value" is enacted in the sphere of culture. This fabricated cultural value can involve a variety of different qualities. It can be a matter of aesthetic value, but it can also be a matter of ethical, narrative, ludic, or creative value. In processes of culturalization, the social is aestheticized, ethicized, narrativized, etc. In the sphere of culture, factors such as authenticity and attractiveness are the guiding criteria, and such criteria cannot be met rationalistically.

The central point is that singular–cultural entities exert a strong affective appeal; they are part of a complex logic of affect. Fascinating individuals and brands, loved ones and idols, works

Practices of worldmaking / Elements of the social	Observation	Evaluation	Production	Appropriation
Objects				
Subjects				
Spatialities	"Doing generality" / "Doing singularity"			
Temporalities				
Collectives				

Figure I.1 Elements and practices of the social

of art and communities, natural landscapes and images, but also enemies and objects of revulsion and disgust – they all circulate in a cultural logic of affects and settle in a non-rational space, which, contrary to what the rationalistic bias of many studies might suggest, is also a special characteristic of modernity. Modernity, in other words, only appears to be fully rational and unemotional. Cultural singularities represent the (mostly positive, but partially also negative) sources of fascination in society. Without them, modernity would be an emotionally neutral, smooth, and well-oiled rationality machine, which is something that it has never been. The impetus behind processes of culturalization is thus different from that which drives rationalization. Whereas the latter, as mentioned above, is concerned with solving problems of scarcity and social order, processes of culturalization are a response to modern society's problems of meaning, identity, and motivation – to the problems, in other words, of who subjects are, what they can identify with, and who they want to be. This is true in general of human societies, the dynamics of which are never fueled by formal rationality alone, but also by the cultural sphere. To borrow the dualistic terminology of Weber and Durkheim, societies receive their primary motivation not from formalized rationality but from their own logic of values and the valuable (from "value-rational action"). This motivation, in other words, does not come from the sphere of the "profane," with its cool factual orderliness, but rather from the affect-laden sphere of the "sacred."[17]

The logic of singularization and culture has its own potentially conflicting dynamic. Far from being free of clashes and contradictions, it is in fact highly explosive (to put it metaphorically). For, in the sphere of culture, value is not only assigned; value is also *denied*. The positive affects of fascination are opposed by the negative affects of rejection. One could say that, in the sphere of culture, some people gain an identity while others lose it or feel threatened by the identity of others; valuation and devaluation go hand in hand. This immanent dynamic of singularities, values, and affects contributes to the conflict between "doing singularity" and "doing generality." Throughout the history of modernity, the relation between the logic of standardization and the logic of singularization has been modeled in different ways. Historically, it is an open question whether rationalization expands at the expense of culturalization or vice versa; whether the two logics are antagonistic or, in fact, complementary to one another. Regardless, "doing singularity" and "doing value" (like their rationalistic antipode) pervade the entire world of the social – that is, all institutional structures and forms of life. Of course, they are especially clear to see in the realms of art and religion, but the aestheticization, narrativization, and ethicization of the social also take place in politics and the economy. These sectors, too, involve promises of singularity and shifts toward culturalization (for instance on the level of collective identities), and they also involve conflicts of valorization (in the aestheticization of consumption and the working world, for example).

Whereas my book *The Society of Singularities* investigates the specific form that the social logic of singularization has adopted in today's late modernity, the focus of my books *Das hybride Subjekt* and *The Invention of Creativity* lies instead on culturalization, and especially on aestheticization, in the history of modernity since its beginnings. With an analytic toolkit that includes the conceptual pairs "doing generality" and "doing singularity" as well as "doing rationality" and "doing value," however, it is possible to go beyond these cases and examine additional aspects of the transformation of modern societies. The toolkit gains a degree of complexity when one realizes that these two conceptual pairs are not strictly coupled together but can occasionally intersect with one another. For, in fact, it should be asked whether "doing generality" is necessarily coupled with "doing rationality," and whether "doing singularity" is necessarily associated with "doing value." These admittedly seem to be the most common and preferred combinations in modern society. The two other logically possible combinations are indeed rare, but they do happen and are interesting in their own way.[18]

Let us look first at the possible intertwinement of singularization and rationalization. In late-modern society, in particular, there are practices in which an orientation toward uniqueness and particularity is not associated with value and affectivity, but rather with rational and purposive programs. These are formal–rational processes that are oriented toward the fabrication of singularities because the latter seem to be "useful." Such is the case, for instance, with the so-called "personalization" of the Internet by means of algorithms, with the production of unique goods by means of 3D printers, or with the singularization of medical treatments by means of individual genome analyses. One could call these examples of "automated singularization."[19] Here, processes of singularization extend so far as to be coupled with processes of rationalization.

In the history of modernity, however, there has also been a fourth logical possibility – namely, a connection between valorization and generalization (between "doing value" and "doing generality"). That which is valuable, in other words, does not necessarily have to be singular, even though this post-Romantic constellation remains especially effective. Under certain circumstances, even the general can be regarded as valuable and can shift, as it were, from the sphere of the profane into the sphere of the sacred. So it is with the culture of the Enlightenment and its universalization of human dignity. Here, subjects are not perceived primarily as being different but, rather, as being equal, and "human beings" are regarded as valuable in and of themselves. In this case, one can speak of a culture of the general in which a cultural act of "doing universality" takes place. The universal can thus appear as a locus of value and can give rise to a universalistic culture that warrants unconditional ethical respect. A clear example of this is the culture of human rights that emerged in the twentieth century.[20]

3.3 Paradoxical temporality

Modern society is characterized by a temporal regime with three main components that coexist in a state of tension: the regime of novelty, increased feelings of loss, and temporal hybridization. Whereas the social regime of novelty is oriented toward the present and the future, the dynamics of loss and temporal hybridization are each concerned in their own specific way with ensuring that the past remains present in the practice of modernity.

In general, the temporal structure of modernity is based on a clear distinction between the past, the present, and the future. In light of the modern imperative for progress, the normal condition of temporality appears to involve not the reproduction of the same from the past into the future – that is, what one could call "tradition" – but, rather, social change. According to this norm, this will ideally be a change for the better; the blueprint for change in modern society is progress. Thus, in the way that it influences social practices in institutions and forms of life, modern temporality fundamentally has the form of what could be called a *social regime of novelty*, an arrangement of social temporality according to the norm of newness.[21] What is rewarded in this regime is not, as was the case in earlier societies, traditional practices, norms, bodies of knowledge (etc.), but rather the new – that which differs from and surpasses whatever has been established. In the modern imaginary, the old

	"Doing generality"	"Doing singularity"
"Doing rationality"	**Formal rationalization**	Automated singularizations
"Doing value"	Cultures of the general	**Culturalization as singularization**

Figure I.2 A four-field matrix of social logics in modernity, with special emphasis on the two dominant forms

should be deliberately suppressed until it goes away, while the new is associated with progress and must prevail, even disruptively if necessary. This is the modern model of "creative destruction" (as Schumpeter called it). As a result of this orientation toward novelty, the modern temporal regime typically turns its back on the past and looks instead at the present and toward the future. For this reason, practices that intensify the present are just as characteristic of modernity as those that deal with the future (in a prognostic or imaginative way, for instance).

The regime of novelty has not only manifested itself in discursive practices, such as the narratives of progress that have accompanied modernity since the "saddle era" around 1770. It has also characterized the majority of modernity's institutional structures – from the capitalist economy's orientation toward innovation to the orientation toward progress in science and technology, from the logic of shock and novelty underlying modern art to the media's orientation toward what is new – not to mention modern politics, which is always oriented toward new reforms (or even revolutions). Finally, forms of life are also dictated by the regime of novelty, given that they follow the imperatives of self-optimization and self-development. The preference for the new over the old can take various forms. Here, one can distinguish between a regime of *finite* perfectibility, according to which it seems possible to achieve a perfect state of affairs at a certain point in time, after which no further development will be needed (this could be called the novelty of perfection), and a regime of *infinite* perfectibility, which assumes that an ongoing succession of innovations will lead, without end, to something qualitatively or quantitatively better (this could be called the novelty of innovation). In addition, there is also a regime of infinite surprise, in which the new is always prized for providing constantly novel variations and the ongoing stimulus of novelty for its own sake (cultural and aesthetic novelty). Depending on its form, the regime of novelty can thus be associated with the social logic of the general and the social logic of the particular. Throughout the history of modernity, these three forms of the regime of novelty have had varying degrees of relevance; in fact, the different versions of modernity can be distinguished in terms of the understandings of novelty – and the orientations toward the present and/or future – that happened to be dominant at the time.[22]

This clear orientation toward the regime of novelty and its progressiveness, however, has a flip side: the modern dynamic of loss, which consists of mechanisms for increasing loss, repressing loss, and processing loss.[23] Theories of modernization (and progressivism in general) systematically ignore this dynamic, but it is impossible to understand modernity and its social conflicts without it. Now, I am not saying that theories of society have failed to take into account the normative or cultural-critical phenomenon of loss (alienation, disenchantment, etc.). My argument is, rather, that modern society *as such* has been propelled not only by a dynamic of progress but also by a dynamic of loss, and indeed that it is haunted by the fear, rage, and trauma caused by loss. This dynamic should thus occupy a central position in any analysis of modernity.

Loss refers to the disappearance of conditions or phenomena in the social world that are not quickly forgotten, but rather remain in focus. Losses are typically regarded as negative because of the emotional connection (identification, possession, etc.) that we have to what has been lost. Grief, in the broadest sense, is the emotion most often associated with loss, but it can involve other feelings as well, such as fear, anger, or shame. The experience of loss can be related to specific events or states of affairs (the death of a loved one, the end of a friendship, the destruction of things), or it can be related to abstract conditions (the loss of status, power, meaning, community, or control). Positive expectations can also be thwarted (a future loss), and an imminent loss can be anticipated (the fear of loss). What is important is that something does not objectively (so to speak) become a loss by disappearing. Such a disappearance can only become a loss through its negative interpretation and effect – that is, via the subjective or social *experience* of loss.

The dynamic of loss confronts modernity with a fundamental paradox. In that modern society is driven by a regime of novelty and progress, it increases the probability of experiencing loss. At the same time, however, it offers hardly any meaningful instruments for dealing with these losses. Modernity's tendency to increase feelings of loss, on the one hand, is opposed, on the other hand, by the tendency to deny these feelings. In modern society, the probability of experiencing loss is so high precisely *because* this society is fueled by a regime of novelty and progress. By devaluing the old, modern society increases the risk that its corresponding disappearance will be experienced as loss. Throughout the history of modernity, there have thus always been new groups of "losers" – that is, people who experience loss.

Loss introduces negativity into the social world, which, driven as it is by the idea of progress, makes no room for it whatsoever. Within the framework of the dominant regime of novelty, in fact, losses have no legitimate place and no possibility of expression. That which has disappeared is simply regarded as obsolete, as something to be forgotten. Modernity is therefore inclined to suppress or deny feelings of loss in a systematic way, so as to make them seem illegitimate. Nevertheless, there have been various ways of processing loss in modernity. There exists a social logic of "doing loss," and it manifests itself in forms of (rationally planned) loss prevention or legal loss restitution, but also in the form of narrative techniques of loss processing, such as mourning or cultural critique; nostalgia, too, is a way of "doing loss," and of course there is also the struggle of victims and "losers" to have their losses recognized by society. The point of all these forms of "doing loss" is that they are all ways of dealing with the emotional intensity of experiences of loss.

The dynamic of loss complicates modernity's temporal structure, but it also complicates modernity's structures of affect and experience. From this dynamic of loss, it becomes clear that, in the modern social world (and despite its insistence on "looking ahead"), the past is kept present in such a way that is neither completely past and forgotten nor handed down as tradition. Rather, it remains present in the social dynamic, which it haunts, in the form of unintended effects and unpredictable reappropriations. This effect, which in many respects counteracts the regime of novelty, applies in a different way to a third context that is central to modern temporality: temporal hybridization.[24] In this regard, my central assumption is that the entire process of so-called "modernization" does not consist of self-contained stages of structural change that make a clean break from the past without preserving any of history's "residue," so to speak. Even the transition from traditional society to modern society was not a "clean cut," and something similar can be said of the transitions between the different versions of modernity itself, despite its overall orientation toward novelty. In contrast to the idea of strict discontinuities, I therefore presume that practices and orders of knowledge that originated from *different* historical eras have been combined with one another and reappropriated at various points in modernity.

It is not sociocultural "purity" – that is, self-containment, homogeneity, and a lack of structural contradictions – but, rather, *hybridity* that is thus a characteristic feature of modern forms of life and institutions.[25] Used praxeologically, the term *hybridization* denotes the combination and mixture of different and in part contradictory practices, forms of knowledge, norms, subject forms, and affectivities with a form of life or an institutional complex. Hybridizations can result from processes of spatial or material–social transgressions, but they can also emerge from transgressions across historical thresholds. This means that, by way of reappropriation, different historical layers can be deposited in present phenomena, with which they interact in unpredictable ways.

There are two reasons why modernity is predisposed to such temporal hybridizations. First, because of its media technology, modernity has been able to keep large parts of the past present (especially from its own history), including practices, subject forms, forms of knowledge, objects, images, sounds, and gestures. All these elements therefore remain available for future sociocultural appropriation, even after long periods of latency. Modern media technologies thus counteract society's efforts to forget the past. Second, the unrelenting processes of opening and closing contingency, the regime of novelty, and the dynamic of loss lead to the active appropriation of the past in the present, or cause the past to influence the present in passive ways. In situations where contingency is being opened up, historical heritage can serve as a critical resource for addressing perceived flaws in society. The regime of novelty paradoxically relies much on the past, which is often reappropriated to make something new. Finally, experiences of loss involve an ongoing reappropriation of the past.

In these ways, elements from various historical periods are regularly drawn upon and inserted into the present social practices of modern institutions and forms of life; indeed, the longer modernity lasts, the more cultural material is available as a historical resource to be reappropriated, or not. To cite a few examples: Even the early stage of bourgeois modernity was not a complete restart – rather, it appropriated elements from aristocratic culture and from Protestant Christianity. The late-modern lifestyle of the new middle class at the beginning of the twenty-first century draws upon elements from the classical bourgeoisie as well as elements from early Romanticism. The democratic systems after the French Revolution borrowed their ideas of statehood from the *Ancien Régime*, while today's late-modern political systems borrow bureaucratic structures from the nineteenth century, reappropriate populist models from the 1920s, or take inspiration from the emancipation movements of the 1960s. In my view, it would therefore be a misstep to focus exclusively on the regime of novelty when analyzing modernity. To do so would be to reveal only half the truth (the "official" truth), because modern society, owing to temporal hybridization and the dynamic of loss, proves to be oriented toward the past to an extent that defies the narratives of most theories of modernization, which tend to discuss modernity in terms of progress alone.

We have seen that the modern mode of worldmaking takes place as a dialectical process of opening and closing contingency that unfolds in a field of tension. One source of tension is the tug of war between "doing generality" and "doing singularity," while another source is created by the coexistence of a temporal regime of novelty, a dynamic of loss, and temporal hybridization. These observations form the basis of a way to analyze modernity that could be called post-modernization theory. In contrast to the claims made in classical sociological theories of modernization[26] – with their focus on key concepts such as formal rationalization, the dynamics of progress, discontinuity, and *posthistoire* – it allows modernity to be seen as an arena of conflict: between rationalization and culturalization, generalization and singularization, hegemony and critique, all within a field of tension torn between novelty, processing loss, and appropriating the past. Such a post-modernization theory of modernity can be used as a research program for empirical analysis in the social and cultural sciences. According to this perspective, modern society does not follow a logic of development, but rather a logic of antagonism or "agonality."

4

The Theory of Society at Work: From Bourgeois and Industrial Modernity to Late Modernity

The general structural features of modernity provide a blueprint for tracing the transformation of modern society from the eighteenth century to the present. In this respect, it is necessary to keep one's distance from two extreme views: from the idea that there is one monolithic modernity, on the one hand, and, on the other hand, the observation that modernity consists of a multiplicity of historical events without any common threads. The task at hand is, rather, to identify the long-term processes that have changed the constitution of modern society. Three historically sequential versions of modernity are brought to light in this way: first, bourgeois modernity, which emerged in Europe during the second half of the eighteenth century as a reaction to traditional, feudal, religious, and aristocratic society, and which became dominant over the course of the nineteenth century; second, industrial or organized modernity, which replaced bourgeois modernity during the early decades of the twentieth century in Europe, North America, and the Soviet Union; third, and finally, the latest version of modernity, which has been developing since the 1980s and can conveniently be called late modernity (or postmodernity, as other authors prefer).[1] The goal of the theory of society should be to ascertain the defining features of the economy, the social structure, the state, the technologies, and the culture of subjectivation in each version of modernity, in order to situate these social formations within the context of the general structures of modernity outlined above.

4.1 Bourgeois Modernity

Bourgeois modernity first arose in Europe. Economically, it spurred the shift from merchant capitalism to industrial capitalism, which gradually displaced the feudal agrarian economy. In terms of its social structure, it coincided with the rise of the bourgeoisie as the ruling class (over the aristocracy), though over time the bourgeoisie would be confronted by the urban industrial proletariat as a social counterforce. On the technological level, the scientific and technical revolutions during the early stages of industrialization provided the material preconditions for this social formation, while the media technology of the printing press provided the background for bourgeois textual culture. With respect to the state and politics, bourgeois modernity established parliamentary democracies, which were governed by the bourgeoisie itself and were thus socially exclusive. This led to the formation of the bourgeois nation state, which (inwardly) entailed a defensive and liberal understanding of statehood while (outwardly) encouraging imperialist expansion in the form of colonialism.

The culture of this version of modernity was steered by the subject culture of the bourgeoisie. Here, a culture of independence, self-responsibility, and sovereign self-control was combined with the cultural models of morality, duty, and self-discipline. This was a culture of morally and individualistically oriented rationalism. It became increasingly secular, and yet it was also challenged by the counterculture of Romanticism – with its ideas of singularity, which pertained to the individual as well as to the collective (peoples and nations). At the same time, the model for the culture of bourgeois modernity was a universalistic, humanistic, social (but very exclusive) culture of the general; it was a culture of education in which the medium of textuality played a defining role. The level of life conduct involved a cultural hybridization with resources from pre-modern culture. Secularization aside, the legacy of Christianity influenced ideas of morality and self-discipline, while the legacy of the aristocracy influenced the ideals of sovereign self-governance.

Bourgeois modernity *opened up* contingency in a historically unprecedented manner that altered all aspects of European (and, later, North American) societies and proved fatal to the feudal, clerical, and aristocratic order of the "old world." It affected politics, the economy, religion, law, science, and – last, but not least – the way in which post-traditional life was conducted. The political revolutions of the time (the French and American Revolutions) can be interpreted as eventful culminations of this open attitude to social contingency. The latter can be associated with the normative standard of progress that characterized bourgeois modernity. This imperative of progress corresponded to the institutionalization of a social regime of novelty. In certain areas of life, this regime was oriented toward the finite novelty of perfection, while in others it was oriented toward the infinite novelty of innovation. The contingency that had opened up against feudalism was ultimately *closed* in a specific way by the bourgeois hegemony. Bourgeois modernity contained the promise of guaranteeing autonomy, but only in a bourgeois form. This new hegemony, however, was soon confronted by critical movements that pointed out its flaws, accused it of being insufficiently modern, and attempted to break open the contingency that it had closed off. Two critical orientations should be mentioned here. In terms of its political economy, bourgeois modernity seemed incapable of dealing with the glaring social inequality that manifested itself in the class conflict between the bourgeoisie and the proletariat. This is the socialist critique. Culturally, bourgeois modernity, with its relatively rigid morality and its rationalism, seemed repressive and alienating, and was charged with stifling individual development. This is the counter-cultural critique, as expressed by Romanticism and the avant-garde.

The particular structure of bourgeois modernity becomes clear from the social logics that were at play in it. In the areas of the capitalist economy, science, and the state, bourgeois modernity ushered forth a surge of formal rationalization. It was committed to "doing generality" on a large scale, especially in capitalist-industrial enterprise, in the bureaucracy of the nation state, and in the institutionalized sciences. In this earliest version of modernity, however, the processes of rationalization were not ubiquitous, because the traditional–agrarian and feudal–religious communality continued to exist to a considerable extent until the beginning of the twentieth century. One could therefore say that the process of rationalization was partial or incomplete during its bourgeois version. At the same time, the gradual erosion of pre-modern traditions was the source of numerous experiences of loss in society – experiences that contradicted all the promises of progress. The loss of community, religion, hometowns, morality, and nature were characteristic themes of social grief. These experiences of loss gave rise to additional – conservative and progressive – forms of critique.

This pervasive yet still limited rationalization took place alongside a characteristically bourgeois form of culturalization. As the aristocratic and clerical culture gradually waned in significance, culture began to adopt the form of the bourgeois cultural sphere, a bourgeois form of high culture that secularized the sacred. At its heart stood the idea of "art as religion." What crystalized in the culture of bourgeois modernity were the enduringly influential structures of a social sphere in which the public, the producers of culture, and singular works of art were forced to confront one another. Producers of culture and their products, in other words, were forced to compete for the attention and esteem of the public.

In bourgeois modernity, the shift toward rationalization, with its radical social logic of the general, was challenged from the beginning by an equally radical social logic of singularization, which emerged from within the bourgeois world itself and turned against it. Romanticism was the "seed-bed culture" (in Parsons's terms) that incubated the radical singularism of individuals, things, places, events, and communities. At the same time, Romantic practices and discourses formed the emotional center of early modernity. Along with other aesthetic subcultures, the field of art provided the institutional space for such a social logic of the particular. Here one finds the first approaches toward formulating a creativity *dispositif*, a regime of aesthetic novelty. Singularism also had effects in the political sphere, especially in the form of nationalism. Within the framework of bourgeois modernity, the social logic of the particular characterized all facets of a legitimate counterculture. It was directed against the prevailing rationalistic model of organizing society, and it challenged this model critically. At the same time, however, this was a *recognized* counterculture that to a certain extent succeeded in influencing bourgeois culture with the ideas of Romantic love, art as a religion, and national consciousness.

Despite facing increasingly severe political and aesthetic criticism, bourgeois modernity was able to maintain its basic structures until the beginning of the twentieth century. Then, over the course of just a few decades, it transformed into a new version of modernity: industrial or organized modernity.

4.2 Industrial Modernity

Industrial or organized modernity, which became dominant in the 1920s and maintained this dominance for nearly 60 years, was based on a mature industrial economy that influenced all of society. In the Western hemisphere, this took the form of industrial capitalism (which, at the same time, was a form of organized capitalism), while in the Eastern hemisphere it took the shape of industrial socialism. What emerged was an economy of bureaucratic corporations. At the same time, the defining economic model was Fordism, which coupled mass production with mass consumption. In terms of its social structure, this phase of modernity eroded the dualism between the bourgeoisie and the proletariat, and replaced it with the comparatively egalitarian and homogeneous structure of a leveled middle-class society. Technologically, industrial modernity was characterized by a further shift toward industrialization that affected the economy and daily life of society as a whole (electrification, automobiles, etc.). In terms of media technology, new mass media (film and radio at first, television later) provided the background for the development of a mass society. On the level of the state and politics, bourgeois parliamentary democracies transformed into mass democracies with mass political parties. The state took on an active controlling role in the economy and in society, and it institutionalized – after a series of elementary crises – a welfare state. In its socialist and fascist instantiations of industrial modernity, the state tilted toward authoritarianism and, in part, totalitarianism. In general, the phase of industrial modernity was characterized by the emerging and then solidifying polarity between the United States and the Soviet Union (the "first world" and the "second world"); at the same time, decolonization was also taking place, and this gave rise to the so-called "third world."

In its Western version, which was led by the United States, the culture of organized–industrial modernity gained its most prominent form in the subject culture and lifestyle of the employee. A culture based on a strong concept of the social, on the collective, and on the social adaptation of an "other-directed subject" (as Riesman called it) was linked to the urban consumer aesthetic of a mass culture that responded to the stimuli of aesthetic superficialities. The social ethos of a strong collective was thus combined in a contradictory way with modernism's "aesthetics of perfect form," and the result was a matter-of-fact, unemotional culture in which even the functionality of technology was transformed into a cultural ideal. Aesthetic countercultures that were originally anti-bourgeois also played a part in shaping this functionalistic rationalism.

In relation to bourgeois modernity, which now seemed obsolete, organized–industrial modernity marked a new shift toward opening up contingency. This, in effect, shattered the old European bourgeois society, a shattering that found its symbolic and material expression to the east and to the west of the center of Europe: in the October Revolution in Russia, on the one hand; and, on the other, in the rise of Americanism – that is, the development of a mass American-style culture in North American cities. During this anti-bourgeois opening of contingency, modernity took on a new form. Industrial–organized modernity was a society of organized masses and a "society of equals" (as Rosanvallon called it) that, in a historically unique way, aimed to control and technologize society while creating an environment of comprehensive social inclusion. In this way, it promised to provide a modern lifestyle for everyone.

Industrial modernity, however, soon became hegemonic itself. With its ideal of conformist white-collar (or blue-collar) existence, which closed off contingency, it was not long before it was, in turn, faced with critical movements of the political-economic and cultural sort. By the 1980s at the latest, which saw the rise of neoliberalism in the West and perestroika in the East, industrial modernity was confronted with the consequences of its social overregulation. Culturally, with the eventful year of 1968 in Paris and Prague, it was challenged by critiques of conformism and the limitation of personal freedom. In the collapse of state socialism – and thus the Eastern branch of industrial modernity, which relied heavily on government regulation – the political, economic, and cultural critiques converged.

These immanent tensions manifested themselves on the level of social logic. Above all, the social logic of the general reached its historically unprecedented peak in industrial modernity. This society was based on the ascent of formal rationalization in all areas of life, from the economy and the sciences to the state and the post-bourgeois lifestyle. It was characterized by total rationalization and mobilization, and this gave rise to a society of equality and uniformity, which, as a downside (or, depending on one's interpretation, a dubious high point), also included the systematic annihilation of people in war and genocide.[2] On the one hand, this thoroughly rationalized society reduced the individual risk of loss and failure by establishing the welfare state. At the same time and to a considerable extent, however, it also produced new experiences of loss. The loss of bourgeois individualism through the rise of mass culture, and the traumatic consequences of modernity's history of violence, which both peaked in this period, are the two central sources of loss during this version of modernity. At the same time, industrial modernity radicalized the dominant social regime of novelty. A logic of unlimited innovation and growth influenced everything from the economy to technology and the state.

In parallel to this pervasive formal rationalization, culturalization also underwent a new round. With bourgeois culture shoved to the periphery, what now flourished was the mass culture of a culture industry that was based on mass consumption and found expression in mass media (film, television). Whereas bourgeois culture is a culture of aesthetic inwardness – that is, it is oriented toward subjectivity – mass culture is a culture of aesthetic outwardness, of visible bodies and things, and not least in the medium of technologically disseminated visuality. Despite its obvious anti-bourgeois tendencies, the post-bourgeois culture nevertheless inherited a few features from the bourgeoisie, so that it is possible to identify a certain type of temporal hybridization. Bourgeois-Enlightenment rationalism's orientation toward order survived as a heritage asset in the matter-of-factness and functionality of industrial-modern culture.

While the social logic of the general functioned as the dominant force in industrial modernity, the social logic of the particular was relegated during this phase to just a few countercultural social niches. These were countercultures whose legitimacy – unlike the case of the bourgeois or anti-bourgeois Romanticism of the nineteenth century – was generally contested by the rationalistic mainstream. Such niches for the social logic of the particular were once again found in the field of art and in aesthetic counter-movements, from the avant-gardes at the beginning of the twentieth century to the counterculture of the 1960s and 1970s. Over the long term, they proved to be influential enough to undermine organized modernity and pave the way for late modernity. Within Fordist consumer capitalism and the visual mass culture, there arose at the same time certain tendencies that allowed the logic of singulari-zation to be "smuggled into" the logic of the general. Consider, for instance, the existence of film stars and the overwhelming spectacle of movies or other mass events, not to mention certain trends in the early creative industries of fashion, advertising, and design. In the Western ("Americanistic") version of industrial modernity, the latter industries provided niches of affectivity with widespread appeal. At the same time, these were social arenas in which the production of cultural and aesthetic novelties was the primary ongoing concern, and thus they did much to shape the modern creativity *dispositif* to come. Even within organized modernity, that is, there were signs that the economy and media technologies, which to that point had functioned as engines of the social logic of the general, could flip sides and become driving forces of singularization. This is exactly what happened in late modernity.

4.3 Late Modernity

During the last quarter of the twentieth century, industrial–organized modernity transformed into a new version of modern society: late modernity.[3] In contrast to the latter, the organized, collectivistic, and unemotional modernity of the twentieth century seemed obsolete. In the economic sphere, a profound shift toward post-industriali-zation took shape. Against the backdrop of increased automation and a new global division of labor, the industrial economy lost its tertiary-sector dominance in formerly industrial societies. The post-industrial capitalism of Europe and North America is essentially a type of cognitive and cultural capitalism (with finance capitalism in the background), at the center of which lie immaterial knowledge work and highly competitive markets for cognitive-cultural goods. At the same time, what has crystalized is a polarized economic and employment structure in which the knowledge work of highly qualified employees, the new professional class, stands opposite to the so-called "simple" services performed by a new service class.

This economic discrepancy between the professional class and the service class has given rise to a new polarized social structure that, having left behind the relative equality and homogeneity of the leveled middle-class society, is characteristic of late-modern society in Europe and North America. The late-modern class structure has, instead, a triadic form. The rise of the new, educated middle class, which benefited from a historically unprecedented expansion of education, stands opposed to the decline of a new underclass – an effect of deindustrialization and the increased need for simple services. Sandwiched between those on the rise and those in decline is the traditional middle class, a vestige of the leveled middle-class society. The parallel nature of these social processes of ascent and decline is just as characteristic of the late-modern class culture as the simultaneous symbolic processes of valuation and devaluation. These two sets of processes have elevated the new middle class into a position of cultural dominance.

The social structure also has a socio-spatial component. Since the 1990s, it has been possible to detect a geographic asymmetry between the prospering metropolitan regions of Europe and North America – as centers of cognitive capitalism and the new middle class – and small towns and rural regions. On the technological level, too, late modernity represents a break from the past. With the digital revolution, industrial technology ceded its all-encompassing formational force to "open machines" (as Simondon called them), which exist in computers and interactive networks. Politics and statehood have changed as well. The corporatist and controlling welfare state has lost legitimacy and has been replaced by a (neo)liberal state based on global competition. The primary goal of this dynamic liberalism – the new dominant political paradigm, which combines elements from economic liberalism and left-wing liberalism – is not social equality, but rather economic and social dynamism and cultural diversity. Geopolitically, the rise of late modernity coincided with the collapse of Eastern European communism (and thus also with the end of polarity between East and West). It also coincided with a shift toward economic and cultural globalization that has dissolved the traditional difference between "industrial societies" and "developing nations" in favor of more complex global inequalities and disparities within the global North *and* the global South.

The culture of late modernity is manifested in the lifestyle and mode of subjectivation practiced by the new, highly qualified middle class, which, again, has become the main driver of social change. This is a culture that revolves around the ideals of subjective self-development, creativity, authenticity, and emotional fulfillment. At the same time, it is tied to the ideal of the attractiveness of individual success in the social competition for attention and recognition. Late-modern subjects present themselves as an aesthetic–economic doublet – as a point of intersection between the processes of aestheticization and economization. The result of this is a psychologized and radically subjectivized culture in which personal fulfillment has become the central measure of one's lifestyle, a culture opposed to the emotionally "flat" culture of organized modernity, which was oriented toward social adjustment.

At the same time, the late-modern subject culture is radically economized in the fundamental sense that it is competitive to an extent that goes beyond mere commercialization. Subjects now move almost universally within constellations of competition, both as "consumers" of other subjects and objects that compete for attention and as "self-entrepreneurs" who compete with others for the attention of third parties. Whereas the life conduct of organized modernity revolved around the maintenance of equality, the culture of late modernity is oriented toward emphasizing differences. It is characterized by its own historical hybridization. On the one hand, the late-modern form of life draws upon elements of bourgeois culture (entrepreneurship, sensitivity, the value of education); on the other hand, its pursuit of self-development, singularity, and authenticity has been influenced to a considerable extent by the chain of cultural–aesthetic counter-movements ranging from Romanticism to the counterculture of the 1960s. In this respect, the late-modern subject forms not only an aesthetic–economic doublet, but also a neo-bourgeois and neo-Romantic hybrid.

Beginning in the 1980s, late modernity brought about a new shift toward opening contingency that affected all of society. This shift led to a sweeping campaign for mobilization and dynamization, a campaign for eliminating the social (economic, cultural, technological) borders that encompassed the entire globe and for dismantling the rigid structures of industrial modernity, which by then seemed obsolete. On the political level, the implosion of communism in 1990 – communism can be interpreted as the zenith of organized–industrial modernity – is the clearest manifestation of this reopening of contingency. In Western countries, it found political expression in dynamic liberalism, while globally it has been reflected in economic–cultural globalization and in the borderless nature of digital computer networks. Influenced as it was by the counterculture of the 1970s, the late-modern opening of contingency also had wide-reaching effects on everyday culture. It caused a shift toward liberalism that led to gender emancipation and liberal parenting, as well as to the aforementioned ideals of self-actualization, singularity, and diversity, which broke free from industrial modernity's ethos of duty and obligation. The imperative of late modernity has been to break down the boundaries and rules that had seemed so immutable in industrial modernity, in favor of establishing the free play of markets, identities, individual emotions, and global currents of goods and symbols.

Yet again, of course, this trend toward opening up contingency in late modernity has been accompanied by specific forms of closing contingency – namely, the establishment of global structures of competition and the establishment of an oppressive (in its own way) culture of performative self-development that produces not only winners, but new groups of losers as well. It took no more than a few decades for new freedoms to be perceived as new constraints. It should thus come as no surprise that new forms of systematic critique would also emerge, sooner or later, within the framework of late modernity. Like those before them, these critiques concern the political and economic system, on the one hand, and private lifestyles and personal identities on the other.

Since the year 2010 in particular, it has been possible to observe a so-called "populist" – largely right-wing, but partially also left-wing – critique of dynamic liberalism, which addresses the social and cultural losers of post-industrialism in the traditional middle class and the new underclass, and which promotes new economic and cultural regulations to counteract the effects of globalization. In addition to this, there has also been much critique of the ecological unsustainability of the post-industrial lifestyle. These critical views have been incited primarily by the existential risks posed by climate change, but they are also related to psychological strain caused by the imperative of self-development. The telos of this critique is not to remove boundaries but, rather, to encourage an intentionally limited form of life that is based on ecological awareness and ethical standards.

In light of its dynamism and liberalism, late-modern society could at first be woven seamlessly into the modern narrative of progress, but it has also been characterized in its own way by experiences of loss. Especially noteworthy are losses of social status, which were brought about by the end of the egalitarian industrial society and the end of industrial modernity in general, which had been organized by national governments and imbedded in national cultures. Yet there have also been individualized losses, which have resulted from people failing to live up to the promise of self-development, as well as ecological losses and thus a fundamental "loss of the future" – that is, the erosion of the previously unquestioned idea that social progress would continue to take place in the future. In its enhanced and self-reflexive sensitivity to loss, late modernity thus differs from industrial and bourgeois modernity, which tended to sweep feelings of loss under the rug. A sensitivity to loss thus goes hand in hand with the escalation of loss itself. Struggles for recognition, in which social groups seek recognition as victims, seem to be just as typical of this phase of modernity as the loss of political utopias. A proactive attitude toward progress has clearly been replaced by a defensive orientation toward prevention, resilience, and the minimalization of loss.

In late modernity, the relationship between the social logic of the general and the social logic of the particular has undergone a fundamental transformation. In place of the conflict between the rationalistic mainstream and counterculture, what has emerged is a pattern of complementarity. The social logic of the general and of rationalization has taken on the role of background structure or infrastructure within a society of singularities, which is characterized by dynamics of attention and valorization in which the social logic of singularities has become a structural-formational force to an extent that is without historical precedent. In late modernity, processes of singularization now operate, for the first time, beyond social and cultural niches. The counterculture has become the mainstream.

The social logic of the general has assumed the nature of an enabling structure for singularities. This is characteristic, first of all, of post-industrial capitalism, whose singularity markets foreground cognitive and cultural goods while pushing the standardized production and normalized labor of (simple) services into the background. It is also characteristic of digital technologies, whose computing capacities and algorithms have digitally unified formerly separate media and provided a universal space of communication for conducting the work of "doing generality," which in turn serves as the infrastructural precondition for the games of identity and difference that take place in today's markets of attention and valorization.

Although the logic of the general is firmly established in the late-modern economy and in its technology on the level of infrastructures, the structural transformation of the economy and that of technology represent – alongside a third factor, the transformation of the social structure and the value structure – the two most important driving forces behind the expansion of the logic of singularization. As the focus of the economy shifted away from the production of industrial and functional standard goods toward the post-industrial production of cognitive and symbolic-cultural goods, the emphasis of the Western economy has moved toward singularity goods that promise uniqueness, authenticity, and attractiveness. The post-industrial economy is a highly differentiated form of consumer capitalism in which the old dualism between culture and the economy has disappeared. The markets of singularity goods are highly competitive, to the extent that it would be safe to call them "winner-take-the-most competitions." With respect to attention, appreciation, and earnings, there is a significant discrepancy between recognized singularity goods and those with minimal singularity capital. The structure of singularity markets – which, far from being restricted to the commercial economy alone, also exist in the competitions to provide better education, better romantic partners, and better cities – is thus a defining feature of late-modern society as a whole. Contrary to what is often thought, cultural capitalism is hardly "soft." In fact, it has proved to be an especially "hard" form of capitalism.

In late modernity, digitalization has provided a second engine of singularization. Digital computer networks constitute a technological *dispositif* that makes it possible to address individual users in their own particular way. This is the dimension of automated singularization. The "window to the world" offered by the Internet is tailored to suit the unique profiles of users. At the same time, the Internet spans the comprehensive space of an attention economy in which individuals or objects can be presented in their singularity – and must be presented as such if they want to achieve a degree of visibility and recognition. In this case, too, there is a fundamental asymmetry between the winners and losers in singularity markets. With the rise of digitalization (and in contrast to the old dualism between culture and technology), the dominant technology of modernity has transformed into a culture and affect machine in which the various cultural and affective goods on offer (stories, images, games) seek to be identifiable and compete for the interest of users, and in which the users themselves have become active producers of such cultural goods. Accordingly, the general public sphere of the mass media has dissolved into personalized media worlds of individual users, on the one hand, and into digital (collective–singular) communities of like-minded people on the other.

The rise of the new middle class is a third factor behind the singularization and culturalization of society. It is closely related to the post-industrialization of the economy and the digitalization of culture. The expansion of university degrees provides the background for the creation of the new middle class. The latter is characterized by the "silent revolution" (as Inglehart called it) of a shift in values: the loss of legitimacy of the values of duty and acceptance, which bound the subject to the general norms of society, and the rise of the values of self-actualization. The values of self-actualization – which infiltrated the mainstream of the new middle class via the counter-culture of the 1970s, and contain elements from a whole series of cultural counter-movements from Romanticism onward – are in turn oriented toward the development of individual particularity and the experience of singularity in the world. In the lifeworld of the new middle class, particularity can thus become a twofold goal, to the extent that one strives for both inwardly experienced and outwardly demonstrated singularity. The singularistic lifestyle, cognitive-cultural capitalism, and the digital culture machine thus mutually stabilize one another while propelling each other on. They have given rise to a social regime of cultural and aesthetic novelty that, in the form of a maturely developed creativity *dispositif*, have established an endless – though more present-oriented than future-oriented – dynamic of newness.

In the wake of bourgeois modernity's high culture and industrial modernity's mass culture, what has crystalized in late modernity is thus a third form of culturalization: hyper-culture. The latter competes with cultural essentialism. The conflict between hyper-culture and cultural essentialism is in fact characteristic of late-modern culture. Hyper-culture is based on constantly transgressing the boundaries between the cultural and the non-cultural, between what is valuable and what is merely profane. In the mode of hyper-culture, the sphere of what society can treat as a cultural resource and what can be an object of cultural (aesthetic, ethical, narrative, etc.) value and affect has seemingly expanded without limits. Here, the line between high culture and popular culture can be crossed just as effortlessly as that between the present and the past or that between different national cultures. Hyper-culture is thus equally supported by cognitive-cultural capitalism, the digital culture machine, and the new middle class. It is based on the cosmopolitan cultural idea that cultures can be combined – that cultural elements from different origins can be fused together to create "hybrid" forms. Hyper-culture has therefore become a resource for enriching the singular identity of the late-modern subject. At the same time, it fits in with the globalization of culture.

In late modernity, hyper-culture is opposed by a new form of cultural essentialism. The latter is based on maintaining rigid boundaries between the inside and the outside, between the ingroup and the outgroup, between the familiar and the unfamiliar. From this point of view, one's own culture appears to be a homogeneous whole and should foster a collective identity. Cultural neo-communities have thus been founded as identity-based communities. Late modernity has seen a variety of such communities, be it on the religious, ethnic, regional, or national level. Whereas hyper-culture is oriented toward enriching the individual subject and his or her uninterchangeable identity, cultural essentialism is anchored in the particular collective and its group identity, which is believed to possess unassailable authenticity. Despite this antagonism, however, both hyper-culture and cultural essentialism operate according to the cultural logic of singularization. In one camp, singularization is directed toward the subject as a unique combination of diverse cultural resources; in the other camp, it addresses the collective as a singular community (with unique origins, religious beliefs, etc.).

4.4 Late Modernity's Moments of Crisis

Every version of modernity has so far followed the same pattern. At the beginning of each phase, there is optimism associated with the opening of contingency; over time, immanent contradictions and flaws become apparent, and the opportunity offered by this opening transforms into a new constraint (into a closure of contingency), which in turn prompts critique and innovation. This is just as true of the rise and erosion of bourgeois modernity as it is of industrial modernity. This pattern is recurring in late modernity as well. Unless all the events of the world have deceived me, the peak of late modernity's early hopeful stage became a thing of the past around the year 2020, and societies have entered a phase in which late modernity itself is undergoing an internal transformation, experiencing a period of stagnation, or perhaps even becoming a new form of modernity (a kind of "post-late modernity").

That a form of modernity has found itself in a state of crisis, in which it is subjected to critique on account of its recognizable flaws and deficiencies, is thus anything but new. As we have seen above, this is in a sense part of the basic structure of modernity. Modernity is essentially a society of ongoing revision, and thus also one of *ongoing crisis*; the recurring process of ebbing and flowing moments of crisis is an integral element of its mode of existence. What is specific to each phase, however, are their respective contradictions

	Bourgeois modernity	Industrial modernity	Late modernity
The economy	Rising industrial capitalism / agrarian economy	Mature industrial capitalism / industrial socialism	Post-industrialism / cognitive-cultural capitalism
Spatial structure	Europe as the center; colonialism	West–East opposition (USA – Soviet Union); "third world"	Economic and cultural globalization
The state	Bourgeois nation state	Control state	Competition state; dynamic liberalism
Social structure	Bourgeoisie vs. the proletariat	Leveled middle-class society	Three-class society; relevance of the new middle class
Technology	First Industrial Revolution	Mass production, mass transport, mass media	Digitalization
(Subject) culture	Culture of the bourgeoisie (individualism, moralism), culture of the general	Employee culture (social ethos and visual aesthetics)	Culture of performative self-development
Rationalization / "Doing generality"	Partial formal rationalization	Mature and dominant formal rationalization (up to totalitarianism)	Formal rationalization as infrastructure
Culturalization / "Doing singularity"	Bourgeois high culture; art; Romanticism as a recognized counterculture	Mass culture; counterculture as a niche	Hyperculture vs. cultural essentialism; singularity capitalism; digital singularization; the singularistic lifestyle
Opening contingency	Against feudalism and the aristocracy	Against bourgeois modernity	Against organized–industrial modernity
Critical movements against closing contingency	Politically: socialism; culturally: the critique raised by artists	Politically: new liberalism; culturally: counterculture	Politically: "populism"; culturally: ecological movements
Social regime of novelty	The novelty of perfection; the novelty of innovation	The novelty of innovation	A mature creativity *dispositif*: cultural–aesthetic novelty
Experiences of loss	Loss of traditional society (community, religion)	Experiences of totalitarian violence	Loss of status ("losers" in modernization); ecological losses; loss of progress
Hybridizations with the past	Christian culture; aristocratic culture	Bourgeois-Enlightenment rationalism	Bourgeois individualism; singularism of aesthetic counter-movements

Figure I.3 Bourgeois modernity, industrial modernity, late modernity – a synopsis

and perceived flaws, which at certain points in time condense and compel structural change. With respect to late modernity, it is possible to distinguish three moments of crisis in particular: a social crisis of recognition, a cultural crisis of self-actualization, and a political crisis. In light of the structural features of a society of singularities, all three can be interpreted as aspects of a *crisis of the general*. Moreover, an additional crisis seems to be emerging: that of the progress-oriented regime of novelty.

The crisis of social recognition, which is characteristic of late modernity, is a result of the expansion of singularity markets into a wide variety of social realms.[4] When singularization begins to mean more than just an opportunity for individual freedom, fulfillment, and otherness – that is, when it begins to form a pattern of social expectations and is institutionalized accordingly – this results in fundamental asymmetries: between those who are appreciated as singular on these markets for recognition, and those who come away from them empty-handed. The singularization of the social has thus led to a pronounced polarization between winners and losers. Winners usually accumulate assets of various sorts, while losers keep adding to their experience of lacking recognition. Typically, a level of social recognition goes hand in hand with a high probability of experiencing subjective feelings of fulfillment and self-actualization. In late modernity, this constellation of winners and losers can be divided into several social levels.

Most basic of all is the economic asymmetry between moderni-zation's winners and modernization's losers on the labor market. The highly qualified participants in cognitive-cultural capitalism – at whose peak can be found "stars" and the employees at top international organizations – can expect considerable gains in recog-nition from their singularity capital, whereas, on the other side of things, the ostensibly interchangeable workers engaged in the normalized labor of the service sector receive minimal social recog-nition.[5] This is the structure of a singularity-based meritocracy that rewards achievement and success as long as they appear extraor-dinary on the market. The high recognition associated with the jobs held by the professional class corresponds to the high probability of successful professional self-development, whereas the opposite is the case for the service class. This professional polarity corresponds to another characteristically late-modern asymmetry, namely that between education's winners – with their valuable degrees, singular profiles, and singular competencies on the competitive market of higher education – and education's losers, with their standard degrees and competencies. Associated with this professional and educational asymmetry is the asymmetry, with respect to recognition and the chances of experiencing subjective fulfillment, between different lifestyles. The new, highly educated middle class can adopt the guiding values of late-modern culture (from lifelong learning to mobility and health awareness) and thus perceive themselves as successful participants in the process of modernization. They are able to singularize (and thus valorize) their lifestyle, and in this way can achieve their inward potential for self-development and receive recognition from others. The new middle class is well aware of how to generate, for themselves and for future generations, the relevant types of capital (linguistic, cultural, mental, physical, and material capital). In contrast, society's appreciation for the life of the old middle class has waned, and the precarious class's form of life seems socially deficient. Individuals in the new middle class can thus experience feelings of self-worth associated with their legitimate uniqueness, whereas those living the lifestyles of the other classes have to struggle with feelings of inadequate self-worth.

Additional asymmetries have emerged on the level of social geography and attention on digital media. Late modernity is characterized by a socio-spatial polarity between the metropolitan regions of cognitive-cultural capitalism (plus the rural vacation spots of the new middle class), which are attractive to newcomers and investors, and regions that have been "left behind." Not only individuals, in other words, but also places and geographical regions can succeed or fail in late modernity. Finally, there is also a polarity between the individuals who exert influence and create visibility on digital media and those who remain invisible and have no influence there. This is a digital divide of a new sort. Nearly all individuals are digitally connected, but most play a passive role in this sphere, while a few are visible "broadcasters" who exert individual or collective influence ("influencers" in the broadest sense). Taken together, all levels create a fundamental polarity between modernization's winners and modernization's losers that has characterized Western societies and their political conflicts since the beginning of the twenty-first century. The rise of diverse forms of populism is an important indicator of this.

A second late-modern moment of crisis concerns the culture of the subject. This is a crisis of self-actualization, which touches the core of late-modern culture.[6] The model of performative or successful self-actualization has been supported above all by the new middle class and by the most influential cultural institutions (media, consumers, management/organization, popular culture), and thus it pervades society as a whole. The late-modern promise of emancipating the subject from the constraints of bourgeois and industrial modernity in favor of a culture that emphasizes the development of individual singularity – a culture of intensive lived experience and emotion – has been confronted by the dark side of a subject culture in which self-actualization is not just a matter of individual opportunity but has become a social norm. For systematic reasons, in fact, a form of life that ties happiness to individual self-growth and the demonstration of singular success – demanding that we all live an "interesting life" – has proven to be prone to disappointment.

The conditions behind this systematic production of disappointment include the volatility of subjective lived experience as a measure of a successful life, the imperative of exhausting all possibilities of existence, and the economization of broad swaths of the social, which has led to the establishment of constellations of winners and losers on a diverse range of markets. At the heart of late modernity's susceptibility to disappointment lies an emotional paradox. Within the framework of a culture of positive feelings, on the one hand, late-modern culture intensifies the emotional life of the subject, which now seems to be the one and only measure of a fulfilling life. In light of increasing disappointments in life and experiences of failure, on the other hand, it is also clear that this culture fosters negative emotions (rage, bitterness, anger, sadness, envy, etc.), though it provides barely any legitimate space in which to express and process such feelings. Late-modern culture no longer simply expects the subject to carry out social duties and behave morally, but instead to actualize the uniqueness of his or her existence, and this has placed the subject under a weight of individual expectations that, in extreme cases, can lead to forms of depression. Alain Ehrenberg has associated just such feelings of depression, which are typical of late-modern culture, with what he calls the "weariness of the self."[7] Cultural critics have accordingly taken aim at the fact that such a lifestyle is psychologically unsustainable.

This social and cultural moment of crisis has occurred alongside a political crisis. Late modernity's political crisis, too, has arisen from the basic structures of the society of singularities. On the one hand, the establishment of digital media technologies has led to the particularization of the public sphere. The mass media of organized modernity, which were based on social inclusion, have been replaced by an individual and collective singularization of public participation. Although the personalization of media access and the formation of politically homogeneous digital communities have revitalized political debate, these developments have also eroded the general public sphere in favor of a plurality of diverse micropublics.[8] On the other hand, the collective identities of particular communities have played an unusually strong role in late-modern politics, as is evident, for instance, in the fragmentation of the party system (the former people's parties of organized modernity) into a multitude of small parties that represent narrow and culturally homogeneous segments of society. This "singularization of politics" has made it difficult to mobilize attention to address problems that happen to be shared by these particular communities.[9] Finally, late-modernity's political crisis also concerns the ability of the state to govern. While it is by no means the case that the competition state has relinquished control, its main concentration now is on fostering economic, social, and cultural dynamism. This is a form of politics bent on removing boundaries in the name of dynamic liberalism, as though there are no alternatives. In a sense, this sort of politics views the global world at large as a vast economic singularity market in which everything revolves around the challenge of creating profiles for unique selling points and geographical advantages. The downside of this is that the social infrastructure of the general has been neglected.[10]

All in all, the crisis of recognition, the crisis of self-actualization, and the crisis of the political can be understood as three aspects of a social *crisis of the general*. This is to be expected of a society in which the social logic of singularities has become structurally formational. Any system of evaluation that relies on the general – in social matters, cultural matters, or political matters – has lost legitimacy and influence in late modernity. All three moments of crisis can be situated into this constellation. In the crisis of recognition, the norms of inclusion and standardized performance that characterized industrial modernity's "society of equals" has been ousted by a high regard for singular types of success. In the crisis of self-actualization, the erosion of cultural bonds forged by generally held feelings of duty and morality, which characterized the ethos of classical modernity, has shifted attention to the aspirations of each and every individual. And, finally, the crisis of the political has resulted from the state's eroding role in serving the general welfare of the people and the general public sphere. In the end, industrial modernity disintegrated because of its overregulation of society and because of its inability to respect singularities. As a mirror image of this situation, the current crisis of the general might turn out to be a test of late modernity's own durability.[11]

In sum, the moments of crisis that have become apparent since the beginning of the twenty-first century can be interpreted as crises of a specific version of modernity that has been developing since the 1980s and has come to be known as late modernity. Like bourgeois and industrial modernity before it, late modernity has clearly entered a state of crisis. It is important to emphasize that this is not an overarching crisis of *modernity* as a whole, but

rather a specifically *late-modern* set of problems; the crises faced
by bourgeois and industrial modernity were of a different sort. No
modern society has relied more heavily on the logic of singularization than late modernity – a constellation that emerged from the
unique and novel combination of post-industrialization, digitalization, and the expansion of education. The problems faced by late
modernity are specific to it.

Nevertheless, in light of the vociferous public discourse that has
concentrated on these problems for more than a decade, it should
be asked whether, in addition to the moments of crisis that are
specific to late modernity, there are signs that *modernity as a whole*
might be undergoing a crisis. There are, indeed, indications that
the idea that has defined and driven modernity from the beginning
might have reached its (practical) limits: the idea of progress. An
awareness of self-inflicted ecological peril, which arose in the 1970s
and has been intensifying since the 2010s on account of the growing
understanding of the damaging and irreversible effects of climate
change, has probably been the most influential political reason for
why the narrative of modern progress has so clearly been called
into question – at least in Western societies.[12] In fact, as I discussed
above, the social regime of novelty, with its normative expectation
for progressive development, was just as much a guiding force of
bourgeois and industrial modernity (in its Western and its socialist
manifestations) as it has so far been of liberal modernity. All
three eras are thus versions of the "project" of modernity, which
involves the ongoing task of improving society in the present and
the future. Both the processes of formal rationalization (with the
aim of optimization and the expansion of rights) and the processes
of culturalization and singularization are motivated by a normative
model of progress.

Of course, skepticism about progress, cultural critique, and an
awareness of the costs of modernization have accompanied the
entire history of modernity. In this respect, however, there are
several indications that this constellation began to condense at the
beginning of the twenty-first century.[13] The debate about climate
change is only one indication of a fundamental shift in the social
relationship between the promise of progress and experiences of
loss, which in a sense have been two sides of the same coin in all
versions of modernity. Accordingly, these experiences of loss have
been articulated more and more (even against resistance), and they
have been fed into the political discourse. Since the beginning of the
twenty-first century, however, what is unusual is that the articulation
of experiences of loss – of losses actually experienced by individual
groups or individuals, but also anticipated losses, and not least the

loss of positive expectations for the future itself – has been moving from the background to the foreground of public debate. Such articulations concern losses of status and future hope experienced by the losers in post-industrial modernization, the traumas of individuals and groups as victims of experiences of violence, the political history of violence, and the losses expected to be caused by ecological catastrophes. By now, experiences of loss have themselves become an element that forms identities, and this baldly contradicts modernity's narrative of progress and those who support the process of modernization.

5

Theory as Critical Analytics

How should the theory of society position itself? What is its fundamental relation to its object, society? By asking these questions,
one enters into the (traditionally rich and ongoing) debate about
the critical orientation of theory. This debate is indispensable, for
without it there would not be any self-reflection about the position-
ality of the theory of society. Max Horkheimer, as is well known,
drew the influential distinction between "traditional theory," which
imagines itself to be distant from its object, and "critical theory,"
which reflects about its own situatedness in society. Niklas Luhmann
coolly responded to this claim (the claim of critical theory's superiority) by upping the ante with systems theory. From this perspective,
critical theory seems like no more than a first-order observation
that approaches society with normative expectations, while only
systems theory is self-reflective in the constructivist spirit of second-
order scientific observation. In more recent discussions, the debate
has gained momentum from Luc Boltanski's opposition between
"critical sociology" and the "sociology of critique." In this case,
Boltanski contrasts the external critique of theorists, who presume
to know better, with an internal critique that examines the forms of
critique employed by real people active in the social world.[1]

In my view, the social and cultural sciences in general (and the
theory of society in particular) should be undertaken as *critical
analytics*, and it is the ideas of just such a form of analytics that have
guided my own contributions to the theory of society. This is related
to approaches that are critical of power and sensitive to immanent
fissures in the structure of society, including the approaches found
in the works of post-structuralist authors such as Michel Foucault,[2]
but it comes from a longer theoretical tradition. Critical analytics
can be placed in the context of the basic assumptions at the heart
of social theory and the theory of society, as discussed above, and
particularly with respect to the modern dialectic of opening and

closing contingency. In my understanding, it takes a third path beyond the two other options of critical social science mentioned above: normative critical theory, and the sociology of critique. It is neither an *external* critique of society in the name of a normative ideal, nor a purely *internal* analysis of the forms of critique circulating in society.

Critical analytics is primarily an analytics of the social, and therefore at its core it is not normatively oriented, which means that it does not operate in the mode of evaluation. In this respect, of course, it contains a slight degree of normativism in its preference for opening up contingency in society. This distinguishes it from the strong normativity of critical theory anchored in social philosophy,[3] which aims to measure society according to certain normative claims and therefore already incorporates, into its social theory and theory of society, normatively connotated concepts as measures of success. Understood in this way, critical theory always runs the risk of squeezing any analysis of society into the straitjacket of its own normative presumptions and thereby unnecessarily limiting the sociological perspective; indeed, its research practices often involve sifting through the social world in an effort to find phenomena that suit (or contradict) its own standards. Here, as it were, sociology is tied to social philosophy. The aforementioned sociology of critique, in Boltanski's sense, arose as a reaction to critical sociology's normative gesture of superiority. By tracing the forms of critique in society itself, the sociology of critique examines the real engines of social change and thus provides an important impulse for the analysis of critical movements. The sociology of critique, however, suffers from a shortcoming that is complementary to that of critical theory: it remains within the perspective of social participants, and thus prohibits a critical view of the unrecognized structural preconditions and consequences of their actions.

Critical analytics, as I understand it, is neither an external nor an internal critique; it is *immanent critique*.[4] What this means is that it does not adopt an external perspective of judgment in order to evaluate whether practices, processes, and structures are correct or incorrect in social-philosophical terms, and it does not make any utopian assumptions about the successful life but instead operates sociologically and analytically on the level of practices, processes, and structures themselves. With its analytical tools, it is not limited to the subjective perspective of participants but rather examines, from the perspective of an observer, the social contexts – that is, the structural preconditions and consequences of action – that are not always transparent from the subjective viewpoint of the actors involved. This type of analytics therefore develops its critical potential within the framework of a particular strategy toward analyzing social contexts both theoretically and empirically. Fundamentally, its starting point is the dialectic of opening and closing contingency, which, as we have seen, is central to the dynamics of modern society. In this regard, it has a clear task: from its perspective, the social and cultural sciences (and thus also the theory of society) are *intellectual tools for opening up contingency*. They work against the obscuration and closure of contingency, which repeatedly takes place in modern society's dominant discourses, as well as in the implicit praxeological logic underlying its forms of life and institutions; they demonstrate that the status quo could also be different, because it depends on man-made factors that can only become transparent through analysis. A critical analytics of this sort can be said to follow a certain set of guidelines:[5]

(1) In often new ways, critical analytics brings to light the restrictive or limiting aspects of what seems to be liberating, rational, and indeed emancipatory in modernity's institutions and forms of life. This can also have a disillusioning and sobering effect. From bourgeois and industrial modernity to late modernity, institutions and forms of life have appeared with the principal promise of enabling and securing (more) freedom. It turns out, however, that gains in freedom are often accompanied by new, more or less subtle, constraints – on account of the standardization, normalization, or recalibration of what is considered "rational" or "irrational," or on account of the establishment of new power differentials, status hierarchies, etc. One task of the theory of society is to figure out *how* this happens.

(2) By means of critical analytics, what appears to be necessary and natural in a given social reality (what seems reasonable, normal, singular, valuable, etc.) is revealed to be unnecessary, unnatural, and contingent upon specific historical and local cultural systems of interpretation. For this reason, it has a strong analytical interest in these specific orders of knowledge, which are embedded in practices and discourses. For this reason, too, it regards historical genealogy as an important tool. The main research question pursued by critical analytics is therefore the following: In which discourses and practices are social realities – economic, political, legal, scientific, quotidian, media-related, etc. – created, and how did these realities come into being? What do they exclude? Such a theory of society also pays close attention to sociocultural conflicts that take place in the public eye or in underground scenes, thereby taking into account critical movements in which established orders of knowledge are up for debate.[6]

(3) That which is seemingly fixed, closed off, and uncontradictory

in modernity's institutions and forms of life is often shown by critical analytics to be contradictory, of hybrid origins, laden with tension, and ultimately unstable. In fact, institutions and forms of life (and, indeed, modernity as a whole) arise with the promise of creating uncontradictory, stable, and balanced orders. In this case, however, the theory of society looks behind the curtains, so to speak, and develops a keen sense for the extent to which these orders might be internally fragile. The analytical–critical interest lies in identifying structural conditions of tension in which social stability seems to be faltering. For this reason, too, historical hybridizations are of special interest, because cracks in the inner structure of society tend to open up where heterogeneous elements have been combined.

(4) Critical analytics assumes that social processes often do not unfold according to the individual or collective intentions of actors; instead, structures emerge that do not correspond to these intentions and can even oppose them. This applies to the unrecognized structural preconditions that govern networks of social practices, and it also pertains to the unintended consequences of participating in these networks. Often, too, these structures and consequences do not correspond to official norms and values. Contrary to its promise to guide social development and organize it in a systematic way, modern society often seems to follow an uncontrollable dynamic of its own, and the patterns of this dynamic need to be worked out.

(5) Regarding the seemingly unwavering progress of modernity – the march of modernization – critical analytics directs its attention to the "flip side of progress" – that is, to phenomena that do not fit into this process and thus often remain invisible in the dominant discourses: to experiences and practices of loss. Instead of concentrating on the progress (and winners) of modernization, it is interested in experiences and articulations of negativity, trauma, suffering, and failure, and it is also interested in the people who have had these experiences: the victims and "losers" of modernization in any of its versions. This also includes future losses and unfulfilled potential. In this way, light is cast on the dark side of the process of modernization, on what has been repressed or unfulfilled, on those who have failed or have been marginalized.[7] The task of any critical social science should therefore be to examine both sides of the modernization process: its hegemonies as well as its experiences of loss.

(6) Finally, critical analytics acts against the tendency to close contingency within its own field – that is, it is opposed to restricting theoretical and empirical scientific work through the use of established and apparently self-evident concepts and methods. Rather, it endeavors to transcend these boundaries to acquiring knowledge

by means of new conceptual tools, new methods, and new or previously marginalized fields of research. It must always ask which contexts or connections are obscured by traditional concepts and theories, and which require new methods in order to be explored. The basic attitude toward new research methods and theoretical impulses should always be that of interdisciplinary curiosity. This is an attitude that is open to approaches that expand or reinterpret the scope of what is sociologically visible, as is currently the case with science and technology studies, global history, affect studies, and analyses guided by the concept of the Anthropocene.

Critical analytics is therefore not derived from social philosophy; rather, it denotes a strategy of inquiry and investigation that is closely connected to the theoretical and empirical research practices of the social and cultural sciences. Thus, it also fits in with my understanding, outlined above, of theory as a tool. In fact, numerous prominent contributions to the theory of society have taken the approach of critical analytics without clearly reflecting about this strategy. Karl Marx's *Capital*, Pierre Bourdieu's *Distinction*, and Michel Foucault's *The History of Sexuality* are three highly different and classic examples of critical social science conducted in this way.[8] They certainly do not fit into the rubric of the sociology of critique (in Boltanski's sense of the term), because they go beyond the horizon of groups of actors and critical movements. Neither can these three books simply be situated within the context of normative and social-philosophical critical theory. Marx, Bourdieu, and Foucault do not primarily evaluate phenomena or place them into a moral context; instead, they let the analysis speak for itself. Their strategy consists in working out how things are not as they seem to be in the official social discourse. Thus, within the framework of his critique of the political economy, Marx systematically demonstrates how, under the conditions of capitalism, value is created and surplus value is appropriated in the production and circulation of goods, and how these processes are obscured by "bourgeois" science and politics. Bourdieu, in his socio-structural analysis, examines how certain dispositions (aesthetic taste, for instance) that seem to result from individuality and self-determination are actually dependent on a cultural habitus mediated through socialization. Finally, Foucault demonstrates how the apparent liberation of sexuality celebrated after 1968 in fact perpetuates, against its own intentions, the cultural fixation on sexuality that had been established in the nineteenth century.

As a general scientific strategy within the framework of modernity's never-ending social dialectic between opening and closing contingency, critical analytics will never run out of work to do.

Its "targets" are constantly shifting. For, in modern society, it will inevitably be the case that contingency will repeatedly open up only to be closed again by one authority or another: bourgeois emancipation begot bourgeois repression, the socialist revolution begot the authoritarianism of real socialism, sexual liberation begot the obligation of sexual pleasure, educational reform begot the stultification of education, the industrial domination of nature in the industrial age begot the dominance of nature in the Anthropocene, the development of the welfare state begot the culture of dependence, the dynamics of competition begot the economization of society as a whole, the opportunity for individuality (in the sense developed by Romanticism) begot the social expectation of singularization, and so on and so forth. New and different constellations will thus always come into the crosshairs of critical analytics. Its unpredictability as a critical approach stems from the fact that immanent critique does not start from a fixed point of view; instead, it is conducted in ever new ways in the mode of critical distance and inquiry.[9]

In favorable circumstances, opening up contingency in the realm of science can have an effect similar to that produced by post-avantgarde art – for the scientific or non-scientific public, that is, it can shake things up by unsettling what is familiar. Critical analytics in the social sciences may not participate directly in the political sphere, but it does have a fundamental political character. It engages in a form of politicization by making previously invisible connections visible, by removing the matter-of-fact veneer from familiar phenomena, and by making them the object of open debate.[10] Although critical analytics itself is not normative – that is, it is not concerned with making normative (ethical, for instance) judgments – it nevertheless involves a sort of minimal normativity, a weak normativity. To repeat, the theory of society, as I practice it, is not a normative social philosophy with a utopian horizon. With its small degree of normativity, however, it is still linked to the Enlightenment project of modernity. The central, domination-critical impetus behind critical analytics is its positive orientation toward contingency itself. This does not mean that opening up contingency in the practices of forms of life and institutions should take place constantly and would always be desirable – whether and where it would be desirable is a matter of political, institutional, ethical, practical, and/or therapeutic debate. After much consideration, one can simply decide to leave things as they are. My point of departure, however, is that the *intellectual* opening of contingency – that is, making social contexts transparent, demonstrating social constraints in what appears to be natural, revealing unrecognized structures, pointing out unintended consequences, exposing unstable social configurations, etc. – is indeed desirable in itself. This is because the intellectual opening of closed contingency is the only way to provide the necessary tools for opening up space for practical possibilities.

Of course, critical analytics in this sense must itself be subject to critique. Bruno Latour has made an insightful contribution to this very debate.[11] His "critique of critique" is aimed at the gesture of iconoclasm and at the related methods of "deconstruction." Deconstruction often results in destruction and in delegitimizing social phenomena by revealing them to be socio-cultural constructions. This sort of critique leads to a situation in which everyone is left empty-handed, because nothing positive remains – except, of course, the norms and phenomena valued by the critics themselves, which are immunized against critique or exempted from it in advance. Latour's counter-proposal calls for a different form of critique: "The critic is [...] the one for whom, if something is constructed, it is fragile and thus in great need of care and caution."[12] Latour's argument is that we should approach modern society's forms of existence – that is, its political, economic, religious, artistic, legal, and everyday cultural practices – with an attitude of appreciation, and that we should treat them not as mere matters of fact to be deconstructed but as matters of concern that should be handled with care. According to Latour, the problem of modern society is that certain complexes of practices and orders of knowledge are inclined, in their values and goals, to treat things in absolute terms: *the* science, *the* market, *the* aesthetic, *the* high culture, etc. This conclusion, however, should not lead one to think that what is valuable in these practices to those who participate in them and shape them (scientists, entrepreneurs, artists, educators, and so on) should simply be destroyed in a gesture of enlightened iconoclasm. Rather, it is Latour's view that the diversity and richness of these values and practices, which constitute modernity, should be preserved.

Latour's critique of critique touches on an important point. In critical analytics, it is indeed the case that a balance needs to be struck, and this again is a question of the "attitude" with which such analysis is conducted. Demonstrating the sociocultural constructedness of a phenomenon by no means entails its delegiti-mization. A loss of legitimacy *can*, as noted above, take place via political debates about one issue or another, but scientific analysis cannot and should not decree such an outcome. Nor is it possible to justify, on the basis of a praxeological understanding of and cultural-theoretical perspective on the social, a *tabula-rasa* approach to critique. The praxeological understanding of the social stresses, in advance, what is both limiting *and* enabling – what is both subjugating *and* empowering – about social practice. From a social-theoretical point of view, it would be too one-sided to see in social practices no more than standardization and the limitation of possibilities. Of course, this inevitably *also* happens, but, at the same time, a world is being actively opened up as well. Moreover, the cultural-theoretical perspective includes that dimension of the social which is not merely a response to problems of scarcity and order, but also to problems of meaning and motivation. Without a doubt, even culturalization ("doing value") involves its share of specific normalizations, devaluations, mechanisms of exclusion, universalizing tendencies, and hidden instabilities. These are things for critical analytics to work out – not, however, by means of a pure "hermeneutics of suspicion" and with the goal of deconstruction, but rather in a way, despite its critical approach, that keeps in mind the qualities that allowed a certain social logic to prevail in the first place.[13] A critique that delegitimized every actual practice of positive freedom in the name of an abstract negative freedom would, in the end, come away with empty hands. In other words, it is necessary to maintain a balance between the critical analysis of contingency closures and an essential openness to value relations and to the enabling side of social practice.

As to what this means in concrete terms (with respect, that is, to the work involved with constructing a theory of society), this can be illustrated with reference to my work on the "invention of creativity" and the "society of singularities." In *The Invention of Creativity*, I reconstructed how the idea of the creative – that is, a model of practice that emerged from social niches and led, above all, to the creative production of culturally and aesthetically new things – was increasingly encouraged and disseminated by various institutional authorities over the course of the twentieth century and ultimately condensed to form a creativity *dispositif* in which the creative practice and lifestyle became the new norm. In terms of critical analytics, the aim of this study is to demonstrate how the opportunity to be creative was transformed by specific mechanisms into a social structure that came to *expect* creativity. On the one hand, I illustrated how the model of creativity came to achieve a hegemonic status in late modernity; on the other hand, I brought to light the contradictions and tensions that characterize the late-modern creative lifestyle. It was certainly *not* my goal, however, to delegitimize the idea of creativity itself, which has unquestionably been one of modernity's greatest achievements since 1800. Rather, my critical concern with the absolutization of the norm of creativity goes hand in hand with my essential understanding of the value

of creativity and originality in modernity. It was my positive fascination with this phenomenon that motivated me to study it in the
first place.

In my book *The Society of Singularities*, too, I also maintained an
attitude that was pro-critical analytics and anti-iconoclastic deconstruction. Since the beginning of modern culture, the orientation
of social practice toward the value of the unique and particular
("doing singularity") has been one of its central sources of fascination. When I reconstructed the structures that arose when this
orientation toward singularity was no longer being cultivated in
social niches but rather came to define, as is now the case in late
modernity, large segments of the social world, my intention was to
bring to light the social asymmetries that this situation has created.
My critical interest here is concerned with singularity as a norm,
with the pursuit of uniqueness as a culturally dominant activity
that devalues the non-singular and the culture of the general, and
with the new contradictions and instabilities that characterize the
singularistic lifestyle. My intention was *not* to wield sociological
analysis in an effort to destroy the value of singularity in modernity.
Quite the contrary. That the culture of late modernity has sensi-
tized human perception to recognize the singular and the inherent
complexity of people and things is, for me, a "matter of concern,"
not a "matter of fact" to be deconstructed. It is precisely *because* I
appreciate the modern value of the singular – as so many others do
– that I found it necessary to take a critical look at how it has been
implemented in society.

In light of the tendency to view absolutely everything through
a critical lens, critical analytics has often been accused of not
offering any constructive solutions, as though its role is to observe
and do nothing else. I do not believe that this is necessarily the
case. Scientific analysis and political intervention may be two
different things, but critical analytics can of course provide a well-
informed background for political interventions – and so it should.
Accordingly, I have never been deterred from employing critical
analytics to outline strategies for formulating alternatives to the
present conditions. In order to break up the ostensible lack of alternatives in a society of singularities, for instance, it makes sense to
strengthen a politics of the general (in the sense of regulatory liberalism), which would work toward developing social infrastructures
and promote "doing universality" in the cultural sphere.[14] And in
order to deal with the enormous intensification of affect in late-
modern culture, it seems reasonable to develop intelligent strategies
for controlling one's emotions.[15] Nevertheless, it is true that the
potential "solutions" proposed by critical analytics have a different

status from those proposed by, say, normative theory. Critical analytics is not concerned with actualizing a universally acceptable political utopia. Instead, its only aim is to formulate *temporary* and *situational strategies*. The work starts where contingency appears to be closing up, and its goal is to open it up again. This work is concerned with the *here and now*; it is not applicable everywhere and for all eternity. Whereas normative theory always approaches its ever-changing object of study – society – with the same set of standards, critical analytics responds to changing social structures and problems with modified strategies.[16]

6

Coda: The Experimentalism of Theory

The act of "doing theory" takes place not only on the production side, but also on the reception side. How, however, should social theories and theories of society be worked on, and how should they be discussed? This question is far from trivial, and it is relevant beyond the context of the present book, which brings together two different theoretical approaches. It pertains to theoretical work in general. From my perspective, there are two ideal-typical ways of dealing with theory: "theoreticism" and experimentalism. As is clear to see, these two approaches are related to the two different understandings of theory discussed at the beginning of this text. If theories are understood as systems, then the approach is that of "theoreticism," whereas if they are understood as tools, the approach is experimental. It should come as no surprise that I argue in favor of the latter.

The "theoreticist" approach, as its name suggests, is an "intra-theoretical" form of reception that has been dominant in the world of science and has accordingly been cultivated mainly by theorists themselves in their dealings with one another, that is, in the realm of "pure theory," be it social theory or the theory of society. The approach is familiar to anyone who has attended academic conferences in which theoretical ideas are presented and put up for discussion, but it can also be encountered in the discussions of theory that appear in newspapers, anthologies, and of course university seminars. The "theoreticist" form of debate assumes that every theory should be interpreted as a "theory-as-system" (in the sense described above). As a result, theory is treated in a way that could be called falsification-oriented. This means that the recipient of a given theory attempts, above all, to identify the apparent weak points where it can be attacked and dismantled. Strictly speaking, the aim is to refute the theory in question, and in this sense the "theoreticist" approach is based on an *eliminatory* attitude: One feels challenged by the theory and, in the best case, can demonstrate that it does not function, meaning that its applicability is severely limited, or even that it should be discarded entirely. With this attitude, in short, one sifts through theories in pursuit of any computational errors that might ideally discredit the calculation as a whole.

This eliminatory gesture is obviously fed from two sources: either from a sort of competition between the producers and recipients of theories, or from a rivalry between theoretical paradigms that has often been brewing for decades.[1] In the first case, the theorist-as-recipient feels provoked by the theorist-as-producer, because the latter has challenged his or her (scientific or quotidian) basic assumptions. The recipient then defends himself or herself against this, often in the form of a counterattack. In debates of this sort, one typically encounters sentences such as: "As they are employed here, the terms X, Y, and Z are unclear," "Dimension A has been overlooked," "The author remains uncritical of B," "The opposition between H and I is too clear-cut," "Assertions J and K contradict one another." In the second case, a given theory is perceived to be an attack on an entire school of theory – as a threat not only to one's own position but also to the entire camp to which one belongs, or to the entire school of thought to which one feels committed in one's theoretical work.

The "theoreticist" attitude (with its eliminatory gesture) has established itself within the field of "pure theory" in such a way that it is often regarded as evidence of academic competence. Those who can identify the weaknesses of a theory and those who know how to parry these objections are considered skillful participants in the scientific world. In my opinion, the "theoreticist" way of engaging with theories – although it often sees itself as a hallmark of scientific rationality – takes place in the spirit of intellectual *bellicosity*. It resembles a war with intellectual arms in which the participants confront one another as enemies, and everything revolves around attacking, defending, eliminating, and holding ground. Despite all the rhetoric about the pursuit of truth, it is mainly about who prevails and who loses. Lest there be any misunderstandings, I should stress that it is, of course, useful to clarify conceptual inconsistencies and work out the internal tensions of a given theory. It is also necessary to point out the blind spots that, of course, exist in every theory. However, when this is done under the banner of bellicosity – that is, with aim of refuting a theory *in toto* – it typically leads to a dead end. This is familiar from many university seminars. For every session, the syllabus will often assign a different (often current) book from the field of theory. If the eliminatory strategy is employed throughout the semester, the participants in the seminar will end up, after several months of intensive work, with empty hands. Mission accomplished. Indeed, a sport has been made out of dismantling every theory with (more or less) good arguments. Perhaps one leaves the playing field as the big winner, with hollow feelings of triumph. Does such an approach, however, lead to a better understanding of the world? If not, what is the point of all this effort?

An alternative to this, as mentioned above, is the experimental approach to theories, which treats them as tools. In his book *The Summer of Theory*, Philipp Felsch discusses a good example of an entire (sub)culture of experimental theoretical work.[2] Here, Felsch describes the reading strategies employed within the intellectual milieu in West Berlin during the 1970s. After the brief dominance of university-enforced Marxism had imploded, the theoretical books published by Merve and Suhrkamp were gobbled up and discussed with alacrity and curiosity regardless of their approach – psychoanalytical, constructivist, post-structuralist, feminist, to name just a few. Then, texts were studied in order to acquire tools for understanding the social world (and thus also for changing it). In short, students and intellectuals undertook an experiment to open up and ascertain the world by means of theory.

This experimental attitude toward theory is by no means limited to the microcosm of the 1970s. Today, however, it is seldom encountered within the realm of "pure theory."[3] Rather, one encounters it primarily in interdisciplinary contexts, but also in the way that certain empiricists and the non-academic public process theoretical work. It is hardly a coincidence that these happen to be three contexts that the theory of society focuses on and hopes to shape: the interdisciplinary field of the human sciences, empirical research, and the cultural and political public sphere. The reason why there is an open and (in the truest sense of the word) curious attitude toward theory in these contexts is obvious enough. In all three, intradisciplinary competition and the issue of status hardly play any role at all. Here, a new theory is not regarded as a rival but, rather, as a potential tool. If one approaches a theoretical text as an interdisciplinary-minded colleague, as an empirical researcher, or as a general reader, one hopes to find in this text a key for understanding society, or something that might stimulate one's own research. The aim is to seek out an instructive point of view, a new perspective in which things appear in a different light. The experimental attitude is not defensive; instead, it is about learning new things. It is not about taking up arms against a competing theory, but rather about welcoming the intellectual possibilities that this theory might open up for understanding and digging deeper into social phenomena. In this light, theory should be understood as an invitation to participate in an intellectual experiment, the goal of which is to achieve a better understanding of reality.[4]

This experiment can be deemed successful if, by means of a new vocabulary, the theory in question offers productive new ways to approach the world. The first standard by which it should be measured is one of not just truth or consistency, but also novelty. Whereas the "theoreticist" gesture is to perceive a new theory as a potential *threat*, the experimental gesture is to see it as a potential source of *enrichment* – not as an attack, but as an offering. It is important to recognize that a new theory does not necessarily delegitimize older or different theories. The experimental mode is not about eliminating worldviews from the field, but rather about *adding* new and interesting perspectives. This is the second standard by which the experimental approach to theory measures its object: A new theory is good if it is attractive and fascinating, and the attractiveness in question here is the very source of intellectual enrichment.

To return to an example mentioned above, a theory seminar conducted in the spirit of experimentalism looks entirely different from one conducted in the spirit of "theoreticism." Now, each new book is treated as a potential source of inspiration, as an opportunity to see certain contexts and connections in new and different ways. It provides an impetus for "thinking without a banister" (as Hannah Arendt called it). Of course, every theoretical approach also has its limitations – and these should be pointed out – but what is more interesting are the possibilities for learning contained within them. Such a seminar should not be a text tribunal but rather a theory workshop in which the goal should be to take theory further. At the end of a seminar led in this way, one is not left with empty hands or with the frustration that "nothing is of any use," or with the hollow confirmation that one has always known everything better than everyone else. Here, one's efforts are, instead, rewarded, because one is left in the end with a feeling of fulfillment. The participants' understanding of the world and their analytical possibilities have been enriched.

As Richard Rorty quite rightly perceived, "theories-as-tools" are vocabularies that help us to see and understand certain things.[5] As vocabularies, they are necessarily limited. Therefore, the best way not to succumb to the one-sidedness of a single theory – to avoid the dogmatism that comes with the territory of focusing on just one "theory-as-system" – is to familiarize oneself with entirely different theories of society (and social theories) and thus to equip oneself with a diverse set of tools for understanding the world. What is needed, in other words, is *theoretical multilingualism*, which means an ability to switch between different theoretical vocabularies in a pragmatic spirit of openness to the plurality of ways in which the world can be approached. From this perspective, theory's toolbox can never be full enough.

Part II

Hartmut Rosa

*Best Account
Outlining a Systematic Theory of
Modern Society*

1

What Is a Theory of Society and What Can It Do?

1.1 The Definition of Modernity and the Problem of Formative Concepts

Since the emergence of sociology as an independent academic discipline at the turn of the nineteenth to the twentieth century, its practitioners have been arguing about what features define modernity as a specific social formation – that is, about what distinguishes modern societies from those that came before it and those that will follow it. In fact, one could say that it was no less than the persistent attempt to answer this very question that gave rise to the great early works of sociological theory, now defined as classical works, and in this way gave the field its identity. Is it the transition from community to society, as Ferdinand Tönnies and many others thought, that sets modernity apart as a social formation – or the capitalist transformation of the economy, as Karl Marx as well as Max Weber (ultimately) suggested? Is the shift from a hierarchical and stratified society to a functionally differentiated society, as Niklas Luhmann (borrowing from Émile Durkheim) proposed in his systems theory, the decisive factor – or do specific processes of rationalization, as identified by Weber and, later, by Theodor W. Adorno and Max Horkheimer, and (again in a different way) Jürgen Habermas, constitute the difference in question? Or is the specific feature of modernity rather to be found in unprecedented processes of secularization or in increased forms of individualization, as observed, for instance, by Georg Simmel in his *Philosophy of Money* and then later identified as a multi-stage process by authors such as Ulrich Beck and Margaret Archer? Or, perhaps, as Simmel likewise suggested early on, did specific interactions between all these tendencies give rise to what we call "modernity"?

The recent debate about the concept of secularization provides a lucid example of how difficult it can be to define one's terms, especially when such efforts are meant to establish clear boundaries.[1] In fact, historical analyses and social-scientific disputes about modernity have shown that none of the aforementioned concepts and processes makes it possible to draw a crystal-clear and historically or geographically unambiguous distinction between different social formations. Not only is it the case that there are still, in modernity, persistent forms and processes of communalization, the gift economy, hierarchical stratification, de-individualization, conflicting rationalities and irrationalities, sacralization, etc., but the reverse is equally true: processes of individualization, differentiation, and rationalization can also be found in earlier historical eras and/or in remote regions of the world whose forms of life are generally *not* understood to be modern.[2] Even with respect to the economic logic of capital accumulation, it can be difficult to identify the point where "non-capitalist" societies unquestionably count as modern, and this is true in historical retrospect as well.[3]

To this definition-related difficulty is added the further serious problem that the common definitions of modernity, and even of the early-modern era, are, without a doubt, normatively charged and reflect ethnocentric biases and limitations, which have been brought to light in recent decades by post-structuralist – and, above all, post-colonial – critiques. This problem can be seen most clearly in so-called "theories of modernization," such as those postulated by Talcott Parsons, and in the different variants later formulated by his followers.[4] They are ultimately based on the idea that the modern American, European, or "Western" social formation represents the goal of social development per se, with the result that all deviations from it are perceived as "backward" or "underdeveloped." This has meanwhile led many leading voices in sociology to suggest that the concept of modernity should either be broken up into a multiplicity of different *modernities*, or even abandoned entirely. For, while the various differences that have been discovered – for instance between a European and a North American modernity or an Indian, Japanese, Chinese, Arab, African modernity, and so on – have continued to add to this multiplicity, at the same time the contours of what, beyond this diversity, could be called their common ground (and thus the justification for using the unifying term "modernity") have become increasingly diffuse.[5]

Abandoning "modernity" as a formative concept, however, would not solve the basic categorical problem of the theory of society, for the central difficulty of identifying social formations as such and distinguishing them from others would still remain. This difficulty becomes immediately apparent in attempts to identify something like "Western societies." Who or what is "the West"? How can it be defined and demarcated from other entities? Can it be demarcated in terms of geography? Does Japan belong to it? Can it be defined historically? This dilemma reappears in efforts to distinguish between a "global North" and a "global South." Does India lie in the North – and are Chile, Australia, or South Africa really part of the South? Is it sensible to distinguish social formations according to cardinal directions? In many places, aren't the differences between urban centers and rural provinces far greater than those between different nation states? Would it then be better to understand global metropolises as a social formation? Even worse, it is entirely unclear what constitutes the core of a social formation. Should we be talking about societies – or about cultures or forms of life? Is there, for example, *one* Indian society, *one* Indian culture, or *one* Indian form of life? In any effort to comprehend such entities empirically, one will yet again encounter a multitude of differences and even incompatibilities; what will be revealed is a multiplicity of languages and religions, social classes and castes, gender positions, everyday realities, etc., and it will be difficult to perceive any formative unity in this multiplicity.

For a long time, sociology itself attempted to solve, or at least mitigate, this problem by adhering to the idea of national boundaries, so that nation states, for their part, were understood as "containers" of specific social formations. More recently, however, the processes associated with the catchword of "globalization" have revealed the limits and inadequacies of this sort of container sociology.[6] Even where it seems possible to draw consistent territorial boundaries, moreover, this does not solve the problem of historical demarcation. If, for example, we were to talk about "German society" (disregarding the interterritorial relations that have always existed in any case),[7] when did it become modern? In the eighteenth century or in the nineteenth century? Or even not until the twentieth century? Or, as Bruno Latour has maintained, has it never been modern at all?[8] Within the social formation of modernity (assuming that the concept should be maintained), is it not necessary to include territorial differences *and* historical differences, so that we would thus have to speak of something like early modernity, classical or high modernity, and late modernity or post-modernity?[9]

The problems of defining social formations within this sea of diversity and contradictions have prompted sociologists and cultural theorists to regard *society* as a diffuse boundary concept,[10] even as an "impossible object,"[11] and to argue that, as a formative concept, the term *culture* (as in "Indian culture" or "the culture of Egypt") should be avoided as much as possible. This, however, is to abandon the idea of social formations as such, and authors such as John Urry and Bruno Latour have accordingly argued in favor of abandoning not only specific and particular formative concepts (such as "modernity" or "the West") but also the general concept of society itself.[12] What is left then, for sociologists, is to trace and follow the specific courses, movements, assemblages, and transformations of people, goods, ideas, and practices, and to analyze their particular constellations.[13] In so doing, sociologists can indeed observe that processes of individualization and de-individualization, differentiation and de-differentiation, democratization and de-democratization, pacification and militarization, economization and sacralization, acceleration and deceleration (and so on and so forth) continue to take place again and again – sometimes at the same time, sometimes not – in the most diverse historical, cultural, and geographic contexts, without having to give rise to any overarching formative patterns. On the level of sociological theory, it is then possible to formulate, on this basis, micro-sociological or ethnographically inspired practice theories (which examine and describe specific social practices in relation to sociality, corporeality, and materiality),[14] or it is possible to trace the historical and spatial interrelations and dissemination of individual cultural artifacts (including certain objects, ideas, or modes of action).[15]

However, as soon as one's attention turns to the overarching contexts of such practices or artifacts – to their structural and cultural connections and backgrounds – then the indispensability of formative concepts comes to light yet again. To me, the attempt of practice theory to fill in the corresponding gap by systematically introducing the concept of forms of life seems even more problematic at this point,[16] because not only do all the difficulties of the formative concepts of culture and society reappear immediately – when (historically) and where (geographically) does a form of life begin or end? – but also because now the aggregate level of practices becomes a problem as well. When everything from marriage to "the South Texan way of life" and capitalism can be called a form of life, how is it then possible to define forms of life and distinguish them from one another at all?[17]

Empirical social research, in particular, which concentrates on analyzing specific correlations, can also get by quite well without formative concepts. It can have little to nothing to do with them at all, in fact, if the objective in question is to study how job commutes and divorce rates are related, or whether there is a connection between religious faith and satisfaction in life, or how the voting patterns of salaried employees are developing in North America, or what percentage of university students in different countries have parents without university degrees, and so on.

On the one hand, it seems difficult to think about society as a formation at all; on the other hand, formation-related macro-sociology, "grand theories," or even theories of society, hardly seem compelling or justifiable unless their criteria of methodological control are (impossibly) made to conform with those of the established natural sciences. Together, this has led to a situation in which sociological theory – understood as systematically thinking about what interacting elements and forces constitute contemporary society and what sort of logics, impetuses, or regularities underlie its tendencies to change – is being practiced less and less around the world (especially outside of Germany) and is in danger of disappearing, at least as an academic discipline.

1.2 Society's Self-Interpretation and the Task of Sociology

The practice of thinking about the current sociopolitical situation will certainly never disappear from social life, given that people – as Max Weber made clear,[18] and as Charles Taylor systematically spelled out[19] – are irrepressibly, and even essentially, *self-interpreting animals*. Not only are we dependent on interpreting ourselves and our world in a formative way (that is, in a way that creates coherence) – in addition, we ourselves and our social reality cannot even be systematically separated from these self-interpretations. Whoever or whatever we are as individuals or as a society – and the world in which we live – depend on our horizons of meaning or our self-interpretations (among other things). Yet this also means that *whoever is able to change the basic concepts of society's self-description and self-interpretation also changes social reality itself*, for this reality is co-constituted by our language. The nature of social phenomena is always in part conceptual; no social institution can be understood or practiced independent of the horizon of interpretation upon which it is based, and such horizons of meaning, in turn, cannot be understood in isolation, because they exist for their part in formational contexts.

What is meant by these abstract concepts can be illustrated with a simple example. In order really to *understand* or *explain* what a person *does* when he or she goes to work in the morning, it is necessary to understand the modern system of paid labor, the concept of work–life balance, the separation of production and consumption, the distinction between politics and the economy, the notion of a career-driven life, the capitalist economy, and the defining features of (late-)modern subjectivity. Without such a horizon of interpretation, which allows us to recognize the contours of a social formation, it might be possible to describe this person's practical activity and determine how it correlates with that of others, but it would be impossible to ascertain its social or cultural significance. Subjects thus always implicitly understand their *own* activity in light of its formation-related cultural significance, which lends meaning to this activity and to their existence. Because such self-interpretation always demands articulation, and because it is always contested, and thus always dynamic, the process of society's self-interpretation, which in part constitutes what society *is* and co-determines its course of development, will never come to an end. If contemporary sociology is unwilling or unable to participate in this process because it lacks any formative concepts, then it will cede this interpretive work to other social authorities: to editorial pages in newspapers, political parties, or religious organizations. This, however, will have serious consequences – for sociology itself, but also for the society or the formation of which it is part.

As regards sociology, the question is what it can really contribute to the state of knowledge if it refuses to reconstruct a formative horizon. Of course, to stick with the example above, it can reconstruct the practice of commuting to work, and it can also determine the statistical correlation between commuting times and divorce rates. In this way, however, it is unable to comprehend the significance of jobs, divorces, and commuting to the subjects in question, and nor is it able to understand the overarching institutional context and its developmental trends. In this way, moreover, it simply has to accept such practices and the institutions behind them as givens, without being able to reconstruct and illuminate their genealogical origins, the logic that led to their formation, and their historical and cultural contingency. It was for this reason, in the famous positivist dispute in sociology during the 1960s, that Theodor W. Adorno and his fellow combatants underscored the reifying tendencies of any approach to sociology that refuses to investigate the formative forces behind social phenomena.[20] Above all, however, any approach to sociology that ignores the theory of society will be unable to establish and explain, on a conceptually sure footing, *that* and *how* life in Berlin at the beginning of the twenty-first century, say, differs from life in Hyderabad at the beginning of the eighteenth century. Without a doubt, such an approach will be able to discover, when analyzing these two milieus, any number of practices that differ from one another, and a number of others that are similar (perhaps there were hardly any commuters in Hyderabad but similar divorce rates, and perhaps there was even a similar correlation between these two rates). In order to determine the systematic significance and weight of such data, however, they have to be integrated into a formative horizon.

To the extent that sociology's task is to elucidate the structural and cultural *contexts* of social phenomena, it would be impossible for it to meet this objective without formative concepts, which aim to conceptualize basic tendencies beyond those of individual and group-specific differences and beyond those associated with the cultural and formation-specific features of a form of life. Without aggregate concepts such as "society," "Christianity," or "modernity," sociology dissolves into (more or less thick) descriptions of phenomena or chains of phenomena, which is to say that it disintegrates into no more than individual observations without any account of their contexts and interrelations. It dissolves, in other words, into a combination of behavioral economics and behavioral psychology. Yet it is precisely such contexts and interrelations that constitute the genuine object of sociology, for even individual phenomena cannot really be understood, explained, or classified without any attempt to comprehend the structural and cultural forces that determine the central developments and changes of a given social formation, and thus define its historical and cultural manifestation. This does not mean that we should disregard the multiplicity or the significance of all the individual, cultural, gender-specific, and socio-structural differences that have led to such a variety of life practices and forms of life. It does mean, however, that we should take seriously the existence and persistence of forces that have a formative structural and cultural effect across all these differences.

If sociology were to refrain from formulating empirically supported and conceptually sophisticated theoretical proposals for how society should interpret itself, it would essentially breach – this is the second sociopolitical consequence – its social contract, which arises from the conviction at the heart of the academic enterprise that modern societies (regardless of whether they are defined in historical, categorical, or territorial terms) are able to influence themselves in a self-reflective way. After all, politicians and religious leaders are necessarily *partisan* by definition, not only in a locally specific sense but also because they each pursue a specific *agenda* that is controversial *within* the social formation in question. They are thus engaged in something quite different from scientifically analyzing the laws or forces that form and constitute society. Instead, their explicit aim is to push this formation in a particular direction or, in other words, to initiate a particular movement within a given formative horizon. Journalists, in contrast, are by definition forced to develop their interpretations on an ad hoc basis and in response to each specific situation. Their work is thus restricted by time, and it is methodologically and conceptually limited as well. As a rule (at least as long as they are working as journalists), they have at their disposal neither the time nor the informational resources to analyze social formations in a systematic and comprehensive manner, and the media which they serve offer neither sufficient space nor time to subject their interpretations to systematic collegial critique.

This therefore raises the rather urgent question of whether the present social formation would really be well advised – in light of today's unsettling ecological, social, economic, mental-health, and political crises – to refrain from marshalling all its available cognitive, methodological, and epistemic resources (in short, its scientific resources) in an effort to develop the best possible interpretation – a "best account" – of its sociocultural condition and its historical situation. This, in my opinion, is the central task of a type of sociology that (also) understands itself as a theory of society. Just such an opinion was formulated, as long ago as 1931, by Max Horkheimer in his inaugural lecture as the director of the Frankfurt Institute for Social Research:

> [T]he question today is to organize investigations stimulated by contemporary philosophical problems in which philosophers, sociologists, economists, historians, and psychologists are brought together in permanent collaboration to undertake in common that which can be carried out individually in the laboratory in other fields. In short, the task is to do what all true researchers have always done: namely, to pursue their larger philosophical questions on the basis of the most precise scientific methods, to revise and refine their questions in the course of their substantive work, and to develop new methods without losing sight of the larger context. With this approach, no yes-or-no answers arise to the philosophical questions. Instead, these questions themselves become integrated into the empirical research process.[21]

What I understand by a "best account," a term borrowed from Charles Taylor, is an attempt to develop – within a given sociohistorical situation, on the basis of all available resources (statistical data, interviews, self-observations, but also constitutional texts, legal rulings, newspaper reports, textbooks, accounts of social movements, literature, film, etc.), and in light of the urgent "cultural problems" (in Weber's terms) that raise the most interesting questions – the best possible proposal for the way in which things (and ourselves) should be interpreted. Taylor's central insight is that an interpretive proposal must, categorically, take the self-interpretations of the actors involved seriously, because these self-interpretations co-constitute the phenomena in question:

> The underlying consideration [...] could be put this way: How else to determine what is real or objective, or part of the furniture of things, than by seeing what properties or entities or features our best account of things has to invoke? Our favoured ontology for the micro-constitution of the physical universe now includes quarks and several kinds of force, and other things I understand only dimly. This is very different from how our ancestors conceived these things. But we have our present array of recognized entities because they are the ones invoked in what we now see as the most believable account of physical reality. There is no reason to proceed differently in the domain of human affairs, by which I mean the domain in which we deliberate about our future action, assess our own and others' character, feelings, reactions, comportments, *and also attempt to understand and explain these.* As a result of our discussions, reflections, arguments, challenges, and examinations, we will come to see a certain vocabulary as the most realistic and insightful for the things of this domain.[22]

With respect to the theory of society, a best account is thus the best possible interpretation of society's situation at a particular historical point in time. What, however, is the *best possible* interpretation? This can be measured by the extent to which it seems plausible to the actors involved in light of the cultural problems at play and in light of their own experiences, fears, and hopes – though, of course, this plausibility must be tested discursively on the basis of all available data and sources of knowledge. This is therefore by no means a matter of *immediately clear* plausibility; like the concept of quarks, a best account in the social sciences can contain a series of counter-intuitive and, say, ideology-critical interpretations or insights that can only be formulated as a result of persistent searching and digging, which reveal contradictions in everyday concepts. In this regard, as Taylor has also noted, sociology is ultimately no different from the natural sciences. The theory of general relativity, for instance, radically clashes with our everyday experiences, and yet it represents the current best account of physics.

In the domain of the social sciences, however, a best account will inevitably be contested. With this approach, it is true, the theory of society certainly does not formulate any "eternal truths." Instead, it offers interpretations that should not be perceived as established knowledge, but rather as *sound suggestions for ways in which society should be (self-)interpreted in light of a given set of specific problems.*

These suggestions are then tested, revised, and expanded in various discursive arenas, in consideration of the experiences and objections of actors from a heterogeneous range of social contexts. The empirical foundation of a best account is not formed by one specific data set; it is not formed, for instance, by evaluating a few statistical surveys or a single collection of expert interviews.[23] Instead, it is a work of synthesis that draws from a multitude of data sources, from which it develops a systematic interpretation of the social formation in question. Its form of empirical verification and control is not that of a strictly controlled methodological study but that of a comprehensive and discursive test of reality. A theory of society formulated in the ivory tower alone can never be a best account, as I understand it. As long as such a theory refuses to be subjected to the perspectives and critiques of society at large, it will never be able to do justice to the experiences, interpretations, and knowledge of all the social actors involved: students, homeless people, entrepreneurs, carpenters, dancers, and so on. Society's experiential knowledge, which is generated in different places and examined from multiple perspectives, will inform any best account worthy of the name. Only in this way is it possible to recognize, and perhaps gradually correct, the inevitable ethnocentrism of one's account and its other limitations, which can arise from one's gender, class, or age. In this sense, public sociology entails more than just introducing interpretive proposals to society; it also means, conversely, that its practitioners should attempt to create their best possible interpretive proposals from the perspectives of a wide range of social experiences and from stores of knowledge based on a wide range of heterogeneous practices.[24]

The suitability and quality of a sociological best account are demonstrated not least, in Niklas Luhmann's sense, by what it enables its readers to see and recognize: by the connections it reveals, by the developmental trends it brings to light, by the problematic contexts it explains, and by the way in which it provides the language with which to describe certain experiences. The quality of a best account is also evident, however, from the impulses it lends to a given discussion about possible alternatives for social action. As a theory of society, moreover, a best account must also fulfill the promise of inspiring social research – that is, of providing it with a horizon and generating research questions to be pursued by empirical studies. As Jürgen Habermas stated in *The Theory of Communicative Action*: "As to what social theory can accomplish in and of itself – it resembles the focusing power of a magnifying glass. Only when the social sciences no longer sparked a single thought would the time for social theory be past."[25] Many works of sociology celebrated as classics today – Max Weber's *The Protestant Ethic and the Spirit of Capitalism*, Norbert Elias's *The Civilizing Process*, Pierre Bourdieu's *Distinction*, Hannah Arendt's *The Human Condition*, David Harvey's *The Condition of Postmodernity*, or Margaret Archer's more recent *The Reflexive Imperative in Late Modernity*, to name just a few – are exemplary for having just such effects. In this same way, the ideas formulated by Ulrich Beck in his book *Risk Society* and those presented in Gerhard Schulze's book *Die Erlebnisgesellschaft* have inspired a number of new approaches and studies in the field of lifestyle and milieu research.[26] Andreas Reckwitz's recently published work *The Society of Singularities* and my own book *Social Acceleration* can also be understood as attempts to provide the conceptual foundations for a best account of society. Because social situations are constantly shifting and changing, however, efforts to produce a best account of them must also be in a constant state of motion and change. As mentioned above, society's desire to interpret itself will never come to an end, and any attempt to fix a single self-interpretation in time will necessarily be driven by ideology.

Even though this type of social analysis relies on narratives or reports of experiences (and even though its plausibility is tested by engaging with just such narratives and reports), it of course also has a distinct – that is, academic – form of its own. Its proposed way of interpreting a given social situation must be based on conceptually sophisticated, theoretically grounded, and empirically supported foundations. Here, however, we encounter a basic problem that has stubbornly accompanied sociology since its earliest stages: the problem posed by the opposition between structural theories and action theories, which recurs again and again in all sorts of variants – for instance in the opposition between macro- and micro-sociology, between methodological holism and methodological individualism, between structuralist and culturalist or materialist and idealist approaches, between *understanding* and *explaining*. My thesis is that all these oppositions – one could also say, states of tension – have *one* common root. They are a result of the fact that social realities can be described *from the inside* and *from the outside*, and yet the descriptions obtained from these different perspectives can hardly ever be made to align. From the outside – that is, *from the perspective of the third person* – social practices and institutions can be studied and described in the same way (or a similar way) as planets, atoms, or the life of plants. From the inside – that is, *from the perspective of the first person* – all "objectivations of life," and thus these very same institutions and practices, can be understood in phenomenological terms espoused by the likes of Wilhelm

Dilthey, Hans-Georg Gadamer, Weber, Taylor, and Habermas, which means that they can be understood in terms of their own horizon of meaning and sources of motivation.[27] On the one hand, the concept of a functionally differentiated society as opposed to segmented or stratified formations, as developed in Luhmann's systems theory, represents a *structuralist* account based on the third-person perspective, as does any Marxist analysis of society based on its class structure. On the other hand, Schulze's diagnosis of the experience society, for example, or Taylor's analysis of modernity in his *Sources of the Self* are ultimately *culturalist* accounts based on the first-person perspective.

Of course, there is now a broad consensus in the social sciences that a best account should be able to unify these two sides – especially with respect to *structure* and *action* – and there has been no shortage of attempts to do so. Examples of such efforts can be found in theories of structuration,[28] for instance, or in the concept of the habitus as "not only a structuring structure [...] but also a structured structure."[29] None of these attempts, however, has managed to provide a convincing solution to the problem upon which a comprehensive best account might be based. As Margaret Archer has rightly observed,[30] all the attempts to unify these two sides suffer from the fact that, despite their intentions, they ultimately deny autonomy or causal power to one side and either attribute action to structural effects ("downward conflation") or, conversely, explain structural formation on the basis of the logic of action ("upward conflation"). Or, as in many variants of practice theory, they dispense with different perspectives entirely by indiscriminately identifying all aspects of a situation as elements of a practice ("central conflation").[31] Archer, for her part, offers compelling reasons for taking the *inherent meaning* or the inherent logic of both levels seriously and for generating explanatory power precisely from their potential conflict.

I therefore agree with Archer that the best account of a social situation must arise from an analysis that considers, from different perspectives and in terms of their respective inherent logic and independent nature, both the structural shape and the cultural constitution of a social formation. Then, however, such an analysis must combine them by investigating the ways in which they interact. Unlike Archer, however, I suggest that this interplay should not be understood simply in terms of the *temporal* difference between structure and action, but rather that they should be regarded as two categorically different elements of the social. In other words, it is not possible to gain an understanding of social movement and social dynamics from the structural and institutional constitution of a social formation, which can be described and analyzed from the third-person perspective. This requires, in addition, a concept of *social energy*, with which it is possible to explain what could be called "social processing." This driving force or energy, I argue, can in turn only be ascertained from the cultural background, namely from the fears and hopes and desires of actors – and thus only from the first-person perspective. What I mean by this can be illustrated with a simple analogy: Let's assume that, in a few hundred years, ethnologists from an entirely different civilization discover an automobile. Simply on the basis of its material components, they would never be able to reconstruct what a car is and means, what it does and constitutes. In order really to understand this thing, they would have to put it in motion. They would have to *drive* it. In the same way, for instance, the class structure of a social formation can be analyzed and represented in minute detail as a structural configuration or – *à la* Bourdieu – as social space. Social *movement*, however, only arises when the (class-)specific self-interpretations of the actors involved are incorporated into the analysis.

The lack of such a culturalist analysis of social energy (and thus of social processing) is clearest to see, in my opinion, in the efforts of contemporary systems theory. The latter can only assert, again and again, that modern society is complex, differentiated, and multi-perspectival, and that every subsystem follows its own *code*. Because, however, the interesting social movements *within* the modern social formation – social struggles, changes in society – take place on the level of the *program*, systems theory fails to arrive at an understanding of social dynamics. For in order to understand the latter, it is not enough to know *that* things are bought and sold in modern society and people are governed and oppose this government; rather, it is necessary to understand *what* is bought and sold and *why*, *with what* program are people governed and *why* do they oppose it, or *what* is considered scientifically true or false and *for what reason*. In the wake of Luhmann, however, systems theory has absolutely nothing to say about this, because it explicitly or systematically excludes the first-person perspective – the cultural driving forces that result from the self-interpretation of actors – from its interpretations.[32]

In what follows, my own proposal for a best account will begin with the structure-related recognition that what I identify as the social formation of modernity can be described from the third-person perspective by means of the concept of dynamic stabilization. Any modern society is characterized by the fact that it must constantly grow, accelerate, and innovate in order to maintain its structure. Structures and institutions, however, cannot grow, accelerate, and innovate on their own. For this, they need a *driving energy*, which they draw from the fears, wishes, and ambitions of subjects, who in turn can only be understood from the first-person perspective (i.e., culturalistically), regardless of the extent to which they may be formed, influenced, and even produced by the structural and institutional conditions in question.[33] The fact that sociology and the social sciences in general not only lack a systematically established concept of social energy, but in fact have *no concept of this whatsoever*, is, in my view, perhaps their greatest conceptual shortcoming. For, without such a concept, society – despite all the emphasis placed on its processual nature and despite all the efforts made to formulate a theory of social change – is almost inevitably made to seem like a static entity.

1.3 Perspectival Dualism and the Three Levels of a Best Account

In the sense of a best account, an analysis of a social formation must, I argue, adopt the first-person and third-person perspective in parallel and distinguish these two sides analytically, while also, however, examining both of them in terms of their inherent meaning, as well as in terms of their interaction and interrelations. Only in this way is it possible to comprehend the constitutional laws and kinetic forces of a social formation. Without a (cultural) understanding of the motivational energies, desires, ambitions, fears, promises, hopes, and threats that this formation generates, its dynamics of social change and kinetic energies cannot be ascertained. However, without a (structural) understanding of institutional reality, it is impossible to grasp the form and direction of these fears and desires. Only by viewing things synoptically is it possible to define the overall character of a social formation, which also constitutes a comprehensive but historically specific form of relating to the world.

Such a definition of a social formation, however, does not become a systematic theory of society until it goes beyond this perspectival dualism and situates itself on three levels at the same time.[34] Here, following the tradition of the *critical theory* of the Frankfurt School, I am of the conviction that the *theory* of society and the *critique* of society systematically and inextricably belong together. A social theory cannot be developed from a neutral standpoint, from a "view from nowhere," so to speak. It is always formulated in the light of urgent cultural problems, which serve as reference points.[35] Critical theory shares this insight not only with Max Weber,[36] but also with pragmatists working in the tradition of John Dewey,[37] with communitarianists such as Michael Walzer,[38] and with French proponents of the *sociology of critique*.[39] Social reflection is a response to the experience and manifestation of practical crises and problems; it arises from the perception *that something isn't right*, that the existing conditions or developments are worthy of critique. It requires a moment of irritation, which challenges a social forma- tion's guiding self-interpretation and selectively steers the attention of researchers, for it is epistemologically impossible to incorporate *all* conceivable features of a social formation into a best account. This moment of irritation – this perception of a disturbance – can be a response to the cultural level just as well as it can be a response to the structural level, but it can also be (and this is perhaps most frequently the case) a reaction to the relationship between the two. In the first case, subjective experiences of suffering or contradictions in society's self-interpretation will lie at the heart of the perceived crisis and will fuel the theoretical critique in response to these situa- tions. In the second case, observed or suspected dysfunctions or structurally inadequate developments will spark the crisis and the corresponding critique.

In a theory of society, it is therefore possible from the beginning to draw a systematic distinction between two levels: the level of *analysis* and the level of *diagnosis* or *critique*. By *analysis*, I mean the systematic identification and definition of the constitutive features and developmental tendencies of a social formation on a struc- tural and cultural level. By *diagnosis*, I mean the identification and definition of apparent missteps, disturbances, or pathologies – that is, the identification of that which is *worthy of critique* according to a given critical standard. In this case, it seems obvious to me that this standard must be related to the diagnosed suffering of subjects (though the subjects in question might not necessarily be aware of this suffering).

What is controversial in critical theory, however, is the third level of a theory of society,[40] which I would like to call the level of *therapy* (I am aware that this is metaphorical, and I am also mindful of all the problems that arise when using such clinical vocabulary). By this I mean the attempt to identify, on the basis of one's analysis and diagnosis, possibilities or points of departure for overcoming the observed missteps and undesirable developments of society. With no more means than the theory of society itself, this can only succeed where such points of departure are inherent to social practice itself – within which, that is, there already appear moments of inner- worldly transcendence.[41] The necessity of incorporating this final step into the systematic schema of a theory of society emerges from the internal constitutional logic of a best account. The best possible interpretation of a historical social formation in crisis must, if it is to fulfill its purpose of contributing to society's self-interpretation, generate suggestions or recommendations or, at the very least – in the sense of Weber's idea that sociology should spur a discussion of values[42] – offer *alternative courses of action* or utopian horizons for shaping the future.

In what follows, I would like to flesh out and color in the ideas that have been presented only abstractly so far. In an effort to formulate my own best account of the modern social formation and its present situation, I will move step by step through the six components that have emerged from the meta-theoretical considerations discussed above. In doing so, I will draw from my previous books *Social Acceleration* and *Resonance*, but in many places I will focus my analysis specifically on *late* modernity in order to provide a best account of the present. As a result, the cultural and, in part, the structural *differences* between different historical phases will necessarily fall into the background, and this might leave the impression that my interpretation, like many others, treats modernity as static, as though whether I was discussing the societies of the nineteenth, twentieth, or twenty-first century would make no difference. In my book *Social Acceleration*, however, I attempted to demonstrate that the logic of escalation or the principle of dynamic stabilization may indeed be a consistent (and defining) structural feature of modernity, but the related (and more or less continuous) process of acceleration has led to major cultural turning points, on the basis of which it is ultimately possible to draw lines between early modernity, classical or high modernity, and late modernity.[43] These turning points are defined by the ratio between the pace of social change and the timeframe of generational change; respectively, they took place at moments of transition from a *multi-generational* to a *generational*, and finally to an *intragenerational*, pace of sociocultural change. Initially, the early-modern relationship to the world was still characterized (in ideal-typical terms) by the assumption or the experience that *the world* as such would remain unchanging, regardless of all the individual and historical vicissitudes that might take place. The assumption, in other words, was that different generations would share the same world. Classical high modernity was then characterized by the idea that different generations should be agents of change. The world of one's parents (or grandparents) was no longer expected to be the world of one's children (or grandchildren); history, as Reinhart Koselleck has shown, was set in motion.[44] This was associated with specific forms of subjectivity, political control, and historical experience. Things changed yet again with the transition to late modernity, which began to emerge in the last third of the twentieth century; which was intensified by the threefold upheaval brought about by the *political*, *digital*, and *neoliberal* revolutions around the year 1990; and which is still ongoing today. Here, the fact that the speed of social change (in the form of a further contraction of the elapsing cultural present) has become intragenerational means that the expectation of stability, as regards the contextual conditions of everyday behavior, has fallen below the generational threshold, and this in turn means that the forms of subjectivity, the mode of politics, and the experience of history have changed yet again.[45] By no means, then, do I understand modernity as a static entity, and nor do I shy away from the fact that the nearly worldwide spread of this social formation has been accompanied, externally, by brutal and bloody colonial violence and oppression, and that it is associated, internally, with multiple forms of racism, sexism, exclusion, exploitation, and marginalization. In order to determine, however, the inherent structural logic and the cultural dynamics of the modern social formation that ultimately helped to bring about these very issues (and other pathological phenomena such as the destruction of the environment), I have decided to focus more closely below on what I regard to be its constitutive and pervasive driving forces.

2

Dynamic Stabilization and the Expansion of Our Share of the World: An Analysis of the Modern Social Formation

In the first section of this contribution, I clarified why, to me, it is insufficient to practice a type of sociology that traces the trajectories, mobilities, and assemblages of things, people, ideas, and goods, and why it is likewise insufficient to practice a sort of quantitative social research that examines individual connections according to the model of the natural sciences – why, in other words, the discipline cannot do without the concept of a social formation (or society). I have yet to explain in specific terms, however, how such a concept can be obtained. What I mean by *social formation* is a formative connection between a particular cultural horizon, which is characterized by a *moral map* – a moral map that defines what is desirable and what is undesirable and therefore creates driving energies in the form of hopes, aspirations, wishes, and promises, along with anxieties, fears, and threats[1] – and a particular structural or societal system of institutions or an institutional arrangement that ensures material reproduction. The interplay between these two components also produces a specific subject form and, in particular, a specific relationship to the world.[2]

It is this interplay that creates the social formation in question, because both sides mutually pervade and constitute one another without being able to be derived from one another. Culture and structure must be understood as interdependent, partially autonomous, and elastically interconnected. This means that changes and developments can take place here as well as there, according to the logic of each side, and thus that there are independent cultural developments and independent structural developments that, within certain limits of elasticity, do not have to cause serious effects on the other side. Contradictions and tensions (between cultural motivations and institutional practices, for instance) can therefore

persist over long periods of time, even though there are constant
reciprocal effects between the two sides in every context of action.
When, however, the contradictions and tensions between the two
levels go beyond the limits of elasticity, this leads to structural or
cultural pathologies that require disruptive adjustments in the form
of formational change. A *structural* pathology develops when social
institutions produce lasting results that seem unacceptable in light
of a society's operative moral map; a *cultural* pathology, in contrast,
refers to a condition in which institutional reality exhausts the
motivational resources of actors or removes any plausible basis from
the hopes and fears that drive society.[3]

For any analysis of a social formation – even of, say, an early
hunter-gatherer society – this means first of all that it is just as
decisive to have an understanding of its means of material reproduction and its institutional structures of coexistence as it is to have
an understanding of its cultural self-perception and its notion of its
relationship to the world. This does not, however, solve the aforementioned problem of how social formations can be delimited from
one another in time and space. In my opinion, the discussion here
suffers from the fact that, in the case of formative concepts such as
modernity, there is always demand for unambiguous definitions and
demarcations, even though such demands are not made (and would
be impossible to satisfy) when discussing objects, or even "natural"
categories such as furniture, colors, or plants. Instead, the linguistic
categorization of such things generally accords with the perception
and distinction of unambiguous prototypes, about whose classification there is no doubt, linguistically or phenomenally. For
example, there are shades of color that are clearly perceived and
identified by observers as red, and others that appear just as clearly
as yellow, *even though* there are of course fluid and difficult-to-define
transitions between these two colors – between red and orange on
the one hand, between yellow and orange on the other – and even
though it is possible to name and identify any number of interme-
diate hues (crimson, pinkish red, bright red, golden yellow, Indian
yellow, lemon yellow, etc.). Yet no one would think to demand that
the terms "red" and "yellow" should be abandoned for this reason.
The same is true of the distinction between bushes and trees, for
instance, or between glasses and cups. Here, too, things become
difficult around the edges, not only because the border cannot be
precisely defined but also because the criteria become uncertain; there
are, for example, very tall bushes and very small trees. Nevertheless,
the prototypical distinction – the clear and paradigmatic examples –
remain uncontroversial.[4] Moreover, this explains why, in light of the
distinction between cups and glasses, there can be so many different

"cup and glass theories." Cups or glasses can be described in terms of their form, their function, their consistency, their transparency, etc., and counterexamples can always be found, such as cups without handles, transparent cups, glasses for hot drinks and cups for cold drinks, and presumably wine cups and coffee glasses; and there are also containers for which the distinction between cups and glasses no longer makes any sense and is simply inapplicable. Yet this does nothing to change the conceptual usefulness and prototypical clarity of the distinction. In this very sense, I believe it is possible to identify a formative context that can be described as modern, regardless of the diffuse nature of its margins and boundaries.

In this overarching sense, social formations are thus characterized by their specific relationship to the world, which is actualized in the formative *interplay* between their cultural and structural factors. As I attempted to demonstrate in my book *Resonance*, it would be wrong to understand the term *relationship to the world* simply as the relationship of people to their world or environment, for human beings and the world are not, a priori, given and then enter into a relationship with one another; instead, they only emerge from their reciprocal relatedness. The relation and the elements related *originate together*. Nevertheless, it can be said, as a sort of cognitive shortcut, that people become subjects and collectively become a society only in relation to a perceived world, and this relationship to the world has, irrevocably, material and institutional as well as cultural and subjective facets. At the same time, this relatedness should not be thought about as a fixed arrangement, but rather as a constant and dynamic process of interaction between subjects and what they perceive to be the world. A relationship to the world is one of dynamic interaction – or, to put it in Karen Barad's terms, one of ongoing "intra-action."[5]

Therefore, in what follows, I will finally examine modernity's relationship to the world in its totality and attempt to provide a best account of its structural constitution and of the driving forces of its culture, which determine the central developmental tendencies of contemporary society and therefore define the modern form of life as a historical and cultural social formation. As already mentioned, this does not mean that I intend to deny the variety or the importance of individual, cultural, gender-specific, and socio-structural distinctions that lead to considerably different forms of life and life practices; rather, my intention is to take seriously the existence and persistence of formative forces that are structurally and culturally influential across all these differences. In accordance with my systematic program for a critical theory of society developed above, what is needed first of all is an analysis of the structural and cultural features of this social formation.

2.1 Component 1: Dynamic Stabilization

Since the publication of my book *Social Acceleration*, I have attempted to demonstrate in a number of studies that the prototypical structural feature of modern societies (and the institutions created by them) is that they are only able to stabilize themselves by remaining dynamic. This means that they can only maintain their structure in the mode of escalation, i.e., that they depend on constant (economic) growth, (technical) acceleration, and (cultural) innovation to reproduce their institutional status quo. Because both economic growth and the increase of innovative achievements can be understood as forms of acceleration, *acceleration* itself can thus be understood as an overall (structural) sign of modernity. This is because economic growth entails producing more and more every year (and this means *faster* production), and it means that more and more has to be consumed and distributed, regardless of how this more might exactly be realized as an increase in value. In a competitive capitalist economy, moreover, there is also the constant pressure to increase productivity, which means accelerating the production of goods and services.[6] Accelerated *innovation*, in contrast, means that technical, organizational, or social innovations have to follow one another in ever shorter intervals of time, and this therefore implies a contraction of the present and the acceleration of social change.[7]

What is specific to the capitalist social formation of modernity is thus *not* growth, acceleration, or increased innovation per se, but rather their *endogenous*, structural necessity. By this I mean that these things must be realized, even if there are no cultural aspirations or environmental reasons for creating such increases. Economic growth, in particular – though inherently related to the other two forms of escalation – is essential for maintaining the functionality of the entire institutional constitution of modern society.[8] In short, without growth, jobs are lost (as productivity rises), then companies and businesses have to close down, which reduces the state's tax revenues, while at the same time the state's expenditures increase in the form of necessary social benefits and infrastructure measures. This, in turn, narrows the scope of policy-making, because the resources are lacking. At the same time, the healthcare system, pension provisions, the educational system, and the cultural sphere will enter a state of crisis on account of underfunding, which ultimately causes the social and political system as a whole to lose legitimacy.

Although it is true, at least on the level of the nation state, that an economy can survive for a long period of time without any real economic growth – the Japanese economy since the 1990s is an example of this – this does not mean that it would be possible to escape the escalation imperative of modernity's formational structure. Without growth, the pressure for rationalizing acceleration and innovation will only become greater, because only in such a way is it possible to maintain the M-C-M' cycle. This simple economic formula sums up modernity's growth principle in a succinct symbolic form. Money (M) is only converted into commodities (C) if there is a realistic prospect for this investment to produce a profit (M') for investors. What compels growth, acceleration, and innovation is therefore not any systemically external pressure to innovate – in the form of population growth, resource scarcity, ecological changes, or a military threat – but rather the endogenous logic of the system itself. As a result, the construction industry, for example, will try to achieve growth even during a real-estate crisis caused by an oversupply of housing and office space; the automobile and airline industries will relentlessly attempt to produce and sell more cars and airplanes, even though there has long been a cultural and political agreement that this is ecologically harmful and probably self-destructive; and the food industry, by continuing to experiment with all sorts of additives, will attempt to turn off signals between the stomach and the brain in order to cause an already overweight population to eat even more.[9] The tech giants, in turn, have found another way to ensure that the number of sold smartphones, tablets, etc., will increase incessantly. They offer customer contracts that stipulate the automatic replacement of devices after a few years. This "escalation game" is therefore driven neither from the demand side (by consumer desires) nor by the curiosity of producers or their joy in creating new inventions. Rather, the cause is the structural constraint that existing jobs, salaries, healthcare, pensions (etc.) can only be maintained by means of constant escalation.

I have pointed out on several occasions that this logic of escalation not only is a feature of the capitalist economy, but also recurs in other value spheres and functional spheres of society. Dynamic stabilization is also a defining feature of the modern scientific enterprise, which (unlike that of non-modern societies) is based not on preserving and passing down traditional knowledge but on constantly expanding the limits of what is known and knowable. The inherent dynamics of this form of knowledge were already acknowledged by Max Weber in his famous lecture "Science as a Vocation":

> [In] the realm of science, [...] we all know that what we have achieved will be obsolete in ten, twenty, or fifty years. That is the fate, indeed, that is the very *meaning* of scientific work. It

is subject to and dedicated to this meaning [...]. Every scientific "fulfillment" gives birth to new "questions" and *cries out* to be surpassed and rendered obsolete. Everyone who wishes to serve science has to resign himself to this. [...] But we must repeat: to be superseded scientifically is not simply our fate but our goal. We cannot work without living in hope that others will advance beyond us. In principle, this progress is infinite.[10]

Just as the self-driving dynamic of M-C-M' represents the heartbeat of the modern economy, a mechanism of *knowledge – research – increased knowledge* (K-R-K') provides the basic motivation of modern science. In a similar way, the art – painting, music, dance, and poetry – of modernity is no longer based on the mimetic principle of imitating nature, or the stylistic principles of "old masters." Its goal is, rather, to *surpass* them in originality and innovation.[11] Finally, the logic of dynamic stabilization has also made its way into politics, in that governance can only be legitimized temporarily through regular elections, whose modus operandi is basically one of candidates competing to outdo one another. The competitors fight for power by making more and more promises (more jobs, better housing, higher income, greater access to early-childhood education). In short, the institutional system of modernity – the market economy, the welfare state, political power, the cultural and scientific spheres, healthcare, pensions – can only be maintained in the mode of escalation and innovation.

My thesis here is that this specific structural constitution, which first emerged in Europe and North America in the eighteenth century, seems sufficiently particular to serve as a formational feature of modernity. On the one hand, it has lent this formative configuration an incredibly high degree of stability, which is not only evident in its continuous reproduction since the eighteenth century but also reflected in its ability to cope with or assimilate a wide range of different cultural traditions. On the other hand, however, this stability is in fact similar to that of a bicycle. The latter remains stable and on course the faster it travels. Yet if it slows down, it becomes increasingly sensitive to shocks and impulses; and if it stops, it will immediately fall down without any external support. For such a social formation, any deceleration therefore entails a structural problem, and a complete standstill proves to be an existential impossibility.[12] The formation will then cease to be. At the same time, however, this speed-generated stability also increases the risk of a (serious) accident.

It seems especially significant to me that this mode of dynamic stabilization requires the permanent mobilization of energy. If growth, acceleration, and escalation are understood in their physical sense, then they can only be achieved by using more of the earth's energy supply. In fact, as the British archaeologist and historian Ian Morris has calculated, the stability of the modern social formation is based primarily on the fact that it has enormously increased its physical energy consumption (especially carbon-based) in the last 200 years. Between the year 1773, when the steam engine was invented, and the year 2000, per-capita energy consumption increased more than sixfold.[13] The compulsion to increase, however, is by no means related exclusively to the consumption of natural resources; it is also related to modernity's social logic of interaction, dynamics of interaction, and speed of interaction. The modern social formation therefore constitutes a "hot society" par excellence (in Claude Lévi-Strauss's terms),[14] and this "heat" is also generated by the use of political and mental energy. As I have already pointed out, the driving energy of modernity cannot be explained with reference to its structural constitution alone. Businesses, universities, or states cannot grow, accelerate, and innovate on their own; for this, they need the active participation of subjects. This, however, is generated *culturally* in the form of motivational fears and desires.

2.2 Component 2: The Expansion of Our Share of the World

Human relationships to the world are always influenced by attractive and repulsive tendencies – that is, by the forces of desire and fear. These two forces constitute the basic forms of our relationship to the world, because they produce desireful and fearful subjects, on the one hand, and because they create attractive and threatening or repulsive aspects of the world on the other.[15] In order to understand the driving energies of a cultural formation, it is therefore necessary to reconstruct, so to speak, the "maps" of fear (what is to be avoided) and desire (what is worth striving for) that apply to it.[16] In this regard, my thesis is that every social formation produces specific horizons of this sort, which explicitly or implicitly define, or at least outline, the form of a good or successful life as well as the abysmal nature of failure. Thus, if we hope to identify the driving energies behind modernity's game of escalation, it is necessary to answer one simple question: What motivates subjects to conduct their lives in such a way as to satisfy modernity's escalation imperative – what do they pursue (what seems desirable to them), and what do they fear (what do they attempt to avoid)?

Now, it does not seem difficult to identify the generative mechanism of fear in the modern and, especially, the late-modern social formation. Via the mode of competition, and in various ways, the imperative of escalation is translated into subjective orientations toward life, where it creates concerns – or even fears – of falling behind or being left behind in the dynamic social order. The logic of dynamic stabilization produces a ubiquitous feeling of standing on the edge of a cliff – or of standing at the bottom of a downward-moving escalator. In order to maintain their position in society, subjects (as individuals or social groups) must constantly – and ever faster – move upward to prevent others from passing them by. It is important to keep in mind, too, that the number of escalators has constantly been increasing. Today, ever more aspects of life require our "social processing," because positions, knowledge, and security are no longer meant to last throughout the duration of a person's life. Jobs, partnerships, friendship, but also investments, types of insurance, technical equipment in hardware and software, and even furniture and the subscriptions to media products: they can all end or become obsolete at any time, and they require constant investments of energy and attention if subjects want to keep up and avoid being out of the loop. In the present, this logic is increasingly focused on the field of *parametric optimization*. In more and more areas of life – the private and the public – parameters of achievement and status are digitally quantified and thus made *visible*, then *comparable*, and ultimately *manipulable* or *improvable*. This applies, for instance, to physical matters such as someone's daily number of steps, length of sleep, or, more recently, blood oxygen levels. The latter is a good example of this sort of activation. Just as, a few years ago, hardly anyone knew how many steps she actually took on a given day, today hardly anyone knows how much oxygen is in his blood. Now, when smartwatches begin to take such measurements, the people who pay attention to them will be ridiculed at first. However, if it turns out that knowing the oxygen content in one's blood "can save lives" by serving as an early warning system for strokes, heart attacks, or COVID-19, it will soon be considered reckless or even socially irresponsible not to collect and monitor this information.

Something similar is taking place all over, in companies, in government offices, and even in schools, kindergartens, and universities, where more and more parameters are collected, compared, and recommended for the sake of optimization (think of PISA scores in schools or impact-factors in the sciences). Whereas Max Weber had attempted to demonstrate in *The Protestant Ethic and the Spirit of Capitalism* that it was initially the fear of eternal damnation that motivated a type of life conduct suited to a dynamically stabilizing economic system,[17] today we are motivated by the "hell" of a bottomless social abyss that will open up and swallow those who are left behind by society, but that also has a grip on those of us who are still managing to run up the downward-moving escalator. The permanent loss of salaried work deprives subjects of their legitimate place in the social order; if they are dependent on the alms of the welfare state, they are allowed to die a sort of social death. For, in the social formation of modernity, gainful employment has become, in a sense, the source of resonance or the umbilical cord of life. In their work, subjects experience themselves, in a self-actualizing way, as part of the social whole; they make a palpable contribution to the success of life and help to maintain its order. In return, they receive strength and nourishment in the form of income; the world sustains and nourishes them in a cycle of resonance. If subjects lose their jobs, however, the dominant cultural self-interpretation – not necessarily on the level of explicit conceptions but in the form of institutionalized self-perception, which is then embodied in the subjects' own perception of the world and themselves – forces them to see themselves as "freeloaders." They are no longer part of the cycle; their income is no longer based on any self-actualizing connection with the world. This way of experiencing the world – based as it is on ideological distortions, which I by no means wish to deny – has physical and bodily dimensions, and it is in fact quite similar to what is known as social death in so-called "archaic" cultures: by failing to contribute to the resonance of their society, people can literally waste away and die without being the victim of any physical assault whatsoever.[18] Such a manner of conceptualizing the self–world relationship, however, does not arise from the structural logic of the social formation alone. To be sure, it is not simply determined by this structural logic; rather, its inherent logic, driving forces, and coherence can only be ascertained from the first-person (cultural) perspective.

This is even more apparent when we turn our attention to the positive, attractive side of modernity. No social formation can exist for long if its driving forces are only of a negative sort – that is, if they create movement exclusively in the mode of fear.[19] A highly energetic formation, which demands from its subjects a constant and ever-increasing expenditure of energy, also needs to offer a positive horizon of promise, a vision of the good life that generates or releases the cultural energy of desire. In this regard, the thesis that I developed in my books *Resonance* and *The Uncontrollability of the World* is that the cultural force of modernity is based on the promise of expanding our (individual and collective) *share of the world*, or expanding the cognitive, technical, economic, and political *availability* of the world and life. Quality of life (and the idea of the good in general) is measured by the horizon of what is attainable, controllable, and available. For this reason, we call a society "developed" when it has sufficient technical, economic, and political means to play an instrumental role in the world; the so-called "development index" is created by calculating just that: a society's technical, economic, and political *share of the world*.[20] For this reason, too, we measure quality of life in terms of disposable income, access to education and healthcare, and social relationships, all of which are understood as resources for broadening the horizon of what individuals can achieve – or for expanding the "sets of capabilities" at society's disposal, to borrow a term from Amartya Sen's capabilities approach, which inspired the United Nations Development Program.[21]

In this respect, it is especially the prospect or promise of broadening horizons that creates motivational energy, and it is the actualization of this expansion that is perceived as a momentary experience of the good. The specific cultural feature of the modern social formation therefore lies in the fact that the essence of the good is not sought and experienced in the *realization* or *fulfillment* of a certain possibility, but rather in the (constant and unlimited) *expansion of possibilities*. This explains, for instance, the cultural significance of the moon landing and nuclear fission, on the one hand; on the other hand, it also explains, for example, the attractiveness of *money* to individual actors, who can literally gauge their share of the world by looking at their account balances. If the account is far in the plus, then the world (of travel, living arrangements, having and doing things) is at one's fingertips; in the case of a billionaire like Elon Musk, even Mars might be within reach. In contrast, a heavily overdrawn account signals that even a bus ticket to the nearest city, a basement apartment in a shabby neighborhood, and a warm jacket in the winter might be unattainable. Yet it is not only economic capital that expands our share of the world; it is also (in Bourdieu's terms) cultural and social capital that determine and increase this share by making certain material, intellectual, and social spheres of the world accessible and available. A whole world of further education and career opportunities awaits a university-bound high school graduate, whereas these same opportunities remain closed off to those whose education ends with a high school diploma. Learning a foreign language, moreover, brings the people and riches of an entirely different culture within our cognitive and communicative reach. Similarly, we will accept an invitation to a party or dinner attended by "important people" with the hope that, by meeting them, whole new social circles might be opened up for us.

When, in a highly dynamic society, the notion of what constitutes a good life has become questionable or vague, when the dominant ethical horizon is no longer teleologically determined and the orientational forms of successful life have become strictly private (for sound reasons of ethical pluralism),[22] it will seem reasonable (if not necessary) for subjects to concentrate, in their life conduct, on accumulating the types of resources that John Rawls called "primary goods."[23] The latter are characterized by the fact that it is always better to have more of them, rather than fewer. This is the case because they determine our share of the world – regardless of whether our life conduct and our future goals are those of a pianist, an internist, or a machinist. Such goods basically overlap with what Pierre Bourdieu identified as the relevant forms of capital: economic capital (money), cultural capital (education), social capital (relationships), and symbolic capital (recognition),[24] though to this list we should also add physical or bodily capital, which – in the form of health, fitness, attractiveness, the ability to cope with stress, etc. – seems to be increasingly important in late modernity. Open any recent self-help book, and you will quickly find this hypothesis confirmed: happiness is associated with increasing (and keeping) these very resources.[25]

The possibility of expanding the horizons of what can be achieved might also explain, in my opinion, a good part of why, across the globe, metropolitan regions have been so much more attractive than rural areas. This is usually explained in economic terms, with reference to the better job opportunities in large cities, but, for the middle classes in developing countries, there are so many disadvantages to urban life, including economic disadvantages – healthcare professionals, for instance, are in greater demand outside of cities, where property prices are lower and where there is less noise and pollution, etc. – that this economic explanation certainly falls short. Young people, in particular, are irresistibly attracted to big cities because theatres, museums, concerts, clubs, shopping centers, sports arenas (etc.) are available to them there, whereas such things are by and large absent from rural life. In short, as Georg Simmel observed, the scope of the world is far greater in large cities. On the one hand, one encounters *within* a metropolis something like the world as a whole in the form of ideas, cultural products, and people from every continent, whereas a village or small town might offer little more than a pizzeria or a kebab stand. On the other hand, big cities, with their international airports, embassies, and consulates, also have the infrastructure and cultural conditions that make it possible to travel to even the most remote regions of the world quickly and with minimal effort.

Finally, if we are interested in identifying the driving forces of modern technological development, the motivation of making more of the world available and thus increasing our share of it again comes into play. The telescope, after all, expands our vision into outer space, while the microscope increases the visibility and accessibility of the material microscopic world, and the endoscope allows us to view and manipulate our bodily innards. The development of high-speed transportation, moreover, is likewise a story of expanding our share of the world, regardless of whether this story is viewed historically (from foot travel to stagecoach to jet planes) or simply biographically. Even by acquiring our first bicycle, we expand our share of the world a bit further, and we do so even more by getting a driver's license, and yet again even more – explosively so – by traveling on airplanes.

The scope of one's everyday life (or the standard cultural scope in general), however, is not measured simply by the state of technological development or merely by economic opportunities, but rather by the interplay between these two factors. An intercontinental weekend excursion becomes within reach when such a trip becomes technologically (and politically) possible and economically affordable. In this sense, the steady reduction of airfares and the increase of tourist destinations over the last few decades have enormously expanded the share of the world available to many people in the "global North." From this perspective, the travel restrictions imposed by the coronavirus pandemic represent a historically unprecedented *reduction of our share of the world* and a dramatic decrease in what is available to us.

Yet the world, which in many respects has become unavailable under the conditions of the pandemic, remains widely accessible by digital means; indeed, the digital availability of social events and cultural content has been increasing rapidly (a process that has long been under way). In any case, the fascination of the smartphone, in particular, and its hold on the attention and motivational desires of subjects from nearly all strata of today's social formation can be explained, in my opinion, by its ability to broaden the horizon of what is socially, culturally, and medially accessible and economically affordable to an extent that is unprecedented in human history. With the help of a smartphone, the whole world is, in a sense, *directly* available to us. With a few clicks or taps, we are able to reach, speak to, and see (almost) all our friends, relatives, and acquaintances; the entire digitalized world of knowledge – all the music ever recorded, all the films, images of current events from every region of the globe, etc. – is immediately accessible. In fact, the modern social formation has thus in some respects realized a moment of *omnipotence*, not only with respect to its collective capabilities, but especially in regard to the *practical capabilities* of subjects, and this, in my opinion, cannot be overestimated. Marx and Engels, astounded by the enormously expanded range of possibilities enabled by the economic and technological developments during the early stages of modernity, asked the following question in 1848: "[W]hat earlier century had even a presentiment that such productive forces slumbered in the lap of social labour?"[26] A best account of the modern social formation would do well to retain this sense of wonder in light of the wealth and possibilities of the early twenty-first century.

3
Desynchronization and Alienation: A Diagnosis and Critique of Modernity

If it is true that the reflexive energy that impels every socio-logical observation and theory is motivated by the perception that something is not right, then it is precisely this moment of aston-ishment (after so much analytical reconstruction) that gives rise to the guiding question behind my best account of the modern social formation: What is wrong with a social formation that is driven by a *desire to increase our share of the world* and whose institutional structure is reproduced *in the mode of dynamic stabilization* (and thus in the mode of constant expansion)? Or, in other words: In what ways does this social formation create its own ecological, social, economic, and psychological crises, which have occurred in late modernity with increasing urgency and acuteness?

In order to answer these questions and thus to formulate a *critique of the modern social formation*, it is first of the utmost importance to understand that (and how) the institutional logic of escalation and the cultural issue of motivation are interrelated. In the previous section, I tried to show that this is the case. Just as modernity's structural mode of reproduction requires, on the one hand, escalation-oriented subjects and the constant intensification of their motivational energy, it also fulfills, on the other hand, their desire for an increased share of the world, though not to the same extent for everyone. In many places and in certain social strata, of course, the imposition of the capitalist logic of accumulation initially led to scarcity and impoverishment, and therefore to a *reduction* of people's share of the world (and it still does so today, without a doubt).[1] That said, the (enormous) increases in global productivity and annual GDPs – coupled with the dramatic devel-opment of technological possibilities – have ensured that this overall dynamic is not a zero-sum game. To claim that the expansion of one person's share of the world is offset by the reduction of another's would simply be false. Even if this were true, moreover, it would do nothing to change the fact that the hope for expanding one's share of the world necessarily motivates even those who have benefited little from these developments and have suffered from the consequences of exploitation and impoverishment.

In this regard, what is important to me here is the insight that the interplay between the institutional structure of modernity and its motivational cultural forces has created a relationship to the world that characterizes the modern social formation as a whole, and can be described in rather straightforward terms, I think, as a *hostile relationship*. The structural pressure for constant escalation (in the form of growth, acceleration, and innovation, as well as in the cultural desire for increasing our available share of the world) makes the world seem, on all levels – on the macro-level of nature, on the meso-level of the political and social world, and also on the micro-level of every individual's self-perception – like a battleground upon which it is necessary to fight and resist. Everything that appears on this metaphorical battlefield has to be identified, defined, dominated, conquered, bought, and made useful.[2] This institutionalized and habituated relationship to the world, however, has problematic consequences on both the structural level and the cultural level, and the urgency of these consequences has become increasingly evident in late modernity. In my view, these consequences have noticeably begun to undermine modernity's existential conditions on both of its formational levels.

3.1 Component 3: Escalation and Desynchronization

The central *structural* problem of the modern social formation is that the logic of dynamic stabilization demands escalatory growth in the substantial dimension of input and output. Even at a moderate annual economic growth rate of 1.5 percent – which is far below the rate of 2 to 4 percent that experts deem necessary for the sustainability of the economic system[3] – a nation's GDP will increase by more than 100 percent over the course of 50 years (at the rate of 4 percent, it will double every 18 years), and such growth will inevitably lead to astronomical increases in output and resource consumption. In the long term, however, this will result in dynamic *destabilization*, because it will become increasingly difficult to achieve additional growth and additional acceleration, which will require more and more physical, mental, and political resources to be mobilized, activated, implemented, pooled together, and used. As we have already seen, a systematic requirement of dynamic stabilization is ongoing ecological, economic, and political *appropriation*, *acceleration*, and *activation*.[4] This state of affairs, I would like to argue in short, has gradually given rise to a four-headed economic, ecological, political, and mental-health crisis, because the pressure to escalate has not only reduced the space for creative possibilities but also endangered and undermined, by means of strain and overuse, the ecospheres of nature, democratic politics, the human psyche, and even the capitalist economy itself.[5]

As I see it, a social formation that is only able to stabilize itself dynamically is unsustainable for the long term. This is because it needs a constantly increasing supply of energy and is thus threatened by complementary phenomena of *overheating* – in the form of the greenhouse effect and an ever more hostile political climate on the macro- and meso-levels,[6] and in the form of burnout on the micro-level of individual psyches. In a number of publications, I have described these phenomena as desynchronization effects, so here I will limit myself to providing no more than a schematic overview of the matter.[7]

The starting point of my considerations is my awareness that not all social groups and forms of life are equally capable of accelerating or being dynamic. This leads to a situation in which accelerating systems and/or actors apply pressure at certain temporal junctions (that is, where different speeds encounter one another and processes have to be synchronized) on all the systems and/or actors that are slower, and this inevitably creates tension and desynchronization effects. Whenever one of two temporally coordinated systems increases its pace, the other will appear *too slow* in a social formation that values speed and depends on dynamism; it becomes a brake, a real obstacle to synchronization. This basic pattern is evident in nearly all social contexts. The rise of social stratification, for instance, can be explained from this perspective. For privileged social strata, the possession of economic, cultural, and social capital is a central resource (for acceleration) from which subsequent generations also benefit, so that the children from these social strata have – from birth, as it were – an enormous advantage over children from less-privileged social backgrounds. Social division is not only handed down, in other words; one can also assume that it will become even more acute from one generation to the next.

Serious and fundamentally unsolvable problems of desynchronization arise, however, not only in the interplay between social strata and forms of life (between geographically bound "somewheres" and globally active "anywheres," for instance),[8] but also at the interfaces between the institutional spheres of society and their respective environments. In fact, I would argue that the four major crises of the late-modern society in the twenty-first century can be described as just such crises of desynchronization. From a perspective that takes into account the overall structural relationship to the world, modernity's social institutions can be situated between the more comprehensive ecological system (as a macro-sphere), and the psychosomatically constituted lives of human individuals (as a micro-sphere). The constant acceleration and dynamization of the social (as a meso-sphere) then imposes increasing stress and pressure on both of these other systematic spheres. On top of this, there are also serious synchronization problems within the meso-sphere itself, because some organizational and institutional contexts are more capable of acceleration than others. As structural problems of the modern social formation, desynchronization crises therefore take place on four different levels at the same time: (1) within a functional system, such as the economy; (2) between functional spheres of society, as in the relationship between the economy, politics, and care work; (3) in the relationship between environmental ecospheres and the socio-technical speed of reproduction and processing; and, finally, (4) at the interface between the psycho-physical processes and needs of subjects and the operational pace and rate of change of society as a whole. This situation has yielded four crises, which I will briefly outline below.

3.1.1 Too Fast for the Economy: The Financial Crisis

On a structural level, the 2008/9 financial crisis – the repercussions of which are still felt to this day – resulted not least from the fact that the transaction speed of financial markets had radically diverged from the real economy's pace of production and consumption. In financial markets, profits can be made from the flow of capital and currency by exploiting micro-second fluctuations; much of the world's trading in stock markets and financial markets is now conducted by algorithms instead of human brokers. Yet the material production of such things as automobiles, houses, clothing, or books – and their consumption in real life, which is not a matter of *acquisition* but one of *use* – is considerably more time-intensive.[9] Because material growth (in annually produced houses, automobiles, clothing, groceries, books, etc.) has become, at least in "affluent" societies, increasingly difficult to generate and is now associated with negative (ecological) side effects, a broad range of financial products were developed that can circulate at nearly the speed of light. The temporal decoupling of the financial economy from the real economy, however, then led to pathological "bubbles" such as the real-estate bubble of 2008, the bursting of which can be explained as the economic consequence of a synchronization crisis. Meanwhile, even many economists have seen the necessity of re-synchronizing these two partial spheres of the economy. To do so, however, would come at an enormous cost – presumably, it could only be achieved by significantly *decelerating* the (financial) economy, though such an effort would contradict the very nature of its formation.

3.1.2 Too Fast for Politics: The Crisis of Democracy

The temporal disparity between society's various spheres of operation is apparent in many modern institutional contexts, for instance when educational processes or care practices simply *cannot* be accelerated at will, despite the pressure to do so for the sake of improving economic efficiency and satisfying political or administrative measures. For this reason, care workers such as doctors and nurses are constantly subjected to conflicting time imperatives, given that they are caught between their professional orientation, on the one hand, and economic or political directives, on the other.[10]

One of the central arguments in my book *Social Acceleration* and in many later studies, however, is that the *political institution of democracy* is also, and inexorably, a *time-intensive* process, which by its very nature cannot be significantly accelerated even with the help of digital technologies. Quite the contrary. Under the conditions of late modernity, in fact, this process has tended to *slow down*. This is because democracy, as a mode of political decision-making, is not simply based on the aggregation of (more or less spontaneous) private opinions about issues by means of a voting process; rather, it is based on the idea of *collectively shaping the political landscape* through a deliberate process of forming public opinion and making decisions. This process involves, first, formulating possible and justifiable positions, but then discussing them and weighing them against each other in a way that the basic democratic consensus among citizens is maintained and the community remains, despite all its differences, recognizable as a common project. In this way, a government's political decisions require constant feedback from *public opinion* as a basis for its legitimacy.[11] This sort of democratic process, however, tends to slow down when the *foundations* of its decisions are contested or become uncertain on account of ethnic, ethical, religious, and political pluralization and de-conventionalization (that is, when the scope of what can be assumed to be a matter of consensus narrows), and it slows down especially when the *consequences* of these decisions become more complex and dynamic as a result of an expanded range of interactions and interrelations. Both of these tendencies have intensified in late modernity, and this is simply due to processes of dynamization.[12]

As a result, desynchronization has widened between the decelerating sphere of democratic politics and the accelerating processes of economic activity, cultural change, and the production of attention-grabbing media content. The consequences of this growing desynchronization are reflected in what has been discussed as a *crisis of democracy* at least since the Brexit referendum, the election of Donald Trump in 2016, and the rise of right-wing populist parties and politicians all around the democratic world (including Modi in India, Bolsonaro in Brazil, and Duterte in the Philippines). In late modernity, established democratic politics is no longer seen as a pacemaker and shaper of social change (understood as progress toward better living conditions), but rather as an obstacle to it or as a form of politics that is predominantly reactive, acting only as a "fire extinguisher" when crises flare. The crisis of the pandemic since 2020 confirms this pattern, to the extent that the actions taken by nearly all states were clearly *reactive*. At the same time, however, nations demonstrated a rather impressive capacity for political action by radically "decelerating" the activity and circulation of all other social spheres, for example by stopping traffic, closing borders, canceling events, and so on. It is obvious that this political action (regardless of the fact that in this case, as in that of the 2008/9 financial crisis, executive government decisions radically curtailed the power of parliaments as the actual centers of democratic action in the name of *time constraints*) runs *contrary* to its own logic and will lead to massively dysfunctional consequences for the institutional order – yet these consequences, one must admit, seem rather desirable in comparison with the potential consequences of the third major crisis at hand, the ecological crisis.

3.1.3 Too Fast for Nature: The Ecological Crisis
Even Niklas Luhmann – who otherwise never tired of stressing that the social formation of modernity, whose core feature in his view is the functional differentiation of autopoietically processing subsystems, becomes all the more stable and efficient the less its chains of operation are disturbed by action – recognized that a central problem of modern society might be that it will undermine its own ecological conditions of existence and thereby destroy itself.[13] This fear, which was expressed more than three decades ago, seems to be coming true today, especially in light of the intensifying climate crisis. What characterizes the rapidly progressing warming of the earth's atmosphere is, on the physical level, no more than a molecular acceleration process. The warming of atmospheric layers entails (like the warming of any gas or substance) an increase in its kinetic energy, which is to say an acceleration of movement on the molecular level. The climate crisis can therefore be understood as an acceleration of the earth's atmosphere (the microsphere) as a result

of socio-technical and economic acceleration processes on the level of society, for which the consumption of carbon-based energy is especially responsible. The physical heat produced by technological acceleration and material dynamization on the ground has ultimately led to climate-changing acceleration in the sky. This process can be described as one of desynchronization because the resulting changes in the climate have been happening too rapidly for many geosystems and ecosystems, thereby inherently disrupting their time patterns, as is clear from the changes in the speed and direction of ocean currents and from the rising number of annual hurricanes.

In fact, I would go so far as to claim that nearly *all* aspects of the present ecological crisis can be understood as desynchronization problems. The much-discussed extinction of species, for example, is not caused by the fact that we fell trees or catch fish but by the fact that we have been cutting down rainforests *at a much faster pace* and emptying the oceans of fish *much faster* than their stocks can regenerate. This discrepancy is many times greater when we compare the rate at which we consume oil or other raw materials with the time needed for these materials to reproduce naturally. Moreover, what we call pollution is only a problem when we generate toxic substances and emissions faster than nature can break them down. Taken together, these forms of ecological desynchronization are clearly not a threat to the planet or to "nature," but they are certainly a threat to the social formation of modernity. Nowhere is the problem of our (hostile) modern relationship to the world more strikingly apparent than in the ecological crisis that this relationship has caused.

3.1.4 Too Fast for the Soul: The Mental-Health Crisis

If ecological desynchronization threatens the modern social formation *from the outside* or *from above*, so to speak (as problematic as the distinction between nature and society might be in epistemological and ontological terms, it defines the formation itself),[14] it is also endangered by the potential mental burnout of subjects *from within* or *from below*. The belief that such a mental-health crisis is upon us is based on the empirically supported assumption that neither inter-subjective nor intra-psychological processes (and thus the generation of subjective motivational energy) can be accelerated at will. Such processes take place at their own specific pace, and any alteration of this inherent pace can have dysfunctional consequences.[15]

When the operative mode of dynamic stabilization leads to the permanent acceleration of society's material, social, and cultural mechanisms of reproduction, this will necessarily have consequences for the psychic constitution (not to mention the bodies and characters[16]) of subjects. The question, then, is how much dynamization individuals can tolerate – especially in light of the specific amounts of time needed for cultures to reproduce themselves through the transmission of values, knowledge, and habitus from one generation to the next – before a situation of dysfunctional desynchronization arises. The psychiatrist and philosopher Thomas Fuchs has described, in the following words, the extent to which the pressure to accelerate weighs down on subjects: "Desynchronization, or falling out of common or world time, is the latent threat against which one must constantly defend oneself."[17] For this reason, late-modern individuals attempt in many ways to accelerate their psychosomatic orientation toward time, for instance by using stimulants such as caffeine, cocaine, and speed, or by taking other medications and supplements that promise to "resynchronize" our consciousness, bodies, and social lives (Ritalin, Taurin, Focus Factor, and so on). Moreover, almost all forms of human enhancement are intended to accelerate bodies and minds that appear too slow in light of the rising socio-technical speeds of operation – whether by "optimizing" whatever seems to be "lagging behind" or by technologically "reconciling" the speeds of humans and machines, as advocated by transhumanists.[18]

At the same time, however, there are alarming indications that *pathological* forms of desynchronization, such as burnout and depression, are becoming more widespread.[19] "In a state of depression," as Fuchs remarks, "all these efforts [to synchronize] fail; the individual falls hopelessly behind, and this disconnection from intersubjective time becomes reality."[20] It is therefore even possible to *define* depression as a form of desynchronization.[21] The World Health Organization itself has meanwhile acknowledged that depression and burnout – alongside other pathological reactions to stress such as eating disorders, sleep disorders, and anxiety disorders – represent the fastest-growing health problems worldwide.[22]

One of the most prominent features of burnout and depression is that they lead to an entirely *undynamic* condition. Those who fall into a state of burnout or depression experience time as standing still – the world and/or the self seem to be "frozen" and deprived of any meaning or movement.[23] "Depressed people suffer from a deceleration and alienation of subjectively experienced time. Their motivational forces weaken, their life's movement comes to a halt, and in cases of severe depression this can reach the point of time itself standing still. The possibilities of the future appear closed and are replaced by a sense of ever threatening and even inescapable doom," as Fuchs summarizes his clinical findings. He then quotes one of his depressed patients: "My internal clock has stopped, while the clocks of others continue to tick. I make no progress in anything I should be doing, as though paralyzed. I fall behind on my obligations. I steal time."[24]

In agreement with such an assessment, authors such as Alain Ehrenberg understand depression as a stress-induced reaction of a desynchronized psyche to modern life's demands for greater speed.[25] Like the ecological crisis of desynchronization, the mental-health crisis also undermines the existential conditions of the modern social formation. Whereas the former underscores the problem of modernity's insatiable need for physical-material energy, the psychological crisis embodied in cases of burnout reveals modernity's equally insatiable (systemic and structural) demand for cultural and subjective motivational energy. It is therefore precisely at this point where we find the decisive interface between the structural and cultural forces of the modern social formation, where their reciprocal effects take place, as will become clear in my discussion of the next component.

3.2 Component 4: Alienation and the Muting of the World

In the section before last ("Component 2"), I attempted to show that the cultural engine of the modern social formation lies in its promise to make the world more *attainable and controllable*. At the heart of this "culturally" critical diagnosis of modernity (in the sense of my sixfold structure of a best account) lies the idea that this promise and its attendant promise of happiness cannot be fulfilled. In late modernity, in fact, these promises run the risk of leading to the exact opposite of their intended results. Once it is made available scientifically and technologically, economically and politically, the world can become radically *uncontrollable* in two ways – externally or internally. Therein lies the central paradox of the modern social formation.

The constitutive (external) uncontrollability of the world is evident from the fact that, in late modernity, it seems as though every effort to expand our technical or social control over things entails, as its downside, the paradoxical feeling of *utter powerlessness*. The result is a constant oscillation between the promise and experience of near-omnipotence, on the one hand, and the experience of radical powerlessness and vulnerability, on the other. A paradigmatic example of this is the development of the scientific and technological ability to split atomic nuclei and harness the energy released from this process. With this ability, modernity indeed reached a new level of controlling the material world by bringing the internal kinetic principle of matter (its "nucleus") within reach, thereby assuming nearly *world-generating* powers.[26] In cultural history, however, this new feeling of control soon gave way to the fear or actual experience of radioactive chain reactions, in the form of bombs or nuclear meltdowns. Against such forces, modern subjects are completely powerless, both individually and collectively.

Interestingly, the paradoxical structure of this experience is repeated, somewhat like a large-scale mirror image, in the late-modern relationship to nature in general. The latter is characterized by a tremendous increase in our knowledge, control, domination, and use of nature's forces and processes, be it in quantum physics, genetic engineering, biochemistry, and semiconductor chemistry, in the development of artificial intelligence, or in many other areas. At the same time, however, what I have described from a structural perspective as ecological desynchronization has led to the widespread conviction that we, as a social formation, are ultimately not making the world more controllable and accessible as much as we are endangering and destroying it. The program of making the world controllable has turned into an uncontrollable practice of endangerment and annihilation, the result of which seems to be that the social formation itself is now at risk of being destroyed by hurricanes, thawing permafrost, avalanches, rising sea levels, heat waves, and droughts, etc. In this case, too, approximate omnipotence has transformed into an experience of constitutive uncontrollability, and therefore one of radical powerlessness.

This paradox, however, is by no means limited to modernity's relationship to nature; it is also based, in my opinion, on the late-modern relationship to history and politics. The basis of the cultural program of making the world controllable is what could be called a "spiritual declaration of independence" from nature and history. In principle, neither the limitations of nature nor the dictates of history (tradition, convention, ancestors, etc.) should have any binding or restricting force. Just as technological developments continue to increase our independence from nature, the idea of *popular sovereignty* and democracy imply the notion that all laws of coexistence – in the economy and education, law and culture, etc. – are politically controllable and therefore (democratically) malleable, and that the historical establishment of such laws has no binding effect. The idea that all power or state authority derives from the people is nothing less than a political claim to omnipotence,[27] even though this idea is contradicted by the experience of radical political impotence – for instance in the efforts to change everyday living conditions in a meaningful way or to combat social inequality, economic injustice, or climate change, in the face of more

complex, more powerful, and faster financial markets, global interconnections, and sociocultural differences. The disparity between the
promise of political controllability and the experience of democratic
powerlessness is, in my opinion, central to the phenomena so often
discussed today in terms of the "crisis of democracy" and "right-
wing populism." Populists promise, with a sweep of the hand, to
make the uncontrollable controllable again. It is no coincidence that
the main slogan of the Brexit campaign was "Take back control!"
For many voters in the United States, Donald Trump's appeal lay
not least in the fact that he simply did things that, according to the
prevailing political consensus, *never could have been done*: utterly
ignoring international organizations and treaties, financial markets,
national courts, the media, and the basic logic of functional differentiation – not to mention his introduction of new tariffs and his
initiative to build a wall between the United States and Mexico, and
so on.[28] Paradoxically, however, such attempts to restore political
controllability led directly to new, late-modern forms of tremendous
political uncontrollability. Whenever highly complex and highly
interconnected bureaucratic entities such as the European Union are
confronted with radical political acts such as the Brexit referendum
or Trumpian solo acts, it becomes apparent that the political world
can return, seemingly overnight, to a state of radical political unpredictability and uncontrollability.

Late-modern subjects, however, experience the transformation
from approximate omnipotence to paralyzing impotence to an
even greater extent in their everyday lives. So it is for high-school
graduates, for instance, who seem to have the world at their fingertips
and who have 19,000 accredited courses of study to choose from in
Germany, and yet, in light of this abundance and the unpredictable
paths their lives might take in a highly dynamic society, they feel
completely incapable of deciding what sort of degree they ought to
pursue. This also applies to health-conscious people who, despite (or
because of) the availability of more and more detailed and extensive
information about the ingredients and effects of food products (of
which there are also more and more to choose from), develop eating
disorders because, despite (or because) of their strictly controlled
dietary behavior, they feel as though they are losing control of their
metabolic interaction with nature.[29] This also applies, moreover, to
the anxieties experienced by pregnant women. Despite (or because
of) the ever new and increasingly sophisticated technical means
for monitoring the bodily processes of both the embryo and the
mother, these anxieties are not reduced but are in fact made even
worse; expectant mothers can come to feel as though they are
self-ineffective – first, because they are dependent on the technical

apparatuses in question; and second, because the bodily processes in question are beyond their control in any case.[30]

The paradigmatic culmination of this tipping point from power to powerlessness, however, can be found in the use of so-called "smart technologies." In a smart home or a smart car, the owner can literally feel nearly omnipotent with a remote control in hand. One click, and the temperature warms up; one push of a button, and it cools down. Light or dark, loud or quiet, red or blue, until the electronic system fails – "One moment please," says a voice from the device or a text on the screen – and one's feelings of omnipotence immediately turn into feelings of radical powerlessness. The light doesn't turn on, the heat doesn't turn off, the music remains loud, and the door remains closed. Unlike in the days of the *partially* controllable, unruly world, here there is no way to make things better with a hammer and a pair of pliers, and brute force will be no help either. "One moment please! One moment please! One moment please! One ..." The rage of late-modern subjects is never greater than when they have *radically lost effectiveness*, when they can accomplish absolutely nothing on their own – other than call for tech support. Even these expert technicians, however, often have no choice but to send a defective device back to the manufacturer.

Thus can be described (in broad strokes) the external paradox of the *uncontrollability* of the world as it is experienced by subjects. Yet there is also an *internal experience* of uncontrollability, which seems to unfold in a manner complementary to increased external controllability, or in reaction to it. "Alienation" – a "relation of relationlessness" (in Rahel Jaeggi's terms)[31] – is the proper term for what I have in mind here, and what I described in my book *Resonance* as the experience of radically muting the world. Once made controllable, the world seems to become elusive in a mysterious way; it seems to become illegible, inaudible, barren, and empty – or, to put it in terms of resonance theory: both *deaf* and *mute*. Alienation is the result of an encounter between the subject and the world in which their *assimilation* fails in a fundamental and lasting way. It can be caused by social injustice or by a lack of resources, but it can also occur, for instance, when a music lover, faced with 50 million available songs on her streaming service, can't find a single song she wants to listen to – or when a high school graduate finds himself utterly incapable of choosing one out of any number of possible destinations for his long-planned graduation trip:

> Parks, capital cities, Helsinki, cats, llamas, Komodo dragons, Galapagos tortoises, nature preserves, local recreational areas, camping stoves, [...] bridges over the Rhein, countries, people,

adventures – all of it nothing but mush. In my desperation I threw open the window and shouted into the complex of town houses: Who flattened the round globe, why are there no valleys or oceans anymore, who uncrumpled and smoothed out the Alps, why does nothing stick out on this earth??? No answer. The destinations of the entire world lay before me with indifference. Now I was tapping into the global whatever. Jetlag. *Weary traveler, lay yourself down* ... Full of nothing, I lay my noggin down on the plastic Pacific.

This is how Rainald Grebe, in his debut novel *Global Fish*, depicts just such a moment of existential alienation.[32] Here, the problem for the novel's protagonist, Thomas Blume, is not that he lacks rational criteria for choosing the best option; his problem is that he feels "no response" from the options at his disposal – that he is not "called" or affected by anything. If the experience of alienation is characterized by the (available and controllable) world becoming bleak and empty, mute and deaf, cold and gray, it can also be said this is a typical feature (or a preliminary stage) of depression. Thomas Blume's psychological disposition, as developed in Grebe's novel, is on the brink of turning into clinical burnout, which is additionally characterized by the fact that the suffering subject will experience himself as cold, deaf, mute, and empty. Burnout is a radical psychological and physical manifestation of alienation – a condition in which it has essentially become impossible to process the world. Of the utmost importance to any diagnosis of the modern social formation, moreover, is the fact that the clinical condition of burnout is accompanied by, in addition to the radically reduced ability to be affected by things, a just as radical loss of motivational energy. Sufferers of burnout have described how they were unable to walk up a flight of stairs or were incapable of lifting a cup to their mouths, even though they seemed physically healthy and thus in possession of their physical energy. Alienation can thus be reconceived as a *cultural disorder* of a social formation that drains the productive energy of desire.

If, however, my thesis is correct that a social formation's institutional processing and modernity's a fortiori escalatory dynamic are dependent on the cultural generation and release of its subjects' motivational energies, then the current *fear of burnout*, which characterizes the *culture* of late modernity, is the symptom of a crisis that also affects the late-modern social formation on a *structural* level. Late modernity would thus be facing, as it were, a *dual* energy crisis – one of which is external and ecological, while the other is internal. The latter crisis, as I have argued, can be explained by the fact that

the promise of modernity – the promise of a controllable, accom-
modating, and pacified world – is dimming and even becoming its
opposite. The end of illusions thus turns out to be twofold. On the
one hand, the world is not becoming more controllable but, rather,
to an increasing extent, uncontrollable and threatening. On the
other hand, however, wherever the world has become controllable, it
loses its *attractiveness* – because every *desire* (as the central positive
impetus behind motivational energy) is always directed toward
something that is *constitutively uncontrollable* and yet *attainable in
principle*.[33] Every love will end if we attempt to bring the beloved
under our power and our control. The phantasm of a completely
controllable world is therefore revealed to be a vision of a dead,
listless, and *un*attractive world that extinguishes desire. Yet desire
will also fade away in a world where the uncontrollable has become
monstrous, which is to say: *unattainable in principle*. In this respect,
the social formation of modernity now finds itself on a perilous
course between Scylla and Charybdis.

4

Adaptive Stabilization and Resonance: A Therapeutic and Transgressive Outline of an Alternative Horizon

Can and should the sociological theory of society propose remedies for the pathologies of a social formation? I have already clarified above why any societal-theoretical best account that is a reaction to a perceived crisis should attempt to develop, at least in outline, a horizon for transforming existing conditions and thus overcoming the crisis in question. This cannot be achieved, however, by providing socio-technological answers to individual functional problems, but rather by presenting alternative designs for what appears to be problematic and worthy of critique in the constitution of the social formation as a whole. In this sense, any proposals of this sort will necessarily be a transgressive moment intended to *transform the social formation* under consideration. Of course, this transgression must already be an inherent aspect of a best account's analysis and diagnosis; transgression must emerge, as it were, from such analysis, which should develop, or at least bring to light, alternatives (in the sense of *inner-worldly transcendence*), from the contradictions and tensions of the social formation. For the older critical theory – as it was practiced by Theodor W. Adorno, Herbert Marcuse, and Walter Benjamin – the central challenge was to maintain a sense that a different form of existence might be possible (and perhaps desirable) in a world that increasingly conceals formative boundaries, thereby limiting the potential to transgress them.[1] In what follows, I would therefore like to explore the options for developing a *different relationship to the world* as a whole by identifying, from the interpretive proposal that I have presented so far, both structural and cultural alternatives, or possibilities for transgression.

4.1 Component 5: Beyond the Escalation Imperative – Adaptive Stabilization

It all seems simple enough. If dynamic stabilization is the problem – because it creates escalatory and insatiable expectations for growth, thereby causing more and more desynchronization – then a different mode of stabilization is the obvious solution. However, such an alternative mode of stabilization or reproduction must not be thought of as static. Because all living things are predisposed to change, and reproduce themselves in states of change, any "freeze" or stagnation of a social condition that inhibits growth, innovation, and acceleration – and thus also the emergence of transformative energies[2] – would be neither desirable nor possible in the long term. Examined more closely, the problem of the modern social formation does not lie in its dynamic character per se, but rather in its intrinsic *demand for escalation*, which has itself become firmly established and ossified.[3] What is needed is therefore a structural and institutional arrangement that is *capable* of growing, accelerating, and innovating when there are *good reasons* for doing so – to meet needs and respond to changing environmental conditions, threats, scarcity, and the like – but does not demand constant escalation simply to reproduce its structure and maintain the institutional status quo. In short, escalation should and must be possible if the matter at hand is one of changing the status quo or reacting to altered environmental conditions, but escalation should not be endogenous and required simply to maintain the status quo. I therefore refer to this mode as *adaptive stabilization*. I do not mean by this that society as it presently exists should adapt to challenges, but rather that an *alternative* social formation should be created. Because the latter, as already mentioned, would not exclude the possibility of dynamic developments or deny the appeal of such developments, especially when it comes to fulfilling social needs, the goal of this alternative formation would not be *degrowth* but rather *post-growth*. The question of whether a society achieves economic growth, high rates of innovation, and increasing productivity (which seems entirely reasonable in regions of the world where hunger – not obesity – is the dominant problem) is conceptually independent from the question of whether it stabilizes itself dynamically or not.

Yet how should such a different social structure look? Sketched out on a theorist's desk, a blueprint for an alternative formation of society can be regarded as the epitome of an illusionary – and, as history has taught us, politically dangerous – fantasy of controllability. In what follows, I will therefore limit myself to three broad ideas, each of which is directed toward the interface between culture and structure identified above: toward the "energy budget," and thus toward the modern social formation's relationship to the world as such.

4.1.1 Metabolic Interaction with Nature

Even the founding fathers of sociology fundamentally agreed that a society's relationship to the world, and thus also the institutional structure of a social formation, is essentially defined by the way in which it organizes its metabolic interaction with nature – that is, how it deals with the resistance that it faces from the world. What this means, however, is that the social formation is structurally and institutionally determined by what is subsumed in sociology under the terms "labor" and "economy." This conviction underlies the main works of early sociology – Weber's *Economy and Society* and *The Protestant Ethic*, as well as Marx's *Capital* and Durkheim's *The Division of Labor in Society*.[4] Equally undisputed is the fact that modernity's dominant social formation at this point is capitalist. All known varieties of capitalism are designed to be dynamic and grow through the process of accumulating capital, which is to say that they are dependent on following a logic of permanently opening up previously uncommodified areas of life. As we have seen, the accumulation of capital systematically compels all three forms of escalation (growth, acceleration, and innovation), and wherever one of these forms fails temporarily or regionally (wherever, say, growth is lacking), then the other two forms of escalation act all the more strongly.

A post-growth society will therefore require a fundamental reform of the economic system, but how might this look? In my opinion, it is necessary for society's structure and culture to "reclaim" labor and the economy – that is, to assign them an (instrumental) place within the form of life as a whole, and not, conversely, to allow the development of this form of life to be determined individually and collectively by the blind pressures of economic growth. By "re-embedding" the economy into the cultural and political world – into the form of life as a whole – the capitalist logic of appropriation and exploitation would no longer be accepted as a structural necessity, though this would not exclude this logic from remaining a socio-economic *possibility* (in certain aspects of life). Decades ago, Karl Polanyi developed several ideas along these lines, which have since been further developed by Nancy Fraser and others.[5] A re-embedding of this sort would make it possible to evaluate, in a critical manner, the attractiveness or unattractiveness of growth, escalation, and innovation, instead of being blindly subjected to their imperatives.

There has been no shortage of suggestions about how to think about such a re-embedding in *institutional* terms and about how it might be practically achieved, but, as a whole, these proposals have so far seemed unpersuasive and difficult to implement.[6] A sense of hopelessness and futility seems to loom over any attempt to develop implementable reforms, and this feeling has largely stultified (at least for the time being) the social energy required to produce transformative changes in society. Instead of making such suggestions myself,[7] I would like to restrict myself here to identifying a central flaw in the dominant institutional formation that might perhaps explain this lack of courage or imagination, and I would like to show how the elimination or correction of this flaw might make it possible to enable the transformation that I have in mind. To do so, it will be necessary yet again to cast a short look at what, fundamentally, constitutes a social formation.

My point of departure is that the basis of every social formation is its relationship to the world. Individually and collectively, people are situated in a world to which they must relate, with which they are always already in a relationship. To be, in Maurice Merleau-Ponty's terms, is *being-in-the-world* (*être-au-monde*).[8] Analytically, it is possible to distinguish two perspectives on the basis of the economic form of our relationship to the world: a *productive* perspective, which focuses on the way in which we *process* the world, and a *consumptive* perspective, which concentrates on the way in which individuals *appropriate* the world. Both in institutional reality and in the cultural perception of modernity, these two sides are radically separated from one another. There are whole worlds, so to speak, between the sites of production (mines, factories, etc.) and the sites of consumption (shopping malls, online commerce, etc.). The flaw that concerns me here is that the economic and political institutions of modernity de facto determine the conditions of production (that is, the way we *process* the world), and yet, semantically (that is, in the way they direct attention, and thus steer the libidinous energies of desire and fear), they operate almost entirely from the perspective of consumption. The *market* model devised by economists, which has been so influential in the age of neoliberalism, is thoroughly based on the perspective of the consumer. It is always about incentivizing consumption; every form of production and every type of market is aimed at triggering the choice to consume (that is, their goal is to create the desire to buy or have a product, service, or innovation). In this respect, *the customer is king* is not just a slogan; it is a formative reality. Accordingly, Clemens Fuerst, who is the current director of the German Ifo Institute for Economic Research, can claim with a straight face that the economy as a whole is exclusively in the service, and under the control, of consumers.[9]

The ideal market, of which economists dream, is one that offers the best possible products at the lowest possible prices. Moreover, the political system, especially in its neoliberal late-modern form, follows this exact same logic in its efforts to control consumption by creating "incentives" – in response to ecological concerns, for instance, this happens when electricity, gasoline, or air travel are made more expensive, and when renewable energy sources are subsidized to be less expensive, or when debates are held about whether ecological "costs" should be integrated into "prices" at all. This applies not only to the individual consumption of "end users," but also to businesses, which, regarding their role in creating a cleaner and more environmentally friendly economy, are themselves treated as consumers and are politically nudged by consumption-based incentives (government efforts to increase or decrease the costs of certain types of labor, raw materials, waste disposal, emissions, etc.). Within the network of modern institutions, actors understand and treat one another as *rational consumers*, even in cases where political regulations influence production processes. It is often overlooked, however, that they are also *producers* who *work* and *identify themselves through their work*, that they are engaged in *processing* nature above all, and that thus they enter into this relationship with nature before they consume it. Labor is thus understood as a purely instrumental relationship.

What is absent here are nearly all the ethical, aesthetic, and democratic sensibilities that are so widely institutionalized on the side of consumers and customers. The central modern values of autonomy, authenticity, and democratic equality (in terms of having equal rights as market participants) are largely actualized in institutions that address subjects as consumers, but hardly at all in the matters pertaining to how subjects act as producers. *What* is produced, *how much* is produced, and *how* things are produced are determined – if not entirely, then to a great extent – by the social formation's escalatory imperatives and by the laws of competition that happen to govern one market or another.[10]

With respect to sociology and history, however, it is no coincidence that societies are identified and defined according to their *modes of production*, and not according to their forms of consumption. One need not be a Marxist to recognize that we define social formations as hunting societies, fishing societies, or gatherer societies, and not as societies of rabbit eaters, fish eaters, or berry eaters. We speak about agrarian societies, industrial societies, or information societies, and not about milk-drinking societies, car-driving societies, or computer-using societies. Contrary to all the prognoses that we live in a consumer or leisure society, moreover, subjects in fact identify themselves even today in terms of their involvement on the *productive* side of things – as architects or stonemasons, as entrepreneurs, bakers, or programmers. They continue to interpret their individual relationship to the world in terms of how they *work with* the resistant world. There is thus a decidedly patriarchal aspect to the division of this relationship into spheres of production and consumption, at least to the extent that this division tends to downplay the *reproductive* side of our relationship to the world, which is just as fundamental for any social formation as its habits of consumption. In any case, the ways in which the institutional structures of our productive relationship to the world are formed are largely beyond the reach of individual and collective participation. This is determined and dominated by modernity's growth imperatives and by the libidinous energies of consumption.

It is admittedly true that the boundary conditions of how we process the world are collectively and politically influenced in the form of labor agreements, protection provisions, etc., but the methods, goals, or quantities of production are seldom considered or discussed in terms of their possible effects on society. Yet the way in which we process the world and relate to it is central to what we are, and if the customer is the *almighty* king, then the producer is no more than a *powerless* subject. I should stress that I am not in favor of returning to the failed model of the planned economy. My point is to draw attention to the fact that a central aspect of the way in which we relate to the world is entirely outside of our reflective, political, and individual control. In this respect, the modern ideals of autonomy and sovereignty are undermined even where the beneficiaries of global inequality happen to live.

Of crucial importance is the fact that consumer decisions are made individually, while the conditions of production can only be shaped or changed collectively. Herein lies another paradox of modern society: the systematic and – quantitatively speaking – increasing individual and institutional *uncontrollability* of production goals, production methods, and thus our productive relationship to the world is compensated for by the constant expansion of the individual and consumer-related horizon of control. It is therefore no surprise that economics and political science proceed from the axioms of methodological individualism – and that the political establishment of social institutions follows these axioms as well, by orienting them toward the desires of individual consumers and toward the actions and decisions of customers, clients, and voters, who are regarded as "rational actors." The question of how to live a good and proper life has become a question of individual lifestyle, and the answer to this question has come in the form of the pervasive *privatization of good*.[11] As a result, theories and practices of *ethical consumption* now attempt to influence the forms and goals of production through the backdoor of individual consumer decisions by introducing moral points of view into the social formation, all with the hope of readjusting our material relationship to the world. It is this context that makes late-modern economics look like a science of domination while making sociology appear to be a science of opposition. Even though the subdisciplines of labor sociology and industrial sociology have lost some of their former influence, the field in general is still steered by the conviction that the collective organization of the sphere of production (and, to a growing extent, that of the reproductive sphere as well) is of central importance to society as a whole. Economists regard the *marketplace* as the center of individual consumer decisions, and treat the paradigm of methodological individualism as nearly absolute, while sociologists tend to regard the *workplace* as central and are inclined toward methodological holism.[12] For a long time, both disciplines overlooked the cardinal importance of the reproductive sphere – which is located, as it were, somewhere in between – though sociologists have done a great deal of work on this issue in the last three decades.

From this perspective, modernity's dominant self-interpretation, which culminates in the idea of *popular sovereignty as a way of autonomously determining one's form of life*, proves to be an illusion. On the one hand, autonomy and equality have no validity in the workplace; as people who "process the world," workers have no say about the means, quantities, and goals of production. As early as the 1980s, Charles Taylor recognized that a historical compromise had been made in the developed modern world: "The compromise consists in accepting alienated labour in return for consumer affluence."[13] On the other hand, however, the autonomy and efficiency of citizens – as people who can determine their own form of life – have increasingly been suppressed in favor of citizens as producers, consumers, and customers. Far from being the result of political deliberation and consensus, social organization and the way in which people conduct their lives in late-modern society seem instead to be the product of the industrial and digital revolutions, on the one hand, and of economic growth imperatives, on the other.

Modern society tirelessly seeks to constitute itself as a consumer heaven; it derives its pride and its feeling of self-worth from its overflowing supply of goods on all levels of life:[14] *The best products at the lowest prices*, tailored to satisfy even the most peculiar individual needs. Who could ask for anything more? Consumer heaven, however, cannot help but be producer hell (not to mention the problems that it implies for the reproductive sphere and the ecosphere), because in the ideal market envisioned by economists, even the smallest deviation from the highest possible quality and lowest possible price will jeopardize a company's market position, and therefore the pressure to rationalize, accelerate, and optimize is unending.

Subjects are formed via their active relationship to the world, and yet in today's society they are addressed almost exclusively as consumers and customers. This sort of relationship to the world has produced not only an overheating atmosphere, a devastated planet, and a towering mountain of garbage; it has also led to a burned-out workforce of producers and reproducers. Above all, however, it has systematically engendered a feeling of alienation (foreseen long ago) resulting from the conceptual and institutional concealment of the connection between production, reproduction, and consumption. Or, as Charles Taylor observed as long ago as 1971:

> A sense of building their future through the civilization of work can sustain men as long as they see themselves as having broken with a millennial past of injustice and hardship in order to create qualitatively different conditions for their children. All the requirements of a humanly acceptable identity can be met by this predicament, a relation to the past (one soars above it but preserves it in folkloric memory), to the social world (the inter-dependent world of free, productive men), to the earth (the raw material which awaits shaping), to the future and one's own death (the everlasting monument in the lives of prosperous children), to the absolute (the absolute values of freedom, integrity, dignity). But at some point the children will be unable to sustain this forward thrust into the future. This effort has placed them in a private haven of security, within which they are unable to reach and recover touch with the great realities: their parents have only a negated past, lives which have been oriented wholly to the future; the social world is distant and without shape; rather one can only insert oneself into it by taking one's place in the future-oriented productive juggernaut. But this now seems without any sense; the relation to the earth as raw material is therefore experienced as empty and alienating, but the recovery of a valid relation to the earth is the hardest thing once lost; and there is no relation to the absolute where we are caught in the web of meanings which have gone dead for us. Hence past, future, earth, world, and absolute

are in some way or another occluded; and what must arise is an identity crisis of frightening proportions.[15]

In order to transform modernity's current social formation into one that is able to stabilize *adaptively*, in the sense suggested above, it will thus be necessary to reorient its political, legal, and economic institutions toward its *productive and reproductive* relationship to the world, and it will especially be necessary to overcome the separation between its atomized approach to consumption, its alienating and externally determined approach to production, and its detached approach to reproduction. This, in turn, will require the actualization of new forms of *economic democracy* that take into account the *reproductive sphere*,[16] extend modernity's promise of freedom to the productive side of the equation, and allow for markets and competition without letting their escalatory tendencies go unchecked.

4.1.2 Pulling the Plug: Turning off Negative Motivational Energy

In the first part of my contribution to this book, I pointed out that institutions and structures cannot create growth, acceleration, and innovation on their own. For this, they also need subjective motivational energies, which means that they rely on the cultural generation of ambitions and fears. Moreover, institutions and structures cannot change themselves on their own. This requires a corresponding degree of transformational energy, which likewise has to be culturally created and steered. Thus, if we want to ask about the possibilities of structurally transforming our escalation-based social formation, it seems sensible to direct our attention to this energetic interface between structure and culture. One driving factor – if not the central such factor – in late modernity's disastrous "game of escalation," as I noted above, is the *fear of social death*, which results from being excluded from the productive–consumptive cycle of resonance between paid labor and income.

In my view, an important step toward transforming the present social formation of modernity would be to pull the energetic plug, so to speak, on unbridled escalation by making this fear disappear, or at least significantly reducing it. This would be the case if subjects could be sure of their social and material basis of existence – that is, if they were no longer forced to defend this basis by participating in a constant competition and struggle for more and more. The aim, in Marcuse's words, would thus be the "pacification of existence."[17] In principle, this has now been made possible by the unprecedented increase in productive forces over the last two and a half centuries, but it has been prevented by systematic constraints imposed by dynamic stabilization. The daily struggle for social status and a sure material footing – socio-ontological *insecurity*, which is unavoidable (within the late-modern social formation), and which is based on the logic of escalation – should be replaced by guaranteed ontological security. One instrument for achieving this sort of adaptive stabilization on the individual level is the provision of a *universal basic income*,[18] which, if introduced in a well thought-out form, would create a secure baseline or floor in a system of *steep and slippery declines*. In their way of life and form of existence, actors could then orient themselves toward *having enough*, which would replace the feeling of *always wanting more but never having enough*. The dialectical dynamic between generating profit and raising wages, between fearing for one's job and increasing one's performance at work, would thus be deprived of its energy supply, so that the structural logic of the social formation would change considerably. In this way, the idea of an unconditional basic income could become the cornerstone of the institutional configuration of a post-growth economy that might be able to fulfill modernity's existential promise of freedom.[19]

4.1.3 Redirecting the Current: The Institutional Reorientation of Positive Motivational Energy

In order for the transformation to an adaptively stabilized postgrowth society to be achieved, however, it is not enough to dry up the sources of negative motivational energy. Social change will remain unlikely, if not impossible, as long as nothing is done on the side of positive cultural motivational sources, which create the energy of desire. This energy is currently devoted, in a one-sided manner, to broadening the horizons of controllability; it is fixated on (economic) growth and expansion (of options and possibilities), and thus it also unilaterally determines the criteria according to which one's prosperity and quality of life are measured. What is needed, therefore, is an alternative vision and an alternative standard for evaluating quality and performance, and, in general, for evaluating the form of institutional realities in business and labor, healthcare and education, sports and culture, etc.

Such a standard will require quality of life to be *conceptually decoupled* from growth, and my thesis is that this decoupling can succeed and be institutionally effective with the help of the concept of resonance, which I will outline in my final section below. On the basis of this new standard, for instance, healthcare facilities, educational institutions, and the agricultural industry would no longer be measured and evaluated (financially or otherwise) by the extent to which they maximize the output of what is available with a minimum input of energy or economic resources; instead, they would be measured according to the extent to which they establish and maintain *axes of resonance* between caregivers and patients, between pupils and the curriculum, between humans and nature. Of course, in all these spheres – and indeed in more or less *every* institution in the working world and public administration – the *formative insistence on escalation* will always be at cross-purposes in new and different ways with the desire for resonant relationships, a desire that is *also* affective and palpable. This happens, for instance, when a nurse feels the silent gaze of a patient but directs her own attention to the clock; when a teacher detects that a student is interested in a subject that is not part of the official curriculum; when a butcher suddenly encounters the pain and suffering of a slaughtered animal. This also happens, however, when a baker feels as though she can no longer do good work because the pressure to speed up and cut costs has become overwhelming; when a journalist or a scientist feels that her publications are becoming worse or more superficial under the pressure to meet quotas or acquire third-party funding; or when an employment agency recognizes the contradictions between the needs of its clients and the administrative directives that it is forced to follow. And so on and so forth. As we have seen, the (alienating) divide between the escalation-based parameters of optimization and the resonant feeling of *being-in-the-world* is often manifested in the form of fundamental *desynchronization*, and this gap can be felt and identified in nearly all of modernity's everyday institutions, even when one is on vacation. This gap or divide can become the gateway or starting point for an institutional transformation toward an adaptively stabilizing and resynchronized social formation.[20] A restructuring or transformation of this sort would not pull the plug on the positive motivational energies of the social formation; instead, it would steer the current of our culture's motivational energy, without which change is impossible, in a different direction. This new direction could lead to a reimagined cultural conception of the successful life, in which, as suggested above, growth (economic or otherwise) would be decoupled from quality of life. By way of conclusion, I would now like to outline how such a conception might look.

4.2 Component 6: Alienation's "Other" – Resonance

With the last component of my best account of the late-modern social formation, I would like to provide, if nothing else, a tentative answer to the cultural crisis that I diagnosed above. We have already seen that such a response will entail a revision of motivational cultural forces – that is, a revision of the prevailing notion of the good life. Interestingly, a recurring symptom of this crisis has been an irreconcilable divide between activity and passivity, between omnipotence and powerlessness, which, as I pointed out in my previous section, is also reflected in the separation between active (but alienating) production and generally passive (but autonomously experienced) consumption. This discrepancy between an active and pathic way of relating to the world was already a theme in the oft-cited passage at the end of Max Weber's work on the spirit of capitalism, in which he fears that the development of modern culture is heading toward "mechanized ossification," with the possible result that the *last men*, "dressed up with a kind of desperate self-importance," could turn out to be "specialists without spirit [=producers], hedonists without a heart [=consumers]." "These non-entities," Weber concludes, "imagine they have attained a stage of humankind never before reached."[21]

This lack of spirit on the part of producers and lack of heart on the part of consumers reveals two aspects of a fundamental problem – namely, a dysfunction in the relationship between subjects and the world. On the one hand, this dysfunction exists in the relationship between working (or researching) specialists and what they are working on; on the other hand, it exists between consuming hedonists and the objects of their pleasure. As a "relation of relationlessness" (to recall Jaeggi's phrase), alienation therefore lies at the heart of both of these pathological phenomena. How, then, should we think about or conceptualize a successful relationship, a *related relationship* (as it were)?

In my view, a successful relationship (to the world) is characterized by the fact that it is mediated between active and passive moments – intentional and pathic moments – in a specifically *mediopassive* way, and that it does so not only in individual experiences but also, and especially, in our socially organized, institutionalized, and thus habituated relationship to the world.[22] The term *mediopassive* (or middle voice), which comes from linguistics, refers above all to a mode of expression that operates in between the active and passive voices of verbs. The middle voice no longer exists in modern Western languages (beyond faint vestiges), but it can be found in ancient Greek, Hebrew, Sanskrit, and in many other languages.[23] It makes it possible to express a way of participating or being involved in an event or activity in which the subject is neither the perpetrator nor the victim – in which, in fact, it is not possible to draw a categorical distinction between subject and object. In such situations, people experience themselves as being neither omnipotent nor powerless, but rather as *semi-empowered*,[24] which means that they *take* part in and are *given* a role at the same time (and thus their experience is simultaneously medio-*passive* and medio-*active*). The idea of the medio-passive concerns a form of *being-in-the-world* in which we are *both* active *and* passive – or *neither* active *nor* passive, but in a state of being beyond this distinction, and perhaps even beyond the distinction between *condition* and *action*.[25] This idea therefore does not apply to forms of interaction and communication that function according to the sender–receiver model, in which we (actively) send out signals and (passively) receive them, in two separate processes. Rather, the relevant forms of interaction here – which are by no means esoteric, but are basically everyday practices – are those in which active and passive moments are inextricably intertwined to the extent that we cannot even say whether we are being active or passive. A good example of this type of interaction is *listening to music*. According to the grammatical form, this is an active experience; and to the extent that we consciously choose to do so (we pick out a certain type of music, turn up the volume, and so on), this is in fact true. However, as soon as we close our eyes and let ourselves be carried away by the music, it becomes rather difficult to say that this is simply an active experience. We are capti-vated and moved by the sounds and melodies, but we also actively follow them and participate in them. (If we happen to be depressed or exhausted, such active participation will be beyond our powers; at such times, we are *only* passively exposed to music and we do not really experience it: this is no more than a "relation of relation-lessness.") In this respect, love is similarly a mixed or hybrid form. According to its grammatical form, *to love* is likewise active, but do we *do* it or does it *happen to us*, or is it simply impossible in this case to separate the intentional from the pathic moments?

For a sociology concerned with our relationship to the world, however, what is even more relevant are forms of interaction that exhibit this mixed form from *both sides*, as it were. *Dancing* or *making music* are good examples of this sort of experience. According to dancers, the most successful moments of dancing are those in which they can no longer say whether they are leading or being led – moments in which the dance seems to develop from somewhere in between this relationship. Here, one would essentially have to say that *the dance dances the dancers* (and transforms them), and this very thought has been expressed poetically on any number of occasions.[26] Musicians experience something similar, for instance, when improvising (though not exclusively when improvising). Over long phases, one of them will set the signals and the other musicians will react, often interchanging roles, but this act of making music will become a living event in the moment when it is no longer possible to say where the impulses are coming from. They will arise from an intermediary space, from the middle, as though *the music is making itself*.[27] If these examples sound a bit too esoteric, think instead of an intensive discussion or a successful conversation. They have the power of coming to life and transforming the participants at the moment when it can no longer be said who is convincing whom, when new ideas seem to develop from the midst of circulating thoughts, so that, at the end of the discussion, neither side has won or lost but rather a new insight has emerged, whose authorship, so to speak, can be attributed to the conversation itself.

I suggest that the opposite of alienation should be understood as a related relationship of this sort. Upon closer analysis, such a relationship has four constitutive moments, which I have grouped together under the term *resonance*. The four elements in question are: (1) the moment of *af←fect* or touch: we are invoked and moved, as it were, by a person, music, an idea, an image, and so on; (2) the moment of *e→motion*, understood as an effective outwardly directed motion in response to something; (3) the moment of *transformation*: when we resonate with someone or something, we do not remain the same; and (4) the moment of constitutive *uncontrollability*: resonance can neither be forced nor instrumentally created, neither accumulated nor saved.

The first two moments make it clear that any resonant relationship involves a reciprocal dynamic of reaching out and being reached, and this dynamic causes subjects to feel connected to the world in an *active* and *intended* way. The arrows used above are meant to symbolize the idea of the medio-passive as motion in two directions, the intersection or middle of which gives rise to liveliness, energy, and novelty. The third moment, which claims that those who participate in a resonant event are transformed by it, is the moment that makes us feel alive, as Bruno Latour has also emphasized on more than one occasion.[28] It presupposes, however, that the other is experienced and accepted as *different*, and that this encounter with difference will also and invariably involve a degree of *tension* and *disturbance*; contact with others entails the risk of hurting and being hurt, and there is also danger in transformation. Resonance is never risk-free.

Nevertheless, it is the need for this relationship of touch and transformation that drives people. In my book *Resonance*, I identified the desire for resonance as the central energetic source of human action – even more important, perhaps, than the drive to satisfy our immediate physical needs.[29] Longing for this sort of being-in-the-world is what ultimately provided the motivational energy underlying the effort to expand the horizon of controllability, and it did so *before* this effort became a structural compulsion. It is based on the hope that the slices of the world with which we can resonate might be found and discovered *elsewhere*, that there is still more to discover and conquer. The program of making the world available, however, is therefore contradicted by the desire for resonance, which leads us to the fourth moment of the resonant event: its fundamental uncontrollability. Resonance can be neither guaranteed nor predicted, neither demanded nor claimed.

On the consumer side of things, capitalism works by redirecting the desire for resonance toward a desire for objects. Commodification offers the promise of resonance, as can be seen in just about every advertisement: *Buy this apple* or *book this cruise, and you will experience pure nature*; *buy this car, and you will experience what it means to have an effective relationship with the world*; *buy these chips, and you will experience true friendship*; and so on. The things made available in this way, however, are of course just *objects*, not the promised *experiences* associated with them by advertisers. In fact, the systemic need for constantly expanding consumption even feeds off the fact that the desire for resonance is consistently disappointed, that the relationship with commodities remains a "relation of relationlessness," and that we are therefore driven to our next act of consumption in pursuit of resonance, because the desire for resonance itself never goes away and cannot be extinguished.

Uncontrollability does not mean, however, that resonance will *never* occur on the cruise in question. It may or may not occur. Resonance can neither be produced at will, nor ever be counted out; it can happen when we least expect it. What is more, uncontrollability also implies that resonance is *open-ended*. Whenever we resonate with someone (or with several people), with an idea, with a landscape, with work, it is essentially unpredictable what *will come out of this*. We cannot know in which direction and in what ways we will be transformed and transform others. As I see it, this is precisely the locus of *natality* that Hannah Arendt numbers among the basic conditions of human existence: the ability to start anew arises from the open-ended and resonant interaction of human beings.[30]

Because parametric optimization can never be open-ended – given that time constraints and competition are veritable resonance killers, and given that the fear of being hurt discourages us from being open to others – the orientation toward resonance in our social behavior sharply contradicts the escalatory imperatives of modernity, as I have explained in detail in my book on the subject. A fundamental aspect of this is that the structurally enforced and culturally motivated program of making the world available creates an aggressive attitude of dominance and control in the ways that we encounter the world. This, in turn, has led to the crises of alienation diagnosed above. The concept of resonance, in contrast, allows for an alternative conception of the successful life, one that is already inherent in the modern social formation and in its aspirations but that cannot be actualized in its current institutions and practices. According to this conception, I think, we should indeed encounter a revolutionary moment of *inner-worldly transcendence*. This is based, first of all, on a shift in focus and a change in attitude. Goal-oriented, one-sided, and active *control and dominance*, which ultimately turns subjects into passive victims, should be replaced by open-ended *listening and responding*, by a dispositional and medio-passive mode of relating to the world. This would make a difference in society as a whole.

In order for it to work, this idea of changing the conception of the good life, which could lead to an institutional and structural transformation of the late-modern social formation (a transformation comparable to that from feudal to modern society), needs to be conceptually expanded in two ways. First of all, it is possible to distinguish four different forms of resonance. People experience their lives as successful when they are able to establish and maintain stable axes of resonance in the following four dimensions: (1) *social* axes of resonance in the sense of responsive relationships with other people; (2) *material* axes of resonance in the form of responsive relations to objects in the world (to the objects we work on, to the furniture with which we surround ourselves, to the plants we care for, or to the musical instruments we play); (3) *existential* axes of resonance that give us a sense of being in a responsive relationship with reality or the world as a whole, however we might define this (as nature, as life, as the universe, as history), and regardless of whether this is mediated through religious practices or experiences of art or nature; and, finally, (4) a *self-axis* that allows us to resonate *with ourselves*, with our body, our emotions, and our personal history, all of which confront us as uncontrollable others.

Regarding *whether* people succeed in establishing and maintaining axes of resonance, however, this does not depend on their individual insight or their good will but rather on the institutional contexts in which they operate and on the practices with which they (must) act. This is because institutions and practices are *intrinsically* linked to dispositional attitudes, which cannot be unilaterally changed without creating institutional dysfunctions that will ultimately destroy either the practices or the subjects. Resonant subjects need a resonant and responsive institutional structure, and vice versa – there cannot be one without the other. On the collective level – this is the second necessary expansion of my concept – a community would need to take shape whose institutionalized relationships to the world are no longer based on escalation and making the world available or controllable, but rather on a medio-passive mode of listening and responding. Because such a community not only would allow for uncontrollability but also would know to appreciate it as a vital aspect of life, it would not feel the need to confront uncontrollability in an aggressive way – and therefore it would not be afflicted by its monstrous return.

How should we think about this? Perhaps it is indeed epistemologically impossible to sketch the contours of a different and better paradigm on top of the blueprint of a dominant paradigm – an existing social formation. Even today, however, it is possible to conceive of a social world that encounters its *uncontrollable other* – both externally and internally – not in the mode of aggression or in the mode of making everything controllable, but rather with a gesture of transformative *listening and responding*. In this case, resonance on the *social axis* means that subjects encounter one another as fellow citizens *who have something to say to each other precisely by virtue of their difference, who want to listen to and reach one another*, and who do not perceive one another simply as competitors or customers, obstacles or opportunities. In the *material* dimension, resonance denotes in particular a relationship with nature in which nature's essences, forces, and dynamics are encountered *neither* simply as something to be harnessed and controlled *nor* as something to which we would simply have to submit. Resonance with nature would in fact entail a reciprocal transformation, but not in the mode of destructive omnipotence and monstrous powerlessness, but rather in a mode of mutually transformative vivacity. Finally, *existential resonance* could arise from a form of political interaction that replaces the false alternative between radical historical independence and the identitarian submission to existing traditions with a relationship based on *listening and responding* to history. Resynchronization would then entail recovering a temporal axis of resonance between the past and the future that might restore life, connection, and energy to the present.

	Structural perspective (third-person perspective)	Cultural perspective (first-person perspective)
Analysis	Dynamic stabilization	Increasing one's share of the world, making the world controllable and accessible
Diagnosis	Desynchronization	Alienation
"Therapy"	Adaptive stabilization	Resonance

Figure II.1 My best account of modernity – a schematic overview

Part III

Modernity and Critique
A Conversation with Martin Bauer

Martin Bauer If I have understood both of your texts in this book correctly, it is possible to detect a remarkable degree of convergence between your positions. Regarding the question of the indispensable form that a theory of society should take, you both argue that such a theory should be designed as historical sociology – which is to say that you both argue in favor of analyzing modern society within the framework of historical sociology. Would it therefore be safe to call you heirs to the tradition which found its most significant expression in the work of Max Weber?

Andreas Reckwitz I would indeed place myself in this tradition. There needs to be close collaboration between the fields of sociology and history, because when we formulate theories about modernity, we have to proceed from the fact that modernity, for its part, already has a history. It is no longer simply what is contemporary. That is, it is not just the historical moment in which we currently live; instead, as an independent epoch, it already has at least 250 years under its belt. With this in mind, it is simply logical and necessary to take this historical dimension into consideration whenever modern societies are the object of sociological theories. For me, this has been central in some of my books, for instance *Das hybride Subjekt*. For this very reason, however, I also have difficulties with the concept of modernity when it is applied in an undifferentiated way and when *one single* – presumably uniform – modernity is attributed certain features, be it capitalism or functional differentiation. In many respects, one has to "work small" with modernity, even if one wants to appreciate late modernity as a special version of modernity with all the ways in which it differs from bourgeois or industrial modernity. Without a strong sense of the historical dimension of this phenomenon, the necessary differentiations would remain baseless.

Hartmut Rosa Despite all the commonalities between our approaches, there are also clear differences. In your work, this historical dimension is more elaborately developed and more important, whereas I am, de facto, driven by a systematic interest. At first, I did not proceed in an explicitly historical way at all. Yet the idea of understanding contemporary society as an independent formation necessarily leads to the insight that processes of social formation are of central importance. That is, one must understand its historical development and trace its genealogy.

However, certain differences in our theoretical approaches arise from our respective concepts of modernity. Of course, I agree with Andreas Reckwitz and historically minded sociologists such as

Peter Wagner that it is possible to identify different phases in the history of modern societies. There is no doubt about that. However, I consider it essential not only to recognize the differences but also to explain what it is that constitutes the common modernity of these phases. To this end, I have identified a principle that is universal to modernity as a whole, which I have described as a genuinely modern logic of escalation. For its part, this logic of escalation has brought about various cultural upheavals. And it is in the diagnosis of such upheavals where our paths diverge, even though we share a common interest in understanding them as precisely as possible.

Martin Bauer So, both Reckwitz and Rosa analyze, in their sociological work, historical processes or the genealogy of social formations. With respect to the history of modernity, Reckwitz emphasizes that we are concerned with a period of more than two centuries and points out that this process, over its course, has also had effects on its own development. How, analytically, should we deal with the complication of observing sociological processes?

Hartmut Rosa The problem arises, above all, when sociology perceives itself strictly as a science of order, or strictly as structural analysis that is content with identifying a structural typology of the social. Take, for example, the approaches of systems theory, which in my opinion operate according to a relatively simple dualism between pre-modern and modern society, in order to claim in the end that essentially nothing changes at all as long as the thing in question is modern – which is to say, functionally differentiated. In contrast, I understand the basic structural principle of modernity as a process. From the outset, I have thought of acceleration as a formative process, and as one that can only be observed as such in light of historical comparisons. Its core feature then led me to the thesis that dynamic stabilization is what structurally defines modernity. My very definition of modernity is thus processual by nature.

In my effort to understand modern society, however, I have also been concerned with developing a concept of social energy, which the social sciences had hitherto lacked. If, for example, one is merely analyzing class structures – as important as these analyses are – one is basically analyzing something like dead matter, and doing so without any dynamic principle that could explain changes in these structures (for its part, moreover, this dynamic principle is itself permanently changing). This is why I'm interested in taking into account the fundamental dimension of process by means of both structural and cultural analysis. The fact that both of us are concerned with processes arises not least from a methodological approach that works with narratives, which, by their very nature, reconstruct forms of development that inherently contain a temporal perspective.

Andreas Reckwitz For me, it is important to demonstrate the varying structural principles at play in different versions of modernity – that is, in bourgeois, industrial, and late modernity. What these different modern eras have in common is that they have all had to negotiate the same fields of tension: the question of opening or closing contingency, the relationship between a logic of rationalization and a logic of culturalization, and the ways of dealing with progress and loss. This is typically modern. That said, the different versions of modernity have each led to different "mixtures" of these factors. In late modernity, for instance, one sees that there has been an extraordinary expansion of the logic of singularization.

This, however, raises the question of what I would call the Foucault problem: How should we understand the transition from one formation to the next? How, in other words, should the sequence of different forms of modernity be depicted in light of the model presented in Foucault's *The Order of Things*, which elucidates the epistemological shifts that have taken place and how one form of knowledge has been followed by another? In very broad terms, I assume that, at a certain point, one version of modernity exhausts itself, so to speak – that it is perceived as faulty or contradictory, and that this perception gives rise to critical movements and innovations that in turn bring about a fundamental transformation. I do not, however, see a single overarching mechanism for such a transformation; in fact, this all depends on historically contingent factors. For example, if one were to ask why the logic of singularization gained prominence in late modernity and what caused this to come about, it would be possible to identify three main factors, each of which emerged during the transitional phase of the 1970s and 1980s. The first factor is the transformation of the capitalist economy – that is, an immanent transformation toward a sort of cultural capitalism that follows its own logic of expansion while more and more new markets are opening up. The second factor is digitalization, and the third is the sociocultural shift that contributed to the formation of a new middle class. These three factors emerged independently, but, interestingly enough, they ended up reinforcing one another. This is why I would never say that there's a single mechanism to explain how we move from point *a* to point *b*. During the 1970s, we had a constellation in which these three factors were simultaneously influential, though I can't exclude the idea that other influential factors were at play as well. Things were different at the beginning of the twentieth century, during the transition from bourgeois modernity to industrial modernity. In this regard, my approach combines sociological structural analysis with historical explication. To understand social change, we therefore have to look specifically at phases of historical transition.

Hartmut Rosa This clarifies the point at which we differ, though I'll immediately concede that these are two different forms of analysis, each with its own justification. You say that we have to take into account historical contingencies because things happen that cannot be derived from the macrostructure. Because I maintain that turning points derive from the structure itself, my analysis obviously proceeds in a different way. In my book on social acceleration, I attempted to demonstrate systematically how transformation results from differences of tempo in the process of social change. My idea was that we initially encounter an epoch in which social change takes place over several generations – so slowly, in other words, that these different generations still live in the same historical world. Next, the generations themselves become the agents of innovation, and this sets in motion a generational rate of change that roughly applies to the period that you call industrial modernity. As I understand things, what is new about late modernity is that the rate of change has accelerated yet again, and that cultural change now takes place *intra*-generationally. This has led to a different self-perception and perception of the world. And because I regard acceleration – or, to be more precise, the logic of dynamic stabilization – as the structural principle of modernity, I can explain – unlike you – modernity's upheavals from this very structural principle without any recourse to one contingency or another.

Andreas Reckwitz Despite Martin Bauer's suspicions that we are both Weberians, these ideas of yours sound rather Durkheimian to me. Durkheim's concept of the social division of labor is based on the immanent mechanics of society, whereas, from the outset, Weber's analysis of social processes is decidedly more historicist.

Hartmut Rosa Now listen here, I'm still the director of the Max-Weber-Kolleg [*laughs*]. But in all seriousness: my research topic is neither the internal nor the external mechanics of society. I am concerned with moments of upheaval or change, which I investigate from a cultural perspective in order to identify differences in experience. How do different rates of social change alter the individual and collective perceptions of this change? Ultimately, I would like to identify different ways of being-in-the-world: What is the cultural experience like when people live in a world that they expect – for good reason – might be different in a matter of three weeks?

Martin Bauer In your case, Mr. Rosa, it is the principle of dynamic stabilization that unites the process that we have christened "modernity." Otherwise, the whole would disintegrate into disparate worlds of experience. In analytic terms, is it this causality of escalation that holds together the identity of modernity?

Hartmut Rosa The identity *of* modernity or identity *in* modernity?

Martin Bauer The identity of modernity – that is, the identity of the phenomenon that concerns us here. About ontological commitments, to which a theory commits itself with its statements, the philosopher Quine wrote: "No entity without identity." For this reason, I ask which entity defines modernity as an epoch. Unlike you, Andreas Reckwitz, as we have heard, deliberately refrains from postulating the existence of something like an identity principle of modernity that has persisted for more than two centuries.

Hartmut Rosa Indeed, I define modernity as a formation that can only stabilize in a dynamic fashion; it systematically depends on growth, acceleration, and innovation to maintain its structure. I would not claim, however, that the cultural self-perception of modernity is predetermined by such a definition. At best, it makes certain self-interpretations more probable and others rather less probable, so that – in a good Weberian manner – one can identify certain family resemblances or elective affinities among the cultural self-thematicizations of modernity and ask questions about different forms of life conduct. The idea of a successful life that one pursues – whether I, for example, decide to follow a normal biographical path in which professional education and starting a family are cornerstones, with the goal of forming a relatively stable personal identity – may depend on the pace of social change, but it is not simply determined by this structural principle. Because I have not followed in the footsteps of Émile Durkheim, but rather in those of Charles Taylor, I am of the opinion that a regime like that of dynamic stabilization never could have been formed or implemented at all were it not tied to a certain way of relating to the world – specifically, a relationship to the world whose goal is to make the world available and controllable. For its part, this relationship to the world is the basis rather than the consequence of modernity's structural logic.

Andreas Reckwitz   I would in fact be extremely cautious with the idea that there is a single entity that could be called modernity. For some time now in sociology, talk of "modernity" has no longer been as self-evident as it once was, for instance in the grand modernity and postmodernity discourse during the 1980s. In this respect, the concept of modernity should be questioned in a fundamental way – whereby it should become clear that any fetishization of modernity is inexcusable. I argue in favor of using the term pragmatically, and thus I rely on a handful of selected features, the overall compilation of which is useful to me as a toolkit. Because, as I already said, I don't proceed from the basis of a single structural principle of modernity, what I see instead are various fields of tension that are characteristic of modern societies. I use these features in my work as tools, so to speak, for analyzing modernity. The first and most important field of tension is the dialectic between establishing order and critique – that is, between opening and closing contingency. A second field of tension is provided by the opposing tendencies between rationalization and culturalization, on the one hand, and between generalization and singularization on the other. Modern societies can radically standardize, rationalize, and "equalize," but they can also be radically oriented toward what is unique or singular. Finally, modern societies are also characterized by a tension between progress-orientation or the preference for novelty, on the one hand, and their often implicit tendency to process losses and their historical heritage on the other. With the help of such a toolkit, it is possible to examine the various phases of modernity in terms of their particular compositions. To what extent does late modernity function differently from bourgeois modernity? And to what extent did the latter function differently from industrial modernity? These are the questions that my approach raises and that I would like to answer.

In this regard, I adhere to a working concept of "modernity," and I see the radicality of modernity in all three of the aforementioned fields of tension. Never before have there been such contingency-oriented, yet simultaneously rationalistic and singularistic as well as future-oriented, societies. At the same time, however, I also make an effort to include the concept of multiple modernities. Shmuel Eisenstadt observed this on the global level, while my concern now is to temporalize it – for it is the case that different forms of modernity exist not only in space but also in time. Communist modernity and fascist modernity, for example, were also versions of modernity.

Martin Bauer   But do you insist on the reality of this modernity, whether as an epoch or as a social formation?

Andreas Reckwitz   In principle, yes, though I'm aware that sociologists will occasionally seem naïve to historians when they maintain that this or that is entirely new to modernity. A medievalist, for instance, will counter by saying that individuality already existed in the Middle Ages. And a classical historian will point out that the opening up of contingency took place in antiquity, not to mention certain forms of democratic participation. For this reason, it is certainly good to have flexible sociological positions – that is, to assume that transitions occur gradually. The concept of temporal hybridizations can also be helpful in this respect. It would certainly be misleading to say that here is the break that brought modernity into the world, before which everything was completely different. Modernity formed slowly, with gradual developments. Why should it be assumed that certain notions of individuality didn't circulate before the beginning of modernity? For good reasons, however, one can maintain that the three aforementioned fields of tension (in their radical and mature forms) are distinctly modern.

Hartmut Rosa   In controversies between history and sociology, many historians do tend to deny that there are any sharply defined discontinuities. Nothing has really ever changed – this is the tenor of their arguments. This or that has always existed. I admit that it's annoying to hear this over and over. That said, the poor historians are also bothered by us, because we sociological theorists of modernity act as though things are entirely new and unprecedented. To this extent, I agree with your assessment of such interdisciplinary encounters.

Nevertheless, I have to ask. It may be undisputed that, between these multiple modernities, there are significant geographical and historical differences, which provide for variance. In the end, however, one would have only variances – or, more precisely, only *differences* – if it is impossible to identify any unifying entity in – or behind – the multitude of these "modernities." If there were no commonality, the concept would fall apart. Now, I understand what you're saying. There are tensions between different poles that define modernity and its different orientations. These are the tensions between opening contingency and closing contingency, between singularization and generalization, and between rationalization and culturalization. Yet another defining feature that you add is that of modernity's expectation for progress, which belongs to the conflicts between wanting something new and defending something old. Because you have suggested as much yourself, I have to wonder whether these four poles of tension can in fact be found everywhere. Is it not the case that every instance of social order is accompanied by the closure of contingency, and, conversely, that life itself gives rise to moments that force contingency to open up again? Isn't it true that disputes about the question of how the general relates to the particular or how the future relates to the past always involve categories that make use of trans-temporal customs of distinction? Aren't these essentially universal and trans-historical principles of tension?

Andreas Reckwitz   Now you're repeating the exact same move that we had just discussed regarding the opinions of historians when you yourself say that all this already existed before. I have to disagree with this thesis, because I'm not interested in an anthropologizing notion of contingency, according to which the freedom to act appeared as soon as *Homo sapiens* emerged – which is to say that the ability to do things differently is somehow part of the natural constitution of human beings.

Only with modernity did the idea emerge that society as a whole is contingent and that the social, in all its aspects, is fundamentally formable and mutable, even in need of being shaped. Only in modern societies can such things be transformed and controlled according to guidelines derived from the idea of progress. In the many tens of thousands of years experienced exclusively by hunter-gatherer societies, societies were never radically transformed, except by external influences such as changes in the climate, epidemics, and things of that nature. In fact, these societies were so static that Claude Lévi-Strauss could refer to them as "cold societies." The radical moment of contingency is characteristic of modernity alone. Indeed, it presupposes that the social as a whole is perceived to be capable of being reconfigured, and in need of being reconfigured. Every social order – be it in the economy, in politics, in governance, in religion, science, or life conduct – now proves to be contingent and ultimately unstable. After contingency is opened, however, this is followed by its radical closure, and this gives rise to orders with totalitarian characteristics, at least in part. Even this inclination toward totalitarianism is typically modern, and this did not exist before.

Hartmut Rosa   An idea is now coming to light about which we can presumably agree without any major dissent. You say that the endogenization of the act of opening up contingency is characteristic of modernity. Yes, I too would claim that the practices of modernity are inherently designed to open things up, though I think it would have to be explained – or established in the first place – where this disposition in favor of opening up contingency comes from. My assumption is that dynamic stabilization, as the structural feature of modernity, is what necessitates this constant need to transgress established practices and the orders associated with them.

Andreas Reckwitz   The leitmotif of modernity is revolution. To such a radical extent, this was not the case in earlier societies; at most, they underwent minor processes of change. In contrast, it is an innate impetus of modernity to open up contingency because things seem to be in need of improvement. I think that the cultural idea of mutability and future progress provides the central background for this orientation toward contingency. Reinhart Koselleck, for instance, worked this out very well in his work on historical semantics. In modernity, moreover, both the process of rationalization and the process of culturalization presuppose this configuration of contingency and this orientation toward progress. In this regard, the three aforementioned states of tension are interrelated.

I would also like to emphasize that modernity's specific orientation can be seen in the field of tension between the logic of the general and the logic of the particular. Of course, one could point to Kant's epistemology and claim that both the general and the particular are at work in every cultural order. We use general concepts and understand the particular with our senses. There is nothing controversial about this. However, modernity generalizes and particularizes in a specifically radical manner. Here, social orders can form that are unilaterally and radically egalitarian and standardizing in a way that would have seemed inhumane to previous societies. Conversely, modernity also tends to allow equally radical processes of particularization, which, at their height, can lead to the singularization of subjects, things, places, events, and communities. Roughly speaking, this is the ongoing conflict between rationalism and romanticism in modernity.

Hartmut Rosa   Then our analyses converge in the observation that there is escalation at both poles, both in the opening and in the closing of contingency. But I think that the increase in particularization and the increase in generalization often happen at the same time. They are two sides of the same coin. Let's take gender norms as an example. As soon as they are no longer coded as binary, we are immediately confronted with social openings of contingency. There's no question about that. Such openings, however, are immediately accompanied by new closures of contingency. Order has to be renegotiated, agreed upon, and reestablished. Gender equality in language and behavior entails doing away with many things that previously seemed to be acceptable. According to my hypothesis, the simultaneity of this opening and closing – this back and forth – is also related to the need to make contingency controllable. When I'm planning a trip to the far North, the organizer should ideally be able to give me a guarantee that I'll see the Northern Lights! I would like to book a certain guaranteed experience, so to speak, even though it is well known that the appearance of the aurora borealis is highly contingent. In this respect, it should be asked whether this is simply a matter of closing contingency. In fact, it would be nice if such liabilities could be regulated so that, when the desired lights fail to appear on the horizon, I can sue someone for damages.

Andreas Reckwitz   This is all very illuminating, as it were, but it's a different perspective. I am not much concerned with the logical connection between opening and closing, but rather in the historical one. For several decades, for instance, we experienced the political dominance of neoliberalism. There seemed to be no alternative, it was hegemonic, and the contingency of thought was thus closed. Then, all at once, a space for thinking critically about things broke open and alternatives came into view. Conversely, yesterday's alternatives can turn into today's hegemonies. In the '68 movement, contingency opened up; the middle-class way of life no longer seemed compelling, and it was heavily criticized. After a certain amount of time, certain elements of the counterculture – the ideal of self-development, for example – themselves became dominant and apparently self-evident. The movement between opening and closing thus forms something like a historical dialectic. For a given span of time, there seems to be "no alternative" to certain patterns of order. During this time, no one can imagine anything being different, as though a limit has been placed on our powers of imagination. Situations of historical conflict, however, bring to light contingencies that can be opened up, whether by critical movements or by innovations. Such openings of contingency may amount to nothing, but it is of course interesting when they sooner or later succeed in establishing new social orders.

Hartmut Rosa   Aren't you talking about two different ideas? On the one hand, something like a pendulum swinging between opening and closing, and on the other hand, a dialectic that can also be understood as a process of escalation?

Andreas Reckwitz   No. What I have in mind is not a swinging pendulum. That would be entirely unhistorical, because it assumes that the opening and closing of contingency happen in the same timeframe. My concern is rather with sequences in a dialectical progression, as I examined, for instance, in my book *Das hybride Subjekt* with respect to subject cultures: A social formation breaks apart, is confronted with its own contradictions and deficiencies, a new order emerges with a different orientation and attempts to fix these shortcomings, and this new order is in turn confronted with its own contradictions, and so on. This is a dialectical movement from problem to solution; it contains the logic of question and answer, if you will. Yet in this regard I am not a proponent of Hegel's or Marx's philosophy of history, which implies that this is somehow an emancipatory process that will one day end in a situation without any contradictions. What I have in mind is rather a dialectic without a telos. It is easy enough to believe that an ecological and more sustainable social formation will solve some of the problems of late modernity – but then new contradictions will inevitably arise, and the game will move on to the next round. Of course, the motif of progress is of central importance to modernity's tendency to open up contingency in its institutional orders and forms of life, but this does not mean that sociological analysis should blindly follow these self-interpretations.

Hartmut Rosa   I don't see things any differently.

Martin Bauer   Your description of the different formations of modernity, Mr. Reckwitz, is based on a structuring narrative. You present a sequence from bourgeois to industrial to late modernity, but you are clearly reluctant to make any higher-level, causal, or explanatory claims. Hartmut Rosa, in contrast, makes a far stronger assertion when he argues that the history of modernity and of modern society as a whole can be explained by the fundamental mechanism of dynamic stabilization.

Hartmut Rosa   Yes, but the mechanism in question always has two sides. In my analytical approach, this irreducible dualism is important to me because it sets it apart from Marxist or Durkheimian theory, which claim to explain the cultural side of things by way of the structural side. I distance myself from this approach. Therefore, when I speak about a social formation, I fundamentally use both sides. What I mean is that it's insufficient to define modernity simply as a form of society that can sustain itself only by means of escalation – by means of growth, acceleration, and innovation, which give rise to an escalatory tendency. Such a definition would have two problems. First, it would itself be static; it would be unable to explain the historical changes and the various phases that have taken place over the course of modernity, which we have discussed. Second, it would lack the energetic principle, which is the latest hobby horse that I've been riding around on. Institutions or structures cannot innovate or accelerate on their own; for this, they need subjects and their motivational energies, and these follow a different logic, a cultural logic. The latter, however, can only be ascertained hermeneutically. I therefore define a social formation in terms of the interplay between its structural mechanisms and its cultural driving moments. Even though their relationship is something like an elective affinity, they do not mutually determine one another. Instead, they coexist in a state of tension.

Martin Bauer   With respect to the development of modern society, how much causal force does Hartmut Rosa attribute to culture?

Hartmut Rosa   This is a difficult question, because I want to avoid purely culturalistic interpretations just as much as I want to avoid any theory of modern social formations in which culture is treated as no more than an epiphenomenon or a "superstructure." This ambition of mine can be derived from my Taylorian pedigree. For a philosopher and social theorist such as Charles Taylor, the basic thing is self-interpretation, and he quite cleverly managed to avoid excessive cognitivism. That is, basic self-interpretations, which are indicative of historical processes or social evolution, do not have to be rational attitudes or mindsets tied to their propositional content. What is meant here are affective and cognitive relationships to the world, which, by combining cognition, affection, and corporeality, encompass more than what is commonly understood by the term *worldview* or *world image*. It goes without saying that such relationships to the world also establish relationships to the self, and that interpretive and cultural moments are constitutive of them. Of course, our relationships to the world are also influenced, reproduced, and in part enforced within and by institutional structures. The concept with which I attempt to integrate structural and cultural moments is thus the concept of our relationship to the world. And to such relationships I indeed attribute causal force.

Andreas Reckwitz   But doesn't your preferred form of analysis belong at its heart to the tradition of sociological theories of modernization? The theory of modernization, especially in the work of Talcott Parsons, has always assumed that there are individual, pervasive, and escalating structural principles *of* modernity, for instance functional differentiation and the generalization of value. Modernity is thus made to seem as though it has a fixed structural core and follows a developmental logic. I've grown more and more skeptical of this traditional theory of modernization. I consider your approach to be a sort of negative theory of modernization. There is a structural core and a course of development – but this might very well lead to our downfall. The basic principle of dynamic stabilization contains a certain degree of self-destructive potential.

Hartmut Rosa   I understand this argument, and there is something to it if I am primarily understood to be a theorist of social acceleration. But there are two central differences between my analysis and theories of modernization, one of which you have already mentioned. It pertains to the normative dimension. For me, modernization is not a positively charged term; I do not describe the process of modernization as a story of progress. Rather, my focus has been on its underbelly or darker sides – it is directed toward the point at which modernization becomes a destructive regime of coercion. In my work, I therefore never regard non-modern social conditions as deficient or backward, but rather as alternatives that could be relevant in the pursuit of salvation. The second difference is that, for me, modernization is not inexorable or irreversible but, rather, a historically contingent process. Unlike, say, Parsons's idea of evolutionary universals, according to which central historical discoveries are irreversible because they create an evolutionary advantage, I by no means believe that all societies must sooner or later become modern or perish. The notion of "recuperative modernization," which was popular after the fall of the Berlin Wall and claimed that the "backward" societies of East Germany will merely have to catch up, was likewise based on the idea that so-called "Western" society, which was allegedly characterized by political democracy, a market economy, mass consumption, and the rule of law, represented the model for historical development. With this model, according to the most radical commentators at the time, we in fact reached the end of history ...

Andreas Reckwitz   ... and you would like to do away with this model.

Hartmut Rosa   Yes! My conception of things really has nothing in common with it. Claiming that the nature of sociality or society dictates the direction in which society is developing is categorically different from insisting that we are dealing with historical phenomena whose future or further development is in no way determined by their past or present.

Martin Bauer   Even if the assumption were true that Hartmut Rosa's sociology of our relationship to the world latently perpetuates the tradition of the theory of modernization, I fail to see in his work or in that of Andreas Reckwitz a science of order in the strictly sociological sense. In other words, neither of your sociological investigations begins with the question: "What makes social order possible?"

Andreas Reckwitz   As regards the capabilities of sociology, I would classify the concept of a science of order somewhat differently, and to this end we have to distinguish between social theory and the theory of society. These are two different branches of theory in sociology. Social theory provides a fundamental vocabulary; it clarifies what the social is, how it coheres, whether one should focus on action or norms, observe communication, interaction, or practices, or operate with "power" as a basic sociological concept. In contrast, the theory of society problematizes societies in their specific historicity; it makes statements about the differences between traditional and modern societies. In light of this distinction, I understand the question of social order's conditions of possibility as one that is social-theoretical by its very nature. And there indeed exists in sociology a certain tradition of understanding social theory as a theory of social order. This is certainly in large part due to Talcott Parsons, for whom the question "How is social order possible?" seemed to be the most fundamental question posed since the classic works of the turn of the century. Here, Parsons speaks of the Hobbesian problem of social order: the puzzle, that is, of how the social can come to be at all, given that all individuals are ultimately selfish. In response to this question, norms come into play. Yet it should not be forgotten that, in Parsons's view, this problem stems from a fear of anarchy, of the chaos of individual egotism.

From my perspective, however, this problem is no longer undisputed today. Since the 1970s, new approaches in social theory have shifted the question, and the decisive reason for this seems to be the insights that have been gained about the temporality of the social. This can be seen, for instance, in Luhmann's systems theory, in which systems are thought about as chains of events. It can also be found in Derrida's post-structuralism – keyword: *différance* – and the latter in turn influenced practice theory, for instance in the work of Anthony Giddens. In terms of the philosophy of history, what lurks behind this is Husserl's temporalization of consciousness. The question is no longer "How is social order possible?" but rather: "How do social reproduction and social change take place?" The question is no longer about how egotism can be overcome, but rather about how certain things can be repeated from time *a* to time *b* and even be made permanent. Some things, however, are not repeated but, rather, emerge brand new. To some extent, this is the new field of tension that characterizes the social: the tension between repetition and innovation. This is why I would no longer think about social theory in terms of classical categories of order.

Martin Bauer With respect to how a younger generation of sociologists understands this problem, do you find Heike Delitz's book *Bergson-Effekte* instructive? In line with what you're saying, the social is here conceived as a process, as a process of becoming that is open to the future, and the conceptual tools that Delitz uses to describe this are the ideas of Henri Bergson and, after him, especially Gilles Deleuze …

Andreas Reckwitz … yes, right, here too one comes across process-based thinking.

Martin Bauer Thus, a former science of order has been transformed into a theory about the dynamics of social life, and this theory requires, among other things, a Bergsonian concept of "duration" in order to temporalize the social without importing natural-scientific notions of time, which ultimately derive from Newtonian mechanics. You, Mr. Reckwitz, follow this impulse by distinguishing between social theory and the theory of society. As it seems to me, social theory then functions as a sociological propaedeutic that answers two basic questions in advance. On the one hand, it provides a socio-ontological definition of what the social is; on the other hand, it determines, socio-epistemologically, the conceptual repertoire with which the social – as a temporalized becoming – can be observed. Hartmut Rosa, if I have read his books correctly, does not acknowledge this division of labor between systematic social theory and the histori-cizing theory of society. Hegel's philosophy might be instructive in this regard. Hegel temporalizes the social like no one else before him. However, he also furnishes all the concepts that describe the social with a historical index, and thus his historicizing theory of society plays a role in answering all the questions that, according to Andreas Reckwitz's proposed differentiation, belong to social theory. Now, shouldn't a sophisticated theory of society take Hegel's enterprise as a guideline and make an effort to integrate social ontology and social epistemology? The goal of this would be to demonstrate how the becoming of the social itself has produced the very concepts and methods that have made it the particular object of sociological theory.

Andreas Reckwitz It's possible to see it that way, even though this form of historicizing has been out of fashion. Over the last 30 years, social theories have instead tended to de-historicize themselves, from rational-choice theory to systems theory and practice theory. This mode of representation, moreover, is repeated in sociology textbooks, which constantly highlight, as methodological alternatives, the abstract dualism of holism versus individualism. But, of course, the origins of certain concepts and their historical contexts can be illuminating. It is clear, for instance, that rational-choice theory derives from bourgeois ideas about the social contract – which is to say, from Hobbes and Locke. The fact that utility-maximizing actors can be conceived and theoretically postulated at all is immediately indicative of a certain sociocultural background. Parsons's structural functionalism, with its rigid systems of norms and values, can in turn be said to "fit" well with organized, industrial modernity. Similarly, post-structuralism and actor–network theory, with their fluid understanding of the social, are well suited for late modernity. The same could be said of practice theory.

Martin Bauer   But doesn't Hartmut Rosa look at the problem differently? Would you not claim that your sociology of our relationship to the world treats (socio-)ontological questions in a way that is different from the praxeological social theory that Andreas Reckwitz prefers?

Hartmut Rosa   In fact, my basic impulse is probably neo-Hegelian. This should come as no surprise in light of my association with critical theory, which, like Hegel, always proceeds from a theory's "temporal core of truth." No theory can be abstracted from its own relationality and situatedness – that is, from its connection to the very historical object that it observes (in a methodologically disciplined manner). In this matter, I would take the side of Taylor or the social anthropologist Hubert Dreyfus and stress that "we are interpretation all the way down." In plain language, this simply means that we have no categories or conceptual tools at our disposal that precede the act of interpretation. Strictly speaking, I would go even further, because I espouse an unreservedly relational ontology. In my understanding, what social entities become and are, how they relate to one another, and how their constellations transform are part of the process that constitutes the social in its relationality. My idea is basically that this is the sort of relational antecedence that gives rise to what seems to be the social, or at least that there is something like co-originality when it comes to relations and the related. In contrast, an antagonistic social ontology – which can be found especially in left-wing discourses, but also, of course, on the other side, as in the works of Carl Schmitt and his followers – postulates that, as social subjects, we are always in an antagonistic or agonal relationship with one another. None of this, however, should be assumed of social actors, who are ultimately addressed here, as well, as maximizers of utility, and it is for this reason that I'm inclined to question and dispel such premises historically. How social actors relate to one another – cooperatively or confrontationally or competitively, for instance – is not an anthropological or ontological question, but rather an element of historically variable relationships to the world.

Andreas Reckwitz With regard to self-historicization, isn't your project of formulating a sociology of our relationship to the world heavily dependent on late-modern ways of living and on the aporias that are typical of them?

Hartmut Rosa Yeah, sure, in a certain sense, of course. If, in 100 or 200 or maybe even 500 years, someone might still be interested in our two forms of thought, it will not be overlooked that they arose from a specific historical context. However, I would agree with Taylor yet again, and say that human beings can do nothing else but constantly attempt to answer the question of what it means to be a human or a being with agency – and to explain what it means to act in this or that way under the specific conditions in question. In Merleau-Ponty's terms, people are thrust into the world, or directed toward the world, and they are forced to interpret themselves and this world. And, in this interpretation, they develop a relationship to the world and with themselves. We are self-interpreting animals, and our self-interpretations are never purely individual undertakings. They have a collective dimension and they are also historically contingent, but they always make use of what Taylor calls "strong evaluations." It would be inconceivable for a self-interpretation to refrain from lending certain things a deeper meaning. In this way, every relationship to the world thus acquires a cultural side. By virtue of such evaluations, we affectively relate to the world. And these two phenomena – the fact that we must interpret things, and that interpretation implies evaluations – I would exclude from historicization and declare to be universal. Acting human beings are always and everywhere self-interpreting animals who orient themselves by means of a map with strong evaluations. These are, to be honest, my two trans-historical propositions. Such maps, moreover, are formed in specific ways – both structurally and culturally – and they constitute our historically variable and also institutionalized relationships to the world. On this level, I am of the conviction that the sociology of our relationship to the world is not simply a theory of late modernity.

Martin Bauer   If one were to ask how Hartmut Rosa, in his sociology, has come to emphasize, along with Taylor and Hegel, that human beings are self-interpreting animals, I would suspect that he was compelled to do so by anti-naturalistic motives. This anti-naturalism is directed against the tendencies of techno-scientific civilization whose underlying metaphysics – how else should I put it? – strives to abolish, once and for all, "unscientific" interpretation and its evaluations in favor of a purely physicalist description of all the realities of the world. Incidentally, I believe that I can also hear just such an anti-naturalistic objection in Andreas Reckwitz's argument in favor of practice sociology. Am I utterly mistaken, Mr. Reckwitz, in recognizing that one of the advantages of praxeological social theory is its opposition to naturalistic simplifications of established subject theories and theories of action?

Andreas Reckwitz   Yes, what you're addressing here is a cultural-theoretical orientation that Hartmut and I certainly share. And this cultural-theoretical or interpretive orientation is central to practice theory as well. In terms of the history of philosophy, what lies behind practice theory is, above all, late Wittgenstein and his concept of language games as forms of life. In addition, one can also think of Heidegger's *Being and Time*. Sociologically, there is not one single practice theory but rather a number of systematic approaches to it, particularly in the work of Pierre Bourdieu and Anthony Giddens, though Theodore Schatzki has attempted to systematize the theory in an interesting socio-philosophical way. This has also played a biographically important role in my life, because, in the mid-1990s, I began my studies with Giddens in Cambridge precisely on account of practice theory. At first, I regarded practice theory as a variant of an interpretive, cultural-theoretical approach, and that was also the topic of my dissertation. Over time, however, I came to find practice theory attractive for other reasons as well. Certain traditional dualisms in social theory can be dealt with quite elegantly with it – not only the dualism of structure and agency but also that between culturalism and materialism. Practices are always anchored in the body, and all knowledge – to offer my own quotation of Taylor – is "embodied knowledge." At the same time, bodies are constantly dealing with artifacts. Without these two material elements, practices are unthinkable. By the end of the 1990s, I had "discovered" Bruno Latour when I heard him speak at Berkeley, and then it became clear to me how well one can really "construct" practice theory in a way that takes artifacts into account. Schatzki himself then also accomplished this.

As it turned out for me, I realized that practice theory can be used extremely well as a tool to work with material and investigate concrete phenomena. There is something de-essentializing about practice theory, given that it dissolves, in a step-by-step process, seemingly fixed entities into "doings," into the specific ways in which the social is fabricated. I had this eureka moment, for instance, while working on my book *Das hybride Subjekt*: What is sociologically interesting is not the self, but rather the "doing subject" and the ways in which such subjects are produced and produce themselves mentally and physically via practices (by means of economic practices or family practices, for example).

Martin Bauer But why are practices social? That is, why are they a genuinely sociological theme? And how is it possible to build a bridge from practice theory to the theory of society?

Andreas Reckwitz Practices are not simply about ways of acting, in the sense of behaviorism. Regulated behavior is only made possible by the fact that actors have incorporated knowledge – that is, by the fact that they act under the influence of something. Bourdieu called this something *habitus*. We are thus dealing with shared orders of knowledge, which create the social out of practices.

Of course, there is the question of how to think about the relationship between social theory and the theory of society. My basic position in this regard is that we use social-theoretical concepts in order to make contributions to the theory of society, but no theory of society can be derived from social theory. One can also fall back on a good social theory as a tool when society itself has changed, and thus when it is necessary to update one's theory of society. In this respect, social theory is a "sensitizing instrument" that makes certain fundamental social phenomena visible or invisible and therefore makes certain assumptions pertaining to the theory of society possible or impossible. How would it have been possible to analyze resonant relationships or singularities if social theory had not produced the concept of affect? Those who rely on a thoroughly rationalistic vocabulary would never direct their attention to such relationships, which are emotionally or affectively charged.

But this is a relatively loose coupling; I do not think that social theory and the theory of society determine one another, as Hartmut assumes. If the connection were too strong, it would reduce the possibilities of analysis and make our analytical tools weaker. A social theory such as rational-choice theory or practice theory or neo-institutionalism or actor–network theory can each provide the background for various theories and analyses of society. One can use rational-choice theory to inform a theory or analysis of capitalism, but one can do the same with practice theory, even though the analysis would, of course, go in a somewhat different direction. I can easily imagine a proponent of practice theory who would regard everything that I've written about modernity completely differently, despite the fact that we share common social-theoretical premises. If they are any good, social theories are analytical tools that can be implemented in a wide variety of ways.

Hartmut Rosa   Rational-choice theories or systems theories – but also structuralist theories – certainly limit the horizon of what can be articulated in a theory of society. To me, however, the problem seems to lie elsewhere. Every theory defines or delimits its object of study – no doubt about that! I agree with you there. Moreover, I by no means wish to deny the utility of practice theories. It's true that anyone interested in gaining an understanding of the social will have to examine practices. But I would not speak of there being a bridge between the material and the cultural, because, according to my understanding, practice theory does not really separate these two sides. Instead, it simply provides a long list of hetero-geneous elements that can contribute to one practice or another. For me, the problem with practice theory is that it allows for too much – basically everything: bodies and spatial moments, but also temporal moments and social moments, moments of knowledge and discursive formations. In order to arrive at a sociologically sophis-ticated diagnosis, however, it is necessary to have certain selection criteria and to draw certain distinctions, among them the distinction between the material and the cultural. My impression is that practice theory does not make such distinctions. It has to borrow them from elsewhere. In order to develop a theory of society, I think that entirely different tools are needed. Practices alone are insufficient, both as the material and as the instruments of analysis.

Andreas Reckwitz   One needs, in any case, certain other tools that are not furnished by the social-theoretical vocabulary. In my perspective, the theory of society can generally not be derived from social theory. This has nothing to do with "practice theory: yes or no?" Rather, things just don't function that way, for two elementary reasons: Social theory provides a generally valid vocabulary; it can basically be applied to any given societies and social forms. In a sense, the concepts themselves do not have a historical index, or at least that is the claim. Habitus or interests or affects or institutions or power exist everywhere. The theory of society, however, must always refer to historical, and thus contingent, states of affairs; it has to know something about specific societies when it forms its concepts. If one regards capitalism as a central feature of modern society, then one must have historically specific phenomena in mind to formulate this concept called "capitalism" – a concept that denotes, in Max Weber's terms, a "historical individual." And this is the reason why no theory of society can be derived from social theory, which is sketched out rather abstractly on the drawing board, so to speak. In order to develop a theory of society, it is necessary to engage with historical and empirical material. In my work, for example, the distinction between "doing generality" and "doing singularity" emerged from my observations of the structures of modern phenomena and certainly not from my readings of Schatzki or Wittgenstein. Practice theory is useful, however, because of its insistence on replacing substances with "doings." This is familiar from social phenomena such as "doing gender," "doing race," and so on. Things are similar as regards my interest in the general and the particular. I find it enormously fruitful to regard these phenomena as "doings," and not simply to postulate the existence of singularities, for instance, but to examine the practices of evaluation or reception that "fabricate" such singularities.

Hartmut Rosa My question concerns perspectives. Which "doings" are important if I want to understand society? Ultimately, we are all constantly busy with and embroiled in a whole abundance of "doings." Let's take your text on the practice of writing! Aren't there already countless elements at play when I simply begin to ascertain everything that goes into this – the desk, the lighting, the pencil, a thousand things, not to mention the content of that which is being written? So, somehow, I have to decide which practices or aspects of practice are really relevant to me in my role as a theorist of society. How do you make selections when trying to understand such practices? That is, do you forge paths that are not made available by practice theory itself? As such, it would be completely okay if such criteria have to be introduced.

Andreas Reckwitz As I said, such perspectives arise not from social theory itself; instead, they are always gained by thoroughly examining the historical and empirical material. This is also true of modernity's three fields of tension, which I've discussed. Even when Max Weber speaks of formal rationalization, for example, he does not simply derive this idea from general concepts, but rather from particular historical phenomena such as Prussian bureaucracies or English factory work. Or when Bourdieu speaks of symbolic class conflicts. These cannot be deduced from his "theory of practice," and they only come into play when he is no longer concerned with Algeria but, rather, with France. That's why I don't really understand this objection. Empirical research, too, always begins with an initial question derived from examining the material at hand. Another example: I've recently been pursuing the hypothesis that a paradoxical way of dealing with loss is a fundamental aspect of modern societies. I think that this hypothesis might help us to understand an important and rather neglected feature of these societies. This is how one makes a contribution to the theory of society. Now, as is my custom, I examine losses praxeologically in terms of "doing loss" – that is, not as purely psychological phenomena but as practices of loss. However, no social theory – practice theory included – can tell me anything about the particular, paradoxical relevance of the phenomenon of loss. To gain an understanding of this, I have to delve into the reality of modern societies and become sensitive to certain contexts.

Hartmut Rosa Yes, that's true, your engagement with loss is exciting. Of course one can raise the question of "doing loss." In order to use it to construct a theory of society, however, I would have to determine which aspects of it are relevant in what ways, and I would especially have to work out how they relate to other practices, such as "doing progress," and what significance they might have to the cultural and structural development of society as a whole.

Andreas Reckwitz Things are no different, incidentally, in the case of rational-choice theory. Of course, the innumerable actors, each operating according to their cost–benefit calculations, constantly have to make decisions. Thus, it would be necessary to explain which of these decisions are important and which should be singled out by researchers and examined more closely. Another case is the social-phenomenological paradigm, with its idea of different horizons of meaning. Once again, the problem arises of which horizons of meaning are relevant, if this or that research question is to be answered satisfactorily. These approaches can be tools for the theory of society – they are not my preferred tools, but they have some similar features.

Hartmut Rosa Now you are listing nothing but micro-theories, while ignoring the problem of how to get from the micro- to the macro-level. First of all, rational-choice theories are themselves micro-theories and have enough trouble articulating their own theory of society. And phenomenology, too, cannot shake the basic

problem of its inability to present something like an actual phenomenological theory of society.

Andreas Reckwitz   Sure, Hartmut, but excuse me – you've seen that
it works and that I've done it in my own books; that is, I've used
practice theory for the purpose of formulating a theory of society.

Hartmut Rosa   That's true, you've done it, and in a fascinating
way, no less. I only mean that, in the theory of society, and in
your work as well, there is always something additional that is not
covered by practice theory, simply because it does not arise from any
praxeologically informed observation. For instance, you talk about
complexes of practices, forms of life, and institutional orders. How
is it possible to define and distinguish these things in praxeological
terms? And you identify four central phenomena of the social –
namely discourses, affects, subjects, and forms of life / institutions.
In doing so, you single out certain elements of practice as belonging
together and as being relevant, but this way of looking at things
is itself, in my opinion, not based on practice theory. In principle,
however, I find this entirely unproblematic, and I only want to point
out that you have not produced your impressive reconstructions of
social developments with the tools of practice theory alone.

Andreas Reckwitz   I think that there are three different problems to
address. First, in my text, I singled out discourses, affects, subjects,
and forms of life/institutions in order to demonstrate how these
familiar phenomena, which are important in my work, can be viewed
from a praxeological perspective. This was not meant to be a schema
or a finite list. One could do the same with all the phenomena of
the social world, for instance with artifacts, with sensual perception,
with images, or with organizations – they can all be reformulated
in praxeological terms. Regarding this theoretical move, I see a
parallel to Luhmann's systems theory, in which common sociological phenomena such as the individual, interaction, or norms
are examined through a communication-theoretical lens and thus
looked at from a new perspective. This is to say that all of these
phenomena and concepts already existed before, but they have now
been viewed in a fresh way. Practice theory is likewise able to "work
through" the whole spectrum of social and cultural phenomena
through a specific lens.
    Second, in my opinion, the dispute about the relationship between
social theory and the theory of society should not be confused with
the dispute about the micro and the macro. A good social theory
can describe both micro-phenomena and macro-phenomena, and

hopefully, too, it can dissolve this strict dualism. Whether this is the case with social phenomenology or rational-choice theory, that would be a different question. But it is certainly true of practice theory. Concepts such as structures (as rules and resources) or the space–time relations in Giddens's work or the social site in Schatzki's work indeed operate on the macro-level, and something similar can be found in Bourdieu's thinking, for instance when he discusses the rules of a game or the power dynamics in a social sphere. But these are, in a sense, universal and ahistorical social-theoretical macro-concepts that are very flexible and applicable to a wide range of societies. In order to construct a theory of modern society, we need more than these concepts; we need to take a leap into the historical specificity of Western modernity, on the basis of which we can then model historically specific concepts.

I wonder, however (and this is my third point), where this idea comes from, the idea that a theory of society can be derived from social theory, or why the two of them have to be so tightly intertwined at all. My suspicion is that this has something to do with our fixation on the authors of social theory and their work, and thus that it's related to the idea of "theory-as-system." For it is indeed the case that these classic writers, whom we discuss in our lectures, often did both: social theory and the theory of society. This is not true of all of them – Alfred Schütz never produced a theory of society, and Ulrich Beck never produced a social theory. But most of them did both. And then there is the inclination to read a system logic into their work, so that the theory of society seems to be embedded, as it were, in social theory, or vice versa. Yet this nexus is only obvious in the case of certain theorists – for instance, in the two German theorists Niklas Luhmann and Jürgen Habermas. If you take the example of "tool theorists" such as Michel Foucault or Bruno Latour, however, this no longer functions. Does Foucault's disciplinary society (his theory of society) follow from his interest in discourses and *dispositifs* (his social theory)? Does Latour's theory of modes of existence follow from his actor–network theory? I think not. If one proceeds by understanding theory as a tool, this opens up the possibility of making entirely different combinations.

Hartmut Rosa   Giddens's point of departure – and Bourdieu's as well – was indeed the structure–agency problem, exactly this dualism. Giddens said that he had to bracket off one of the two sides if he were to do any serious work, whereas Bourdieu developed both a structural theory – namely, his analysis of the distribution of capital – and a theory of action: his idea of habitus. Thus, he clearly demarcated the two sides of the dualism in question. I do not see this sort of systematic architecture in your work.

Andreas Reckwitz   Yes, but I'm also not writing a comprehensive social theory like Giddens's *The Constitution of Society* or Bourdieu's *Outline of a Theory of Practice*. I don't see that as my task. I'm a participant in the field of practice theory, with which I work and which I accentuate in my own particular way. There's no reason to reinvent the wheel over and over again. Practice theory already exists, for instance in the work of the two authors just cited, who remain important inspirations to me. Of course, social theory will always be further developed and reaccentuated, especially in terms of the issues that are pertinent to the theory of society. Hartmut, we've been talking this whole time about the place of practice theory in my work, but I have to say that I fail to see any clearly accentuated social theory in your own work.

Hartmut Rosa   Objection! I have to refute this. I have attempted to account for both sides – the structural side and the action side – and have done so through the idea of "perspectival dualism," a concept introduced by Nancy Fraser. My goal has been to provide two accounts that in fact address structural problems as well as action-theoretical problems. A complicated undertaking, as I readily admit. Perhaps we can come to an agreement by focusing on the key term "anti-naturalism." That doesn't mean that we would have to exclude or ignore scientific knowledge per se – they can certainly be included in our attempts to provide a best account of our action.

Martin Bauer   At this point, we can set aside the controversy concerning the relationship between social theory and the theory of society and say that it is ultimately an open question. Regardless, you seem to agree that a social theory makes certain (social-)ontological commitments as soon as it defines the material that constitutes the social. Let's turn to the question of the generalizing perspectives that are needed by a theory of society when it thematizes the historicity of social formations. Does such a theory need to offer a critical perspective under which society as a whole or individual social phenomena could be normatively judged?

In this respect, Andreas Reckwitz argues for abstinence. Although his understanding of the theory of society requires a historicizing appraisal of modern sociality, the social-historical narrative that he has crafted with the aim of differentiating between bourgeois and industrial modernity, as well as late modernity, does not recognize any sense of direction in the historical process. There is no teleology, in other words, that dictates this sequence of different versions of modernity. There is no overarching purpose that can explain this sequence; it is, rather, a series of contingent events.

Andreas Reckwitz   But this observation has nothing to do with the question of the sociological critique of society.

Martin Bauer   It does to the extent that Hartmut Rosa, unlike you, identifies a sense of direction that is of some importance to his critique of modernity.

Hartmut Rosa   Yes, but not as a sort of *historical* teleology but, rather, as a *formative* teleology. Within the given formation of modernity, it is possible to recognize a direction that I indeed find worthy of critique. Only I would not call it a telos. The philosophy of history is not my concern; what I see is, rather, a process logic that, in my understanding, is characteristic of the formation in question.

Martin Bauer   What you have described as modernity's structure of dynamic stabilization brings to light a mechanism that in part causes different historical processes and therefore also makes prognosis possible.

Hartmut Rosa   Yes.

Martin Bauer   And from this possibility of prognosis, which your theory of modernity offers, arises the need for intervention, even the need for drastic interventions in the interest of the self-preservation of our species.

Hartmut Rosa   I would say so, yes.

Martin Bauer   I've been interested in clarifying this matter, because it's fundamental to your conception of the theory of society and it illuminates how you anchor your critique of modernity within theory itself.

Andreas Reckwitz   Of course, our respective models of critique depend not least on how we understand history. But we should first address the differences that distinguish our understandings of social critique, even though in this regard we share the presupposition that critique should play an indispensable role in any theory of society. According to Max Horkheimer's argument in his essay "Traditional and Critical Theory," science has to reflect about its position in society. We should not think that we can adopt a neutral or, as it were, extra-societal position of observation. At the same time, however, I do not take the side of critical theory, especially as it is represented by some of the proponents of the Frankfurt School.

This has been the case since my student years in the 1990s. At that time, the theoretical approaches of Habermas and Luhmann were hegemonic in Germany. With both of these positions, however, I was discontent for various reasons. I was unable and unwilling to join one camp or the other, and instead I found the approaches of Bourdieu and Foucault, which were still receiving less attention at the time, more interesting. What I found increasingly problematic about Habermas's communication theory, however consistently constructed it may be, was that it seemed too normative as a critical theory of society. This is a grand social philosophy, but its sociological analysis is stuffed into a normative straitjacket from the outset. The danger in this is that it can lead to analytical dead ends. One always knows what to look for – namely, the ideal of communicative rationality, which is, as expected, undermined by social realities. The paradoxes of the social are hardly given any thought at all. Against this backdrop, it is also difficult to account for new phenomena in society, whether it's new forms of life or digitalization, and these can manifest themselves in surprising ways. I think that it's important for sociology to allow itself to be surprised by new phenomena and try to understand them without proceeding from a preformulated and normative analytical framework.

As I see it, the task at hand should be to implement a form of critical analysis that operates with few normative stipulations. In this regard, I have followed with great interest the alternative approach that Luc Boltanski has formulated in his sociology of critique. He has distanced himself from critical theory by identifying, in strictly empirical terms, which practices of critique really take place in contemporary society. Boltanski's effort to examine critical movements that open up contingency in their own specific ways is commendable, but here the problem is that, empirically, his sociology of critique is concentrated entirely on the perspective of participants. His research is really only focused on which actors and groups of actors are practicing which types of critique.

I have attempted instead to pursue a third option, which, following Foucault, I call critical analytics. By this, I mean a mode of sociological analysis that deciphers what is ostensibly self-evident in its contingency, makes this contingency apparent, and therefore also makes transparent certain social contexts that do not appear in official representations of reality. I think that this type of critical analysis, which does not evaluate itself but lets its analysis speak for itself, as it were, is quite common, not only in Foucault and Bourdieu or in cultural studies, but also in Marx or in some of the authors of the early Frankfurt School, but it is seldom foregrounded. To give a concrete example: The book that I wrote about creativity is about how, historically, both creativity, as a social imperative, and also the creative subject, whose existence is often taken for granted, were only able to develop in particular social and cultural contexts. Creativity is frequently assumed to be a quasi-natural characteristic of human beings, but my concern was instead to reconstruct a genealogy of the social fabrication of creativity. At a remove from its object of study, this form of critical analytics documents the contingency of the creativity discourse and its social effects without any intention of critiquing creativity or the creative subject as such.

Hartmut Rosa   Although I consider myself a critical theorist, I can partly agree with your objections to critical theory. The problem was that its criteria of evaluation were rigidly fixed, and these criteria determined, according to critical theory, the issues from which people suffer. It was assumed that society's pathologies were known and theoretically established, and thus all that was needed was to categorize the phenomena in question, instead of taking their social reality seriously. In my sociology of our relationship to the world, I therefore attempt to take a different approach. My initial question is not normative but descriptive: What is really happening? What sort of relationship to the world emerges within a given practice or in a particular form of action or structure; what sort of relationship do subjects consider desirable, and which do they avoid? To this extent, I share with you a strongly descriptive interest.

Beyond that, however, I also try to take the first-person perspective as seriously as possible. What are the hopes and desires of subjects directed toward? What do they experience as successful? What as unsuccessful? Only the answers to such questions can provide starting points for critique. One can then justifiably say: People, look here, these are the things that, according to your own perception, aren't going well and should possibly be changed. This method also provides an independent analytical approach to the possibilities and practices of critique. In principle, I feel a sense of solidarity with the first-person perspective, with its point of view, and I do so in the firm conviction that theory fundamentally arises from a critical impulse – namely, from the feeling that *something's not right here, something's a little off*. It has long been my mantra that sociological theories, and perhaps other theories as well, ultimately spring from a sense of irritation or concern. Even Luhmann's theory originated from his feeling that many of the self-descriptions circulating in society were simply not right. Therefore, I believe that every analytical interest is always accompanied by a critical interest. For this reason, too, I maintain that the standard of critique cannot be gained externally and that phenomena should not be approached from the outside. "I'll tell you what you should really do or think" – this is not my attitude. No, things that are problematic come to light via practice, and I attempt to describe them.

Martin Bauer   But how does a sociologist gain access to the internal optics of suffering subjects? And even if, historically speaking, every theory's context of discovery includes a certain degree of emotion – a subjective feeling of irritation – I'm surprised by how aggressively you promote the first-person perspective. Doesn't such a methodological maxim, to put it cautiously, conflict with the idea of sociological enlightenment and its claim to objectivity?

Hartmut Rosa   I would indeed like to practice theory from a first-person perspective, and by no means do I want to be a social scientist who operates according to the motto "I now know how things are and wish to enlighten people." Honestly, this is why the idea of enlightenment bothers me a bit, unless one understands enlightenment primarily as self-enlightenment. As I've said, the concept of the best account is central to me. That is, I present a draft of an interpretation, which phenomenologically starts with the first person, with me. The attempt to turn this interpretive offering into science then unfolds, necessarily, in a dialogic manner. I present this offering as an invitation to an ongoing conversation. According to my self-understanding as a sociologist, I am paid to do exactly this sort of interpretive work. In doing so, moreover, I attempt to include all available material that is relevant to producing a best account: data from empirical social research, as well as literature or films. What I need to clarify and understand is the substance of these sources and what sorts of experiences and relationship to the world are expressed in them. In light of the material that he or she has gathered, the ambition of the interpreter should be to propose an interpretation with a broad and clearly contoured horizon and to ask the following question: Hey, people, can it be that we really desire this or that thing and are in fact suffering from these other things? So begins the discussion. It is not the case that I want to publish some sort of positive knowledge and present it to the outside world. Instead, the account that I offer has to prove itself in the discussions and disputes that it incites, for instance in my discussions with garbage collectors or homeless people in Brazil or with university students and pupils in India – discussions that I've actually had. Such dialogues are anything but uncomplicated, but I would say that they are overdue and that the type of social science that I endorse can only function in this way. The decisive point of phenomenology lies in deducing, from concrete experiences, what is individual and specific, and then in revealing, on the basis of this knowledge, a generalizable structural core. This can only be done through a mixture of introspection and dialogue, though it can of course be the case that the introspection of an interview partner might serve as one's starting point or base material.

Andreas Reckwitz   Back to your idea of critical theory – that is, to your understanding of resonance and how you emphasize it. Is it safe to say that, in terms of how your theory is constructed, resonance is to you what communicative rationality is to Habermas or recognition is to Honneth?

Hartmut Rosa   Yes, one could say that.

Andreas Reckwitz   In that case, you are making an emphatic appeal for the participant perspective. And, of course, it is possible to ask empirically: Do participants, in their interactions and social relationships, feel something like resonance? My impression from your book on resonance, however, was that you simultaneously adopt an observer's perspective in order to ask whether such reported experiences really amounted to resonance. So, in other words, you require a stable criterion for success, and yet otherwise you place yourself entirely at the disposal of the subjective perspective.

Hartmut Rosa   Yes, you're raising a point that is as important as it is sensitive. However, I have a strong intuition that I can solve the problem at hand. Am I able to recognize from the observer's perspective whether resonance is occurring or not, or do I have to rely on the information provided to me by subjects? Let's take our conversation as an example! I would guess that both of us have a sense of whether and when this was a good conversation. That is one side of judging success. I can say that our conversation was resonant if, thanks to our exchange, I have come up with ideas that I hadn't thought of before – when I feel that, yes, he had a good point there, and when, at the same time, I have the impression that my arguments have likewise reached you and have influenced your position in one way or another. Both participants will regard their conversation as positive when they share the feeling of having reached one another and set each other's mind in motion. Of course, the possibility can't be discounted that only I might feel that our conversation had genuinely been resonant, when in fact I was only doggedly repeating and discursively rehashing what I always say about certain topics, while you never had a chance to get a word in. There could be a camera filming our conversation, however, and the recording might clearly and undeniably indicate this. It could refute my claim that our conversation was really resonant. In the end, a resonant relationship is always two-sided; there is, on the one hand, the experiential dimension of the subjects, while, on the other hand, there is also an objective event. The structural analogy to theories of alienation comes to mind. Here, too, there are two sides involved: alienation as subjective lived experience, and alienation as an objective social relationship. Yet it is possible to keep both sides in view if one thinks in terms of the "perspectival dualism" to which I am methodologically committed, as I've already pointed out. In short, what counts as a resonant experience can only be understood from the first-person perspective, but whether a resonant relationship exists can in principle (also) be recognized, and perhaps even measured, from the third-person perspective.

Andreas Reckwitz As it seems to me, the concept of resonance fulfills two functions for you. On the one hand, it functions as an analytical concept; on the other hand, and at the same time, it serves as a touchstone for your critical theory. But doesn't this dual function lead to certain difficulties? Shouldn't a critical theorist feel irritated, at least occasionally? Let's take the example of a mass event like Goebbels's famous and notorious speech at the Sportpalast in Berlin. Here, it's possible to see resonant relationships in many respects; there are affects galore. It is a significant insight, I think, to recognize that fascism is not a rational phenomenon, but rather functions by means of affects and emotions. Now, however, it is also easily conceivable that Goebbels's audience perceived these affects as positive resonant relationships. If their "first-person perspective" is somehow a crucial factor for any critical theory of resonant relationships, then I would have to say that this theory has a serious problem.

Hartmut Rosa For me, however, resonance means more than simply being affected …

Andreas Reckwitz Sure, but then you say that it might as well be called resonance …

Hartmut Rosa … but no one does that, Andreas. In everyday experience, no one says "I had a resonant …"

Andreas Reckwitz ... but their eyes are gleaming, and this was unmistakably captured by the camera.

Hartmut Rosa Yes, I agree with you. The example of National Socialism has bothered me profoundly. When I was first developing my theory of resonance, a participant in one of my discussions about it once said to me: "Just hearing the word *resonance* sends an ice-cold shiver down my spine because it makes me think of those fascist mass demonstrations." That's when I first started to grapple with the issue, and then I modified my theory by introducing the distinction between resonance and echo, which I modeled on Helmuth Plessner's differentiation between resonance and sentimentality. This is what I mean when I say that theory has to be further developed dialogically.

Andreas Reckwitz So, ultimately, you have to express yourself as an observer and, in a sense, set the record straight by pointing out that, as participants, people may indeed have been affected and may have found the events great, but this is in fact not real resonance but, at best, a feeling of pseudo-resonance.

Hartmut Rosa As I've said, both perspectives are important to me. We are back at the example of assessing a conversation and the possibility that the respective perceptions of the participants in this conversation might not be in alignment. It is similar in the example of the Nazis, because the resonant relationship, the particular quality of which I've attempted to demonstrate and understand in my work, does not materialize there. According to my definition, resonance is a movement that consists not only of affects but of four elements: affects, self-effectiveness, transformation, and open-endedness or uncontrollability. At the Sportpalast in Berlin, I would have missed out on three of these four elements. The question would be whether the discrepancy can be so radical that people could say that, for them, it was an *experience of the good life*, whereas I as an observer would have to contradict and correct their own self-interpretation. But let's simply look at right-wing populists. What has created them? Resentment, aggression, and rage. From the first-person perspective itself, that hardly qualifies as a successful life, even if their gleaming hate-filled eyes are everywhere to be seen.

Andreas Reckwitz But aren't we thus faced with the situation that resonant relationships first have to be observed empirically, in order then, in a second step, to be classified as good or bad from an ethical point of view ...

Hartmut Rosa No, I have to disagree, though I'm quick to acknowledge that this is the most hotly contested point of resonance theory. Many people have advised me not to define resonance as something good per se or even as the good, but instead to distinguish between positive and negative resonance and introduce an additional ethical criterion. But I'm against doing so, even though I'm aware that it's a sensitive matter. To me, the crucial question seems to be whether affects such as hate, rage, and murderous desire can really be experienced as successful resonances. Let's assume that I just heard a speech like Goebbels's and I leave the Sportpalast with the desire to kill all sorts of people: Jews, disabled people, homosexuals, Russians, communists. My question would be whether someone with such an attitude could seriously say: "For me, this is the good life." To be honest, I think such a statement would be impossible.

Andreas Reckwitz But aren't resonant relationships one thing and notions of the good life another? In the social world, many things happen that participants regard to be successful, even though the event in question might be deemed worthy of critique from a social-philosophical or ethical point of view. Throughout the presentation of your theory, you nevertheless attempt to skirt around this divergence. Like Habermas's effort to formulate a normative theory of communicative rationality, your own efforts do not seem to be especially welcoming to paradoxes. Is it not possible to detect a certain tendency in your work to create unambiguous relationships while overlooking the paradoxes that are unignorable in everyday practices and experiences? It may be that resonance is experienced as successful and that you, as an outside observer, agree with this perception, but what happens when the participant and the observer disagree about this?

Hartmut Rosa It is true that presupposing feelings of success is a theoretical assumption that could be called normative. I understand this as a proposed interpretation that needs to be proved but that might, of course, turn out to be wrong. This proposal can be challenged from both the sides that we've been discussing here. From the first-person perspective, someone could convincingly argue that he or she experiences resonance as something bad and does not seek it out at all. Interestingly, hardly anyone has said this, even though there's, of course, a psychological mechanism whereby subjects, in response to traumatic events, can develop certain tendencies to avoid such experiences because they associate being touched with being harmed. Instead, what I repeatedly encounter is the objection that there are ethically undesirable resonances. In my opinion, however, the criterion of undesirability is itself a "deaf response to resonance." I think that racism and sexism, for instance, are structural examples of such deaf responses to groups of people whose voices have been muted, and if there's a strong animal-rights movement today, I think this has been motivated by the fact that we can perceive, as Adorno remarked long ago, an appeal for resonance in the eyes of cows being slaughtered or in the barks of landmine-detecting dogs.

Martin Bauer   Let's return to our initial question – that is, to the problem of whether a theory of modern society must be critical, and from where, as sociology, it draws its criteria for critique. It's become clear that Hartmut Rosa's approach is based on the success of resonant relationships – that is, primarily on information gained from the first-person perspective. Andreas Reckwitz, in contrast, relies on a method which he calls critical analytics. The aim of his genealogical approach is to dissolve the given positivities within society. And if the hallmark of modernity, as he stressed earlier, is revolution, then it is probably revolutionary of a sociologist to ask, in light of such positivities and following Foucault, how they were historically formed and which heterogeneous forces were at play in their creation.

Andreas Reckwitz   Indeed, as it seems to me, my understanding of critical analytics fits seamlessly into my approach to the theory of society and into my general sociological concern with modernity. Critical analytics is on the side of opening up contingency. If one assumes that modernity unleashed a dialectic between opening and closing contingency, then the role of the human sciences – not least sociology and the theory of society – should be to work toward opening up contingency. This is on a theoretical level, of course, because it remains a practice within the science of sociology to expose, by means of genealogical reconstruction, the constructed nature of creativity, singularity, and other social phenomena and entities. In this respect, a residual degree of normativism remains, even though I profess to practice a non-normative type of theory. It should be clear that critical analytics cannot operate without a minimal degree of normativity. This consists in being engaged on behalf of opening up contingency – and this in itself is modern.

This is not to say, however, that every social act of closing contingency is bad per se and that every closed contingency needs to be opened up. Of course not. This is itself a political or ethical question. On a theoretical, intellectual, and cognitive level, the issue is, rather, to clarify the constructed nature of the object of analysis at hand, the structures and genealogies that enable it, the implicit norms with which it operates, and the seemingly – but only seemingly – valid notions of rationality that underlie it. The consequences that such an effort might have in the non-scientific world is another matter. This is a question of political discourse, which can of course be intellectually informed. On the basis of critical analysis, informed decisions can be made if the public has been made sociologically aware, and if unseen connections have been brought to light. In order to assess, for example, whether the social logic of singularity is negative or positive, it's important to understand how the game is played. The truth of the matter is that the social logic of singularization typically operates behind the back of actors, who often believe that things are "really" unique. It is hardly necessary to conclude from this that institutions or forms of life should no longer want to engage in singularization. In the end, it might also happen that a decision is reached along the lines of, well, now we know how it functions, and everything seems to be fine. Now, at least, we would be dealing with a practice that has been thought about in the public sphere. In this sense, sociology is not prescriptive; it does not demand that this or that should be done or that this or that contingency should be opened up. A sociologist might write a critical analysis of the mechanisms of cultural capitalism, but this does not necessarily mean that cultural capitalism should be abolished. It is rather a matter of opening up new possibilities in the medium of analysis, or of demonstrating possible forms of intervention. Whether society finds these suggestions useful or reasonable is another question entirely.

Hartmut Rosa   In other words, the aspiration to open up possibilities, to broaden the horizon of possibility – this is a modern phenomenon, as you would also say ...

Andreas Reckwitz   ... exactly ...

Hartmut Rosa   ... and therefore, of the two poles within modernity, as you see them, you take the side of opening up contingency, right?

Andreas Reckwitz   On the theoretical level. As a politically thinking person, I would of course say that we have to create institutional orders that satisfy certain standards. As a sociologist, in contrast, I operate within the scientific or intellectual realm, in which I work analytically to demonstrate how things are socially constructed. This does not mean that I would refrain from making normative comments about my findings. The boundary between analysis and political opinion can be crossed, but one has to be aware that, by doing so, one has shifted from one genre to another. If the logic of singularization has gone too far, to the extent that only singularity matters – that is, to the extent that the standards of the general have entirely been pushed into the background – then I can speak up politically and say, okay, under these conditions, we should probably focus on "doing universality." This gesture, however, would be a political intervention, which is of course permissible but not necessary. Other actors might draw different conclusions from the same diagnosis.

Hartmut Rosa You draw a line between scientific analysis and political opinion, and you refer to the separate spheres of science and political discourse, as many people do, because it's plausible enough. In contrast, I attempt to provide a best account of things in which I bring together the political and the normative …

Andreas Reckwitz … which is typical of the tradition of critical theory, in which the one follows from the other.

Hartmut Rosa Actually, yes. My analysis articulates a critique of the modern social formation as a whole – of both its sides: its structural logic as well as its cultural horizon. The structure and culture of this version of modernity, as I argue, are moving in a direction that is worthy of critique. And if this critique is taken as a sociological position or opinion, which it in fact claims to be, then strictly speaking it requires something like an extra-formative point of view. I read your work differently. In Charles Taylor's terms, one could say that I'm on the side of modernity's detractors, or at least that I'm one of modernity's critics, but I don't think that you do this when you explain that you operate on one side of modernity's horizon – that is, on the side of opening up contingency.

Andreas Reckwitz Yes, I operate within this ambivalence of modernity. When I take a stand and say that we should consider the direction in which everything is going, the position that I take always tends to be that of contradicting the dominant logic – and this is typical of the logic of modernity, according to which any closure of contingency is responded to by a critical opening of contingency. If one observes that the logic of singularization is running rampant, it is logical to object to this in favor of the general. If we were living in the middle of the 1960s – that is, during a peak phase of industrial modernity – the critique would have to take a different direction and argue for promoting differences and singularization. Or let's take the key word "affectivity"! My suspicion is that late-modern culture is too reliant on affect and being affected, a view that probably represents an additional difference between us. I would be in favor of cooling things down in this respect; a degree of de-emotionalization seems necessary. Conversely, I certainly would have taken the other side during the emotionally subdued years around 1960, when I would have argued in favor of more emotionalization. Viewed in this way, critical analytics, as I understand it, has moving targets. Because history changes, critique has to change along with it.

Hartmut Rosa When I look at your three bipolarities – that is, rationalization versus culturalization, generalization versus singularization, closing versus opening contingency – my impression is that the moving targets pertaining to the first two oppositions arise from your conviction that balance is necessary, whereas, in the matter of contingency, you are firmly on the side of opening. But wouldn't you also say that, in some situations, we need contingency to be closed? I'm thinking of legal regulations such as labor laws and rent protection. Neoliberalism, in particular, always claims that it is in favor of opening up contingency in so many areas of life.

Andreas Reckwitz Certainly, but in its own way it has also managed to close contingency ...

Hartmut Rosa ... yes, on the flip side of things, but ...

Andreas Reckwitz ... marketization, this is a new straitjacket. The gesture of opening things up, of creating necessary dynamization, and of overdue deregulation was meant to break apart ossified structures and lead to openings of contingency, but then it led to the ubiquity of the market. It happens to be a neoliberal prejudice to think that rent protection, for example, closes contingency, but the opposite is true. In opposition to neoliberalism, it in fact opens up contingency; it makes it possible to conceive of a different infrastructural order, for instance.

Hartmut Rosa It should thus be asked when and where contingency should actually be evaluated in normative terms. Perhaps every move includes both sides, and every decision goes hand in hand with a closure of contingency.

Andreas Reckwitz We have already gone over this aspect. In purely logical terms, one can certainly say that this is the case, but historically it's possible to distinguish phases more inclined toward opening from phases more inclined toward closure. The ongoing impulse to revise the status quo is a feature of modernity: Things must not go on as they have been; there are questionable constraints, injustices, and tendencies toward alienation that must be eliminated. Such tendencies toward opening contingency flare up at certain points, and the flip side to these openings is, after a certain amount of time, a new closure. Critical analytics has to be sensitive to precisely this dialectic, according to which what was once liberating can at some point turn into something repressive and problematic.

Hartmut Rosa   I think you need the perspective of actors for that. Here, again, I see some common ground between us, but also a difference. Where you talk about opening or closing contingency, I speak of controllability and uncontrollability. It is my conviction that the movement of modernity – one of its fundamental interests – is aimed at broadening the horizon of controllability or availability under which subjects can act. From this perspective, contingency is a matter of the third-person perspective. Whether contingencies are increasing or decreasing – this can be observed from the outside. Yet the crucial point about modernity's development, as well as in your diagnoses of it, arises from the perspective of subjects alone. Their question is not whether contingency has somehow increased or decreased; instead, their question is whether more or fewer things are available to them.

Andreas Reckwitz   But this seems to be a completely different question to me. I am not primarily concerned with whether contingencies are increasing or decreasing. My concern is rather with processes of closure and how they're related to hegemonic strategies.

Martin Bauer   But doesn't your argument for the revolutionary principle of modernity furnish your genealogical concept of critical analytics with a degree of libertarian emphasis?

Andreas Reckwitz   There is no such emphasis whatsoever.

Martin Bauer   That's a given, Mr. Reckwitz. Unlike me, you are fortunately never emphatic …

Andreas Reckwitz   [*laughs*] I would rather speak of minimal normativism. Emphasis sounds too aggressive to me.

Martin Bauer Nevertheless, my impression is that you represent a libertarian position, however "detached" it might be. Is this not the case?

Andreas Reckwitz "Libertarian" is itself not such a simple term. There are also so-called "libertarians" in the United States, but that is certainly not what I mean. Yet it is a position in favor of opening up new possibilities, and this applies to institutions and forms of life alike.

Hartmut Rosa In principle, I am very sympathetic to this position. Motivationally, I would say that I stand with you on Foucault's side, although, as someone whose intellectual socialization took place in the environment of critical theory, I used to think that he wasn't interested in normative problems and that he didn't have any normative criteria at all. Later, I realized that when Foucault deals with transgression – when he discusses moments of transgression in which unexpected possibilities suddenly open up – he brings into play not only freedom, but also the same dimension of experience that I interpret as success.

Andreas Reckwitz Though such motives are admittedly rather hidden in Foucault's work. The minimal normativism that I have in mind is certainly related to the modern concept of freedom, which, as argued in Richard Rorty's book *Contingency, Irony, and Solidarity*, is the freedom to be conscious of contingency.

Martin Bauer I find it instructive how, in the context of your theory of society, this keen awareness of contingency leads to a type of critical analysis that envisions sociological enlightenment primarily in terms of local intervention ...

Andreas Reckwitz Precisely ...

Martin Bauer You are reacting to a particular historical constellation and would resist any attempt to go beyond this local intervention ...

Andreas Reckwitz ... exactly. Any such intervention has to be local and situational, because, at any other place or at any other time, a different set of circumstances would be worthy of critique.

Hartmut Rosa I understand that well. Regarding my own theory, in fact, I'm always on the fence about whether my intentions might be too broad, as though I've been driven by an idea of salvation, the utopia of a world in which everything is resonant. I have to reproach myself from time to time for such excesses, which could easily be misused politically. Yet, as long as there's no miracle – what do I know, maybe the savior will come and fix everything – I'll, of course, have to assume as a sociologist that no completely resonant world awaits us. On the contrary, I think this is impossible for conceptual reasons alone. So, perhaps this is another point of convergence between us? In any case, the task of the social sciences and of the human sciences as a whole, in my view, should be to analyze impediments to resonance and moments of alienation in a concrete and localized manner. I'm not even remotely interested in abstract and untenable complaints about how everything was better in the past. Repression – that is, circumstances that impede resonance – has always existed, especially under paternalistic and authoritarian regimes. And, today, the repression of resonance takes place in different situations and in different venues. So it will remain a never-ending and always current task, just as you said, to reformulate the basis of interventional critique. The critique of resonant relationships does not come from nowhere.

Andreas Reckwitz   But you are already working with an aggressively normative standard. The critical analytics that I've been talking about proceeds differently and is not oriented in that way.

Martin Bauer   In Hartmut Rosa's work, one can clearly see traces of Weberian neo-Marxism, as formulated by the Frankfurt School, with recourse, incidentally, to the early Georg Lukás. Nor will the "iron cage" that Rosa's theory illuminates be entirely unfamiliar to readers of Horkheimer, Adorno, Marcuse, and others. Nevertheless, you've opened up new and hitherto unexplored fields of observation for critical theory, not least via Charles Taylor. And what you regard to be worthy of critique there finds its expression in a different dimension, and not always in the local and situational interventions that Andreas Reckwitz considers sociologically justifiable.

Hartmut Rosa   I think we can agree on that.

Notes

Introduction

1 Jean-François Lyotard, *The Postmodern Condition: A Report on Knowledge*, trans. Geoffrey Bennington and Brian Massumi (Minneapolis: University of Minnesota Press, 1984).

2 Yuval Noah Harari, *Sapiens: A Brief History of Humankind* (London: Harvill Secker, 2014); Yuval Noah Harari, *21 Lessons for the 21st Century* (London: Jonathan Cape, 2018). For a similar approach, see Robert L. Kelly, *The Fifth Beginning: What Six Million Years of Human History Can Tell Us about Our Future* (Oakland: University of California Press, 2016).

3 David Christian, *Big History* (New York: DK Publishing, 2016).

4 Thomas Piketty, *Capital in the Twenty-First Century*, trans. Arthur Goldhammer (Cambridge, MA: Harvard University Press, 2014); Thomas Piketty, *Capital and Ideology*, trans. Arthur Goldhammer (Cambridge, MA: Harvard University Press, 2020); Branko Milanović, *Global Inequality: A New Approach for the Age of Globalization* (Cambridge, MA: Harvard University Press, 2016); Shoshana Zuboff, *The Age of Surveillance Capitalism: The Fight for a Human Future at the New Frontier of Power* (New York: Public Affairs, 2019).

5 Pankaj Mishra, *Age of Anger: A History of the Present* (New York: Farrar, Straus & Giroux, 2017); Maja Göpel, *Unsere Welt neu denken: Eine Einladung* (Berlin: Ullstein, 2020).

6 Zygmunt Bauman, *Modernity and Ambivalence* (Cambridge: Polity, 1991); David Harvey, *The Conditions of Postmodernity* (Oxford: Blackwell, 2000); Scott Lash and John Urry, *Economies of Signs and Space* (London: SAGE, 2002); Anthony Giddens, *The Consequences of Modernity* (Cambridge: Polity, 2015); Manuel Castells, *The Information Age: Economy, Society and Culture* (Oxford: Blackwell, 1996–8).

7 It seems as though the tendencies of our European neighbors in France are similar to those in Germany. The fragmentation of the discipline has not fully discouraged French sociologists from contributing to the theory of society. Consider, for instance, the sociological tradition established by Pierre Bourdieu, the prominent books by Luc Boltanski, Laurent Thevenot, and Ève Chiapello, not to mention Bruno Latour's monumental book *An Inquiry into Modes of Existence*, and the work by Bernard Lahire and Alain Ehrenberg. The Israeli sociologist Eva Illouz, whose books provide an important contribution to the theory of late modernity, has been strongly influenced by the discourse in France. The establishment of independent research institutions, the interdisciplinary orientation of the *sciences humaines*, and the prominent role – even more

prominent than in Germany – of public intellectuals in France clearly smooth the way for French sociologists to work on large-scale theories of society.

Part I Reckwitz: *The Theory of Society as a Tool*

1. Doing Theory

1 The English term *social theory* normally encompasses both social theory and the theory of society, but it is important not to blur this distinction.

2 Conversely, social theory operates with, in its own way, a particular form of empiricism, a specific and ultimately pre-scientific experience of the social world – for instance, an experience of action, roles, power, understanding, or practices. See Stefan Hirschbauer, "Die Empiriegeladenheit von Theorien und der Erfindungsreichtum der Practice," in *Theoretische Empirie: Zur Relevanz qualitativer Forschung*, ed. Herbert Kalthoff et al. (Frankfurt am Main: Suhrkamp, 2019), pp. 165–87.

3 It is therefore no coincidence that social theories such as pragmatism, phenomenology, or post-structuralism transgress the boundaries between sociology and philosophy.

4 In contrast to the notion of modernization theories, which have long been influential in sociology, I do not proceed from the assumption that modern Western society represents the "normal case" that will eventually be found throughout the world without any variation. Modern Western societies are, instead, a highly specific constellation, a highly specific network of practices at a particular time and place in human history. As Dipesh Chakrabarty has argued, it is high time to "provincialize" Europe (and North America), that is – to see there nothing more or less than one specific path of development among others. This does not change the fact that certain elements of European and North American modernity – such as capitalism or science – have been borrowed and processed to various ends outside of this narrow geographical context. As Shmuel N. Eisenstadt pointed out, global society has the character of a complex of "multiple modernities" that intersect with one another and produce hybrid forms.

5 In recent decades, this rather ambitious option of producing a general evolutionary theory of human history has not been *en vogue*. Now, however, it seems to be attracting interest again. See, for instance, Davor Löffler, *Generative Realitäten I: Die Technologische Zivilisation als neue Achsenzeit und Zivilisationsstufe. Eine Anthropologie des 21. Jahrhunderts* (Weilerswist: Velbrück, 2019). The topic of global interconnections has also been a prominent feature in recent books on global history. See, for example, Sebastian Conrad, *What Is Global History?* (Princeton University Press, 2016).

6 The term *modernity* means different things in different disciplines. For example, there are clear and wide differences between the way in which sociology understands modernity and the way it is used in art history. The former understanding is based on the structural changes in society that have taken place since the eighteenth century, whereas the latter understanding overlaps with modernism, which began with the avant-garde artists around the year 1900. For a discussion of such terminological differences, see Krishan Kumar, *From Post-Industrial to Post-Modern Society: New Theories of the Contemporary World* (Oxford: Blackwell, 1995), pp. 61–89.

7 As a concept, a "diagnosis of the times" (*Zeitdiagnose*) is not restricted to academia. It implies the genre of a publicly persuasive *description* of contemporary society that can also take on the form of an essay. This distinguishes this genre, however, from a theory of late-modern society, which is a subdivision of the *theory* of society. The latter pursues decidedly theoretical interests – and

therefore an interest in systematic concepts, in comprehensive synthesis, in explanatory hypotheses, and in empirical research programs.

8 On this topic, see Hans-Peter Müller, *Krise und Kritik: Klassiker der soziologischen Zeitdiagnose* (Berlin: Suhrkamp, 2021).

9 In light of the praxeological social theory that I employ, it is possible, for instance, to develop various perspectives on the theory of society. This variability of possible theories of society also applies to other social theories, for instance to rational-choice theory, social phenomenology, actor–network theory, or neo-institutionalism. Conversely, it is also true that certain theories of society presuppose certain social-theoretical concepts, without which they would not even be able to "function." Norbert Elias's *The Civilizing Process*, for example, has as its basis a social theory that relies on a sociologically strong concept of affects. Between social theory and the theory of society, there thus exists a loose – but not strict – connection.

10 On the importance of metaphors, see Susanne Lüdemann, *Metaphern der Gesellschaft: Studien zum soziologischen und politischen Imaginären* (Munich: Fink, 2004). On the significance of narrative patterns in general, see Albrecht Koschorke, *Fact and Fiction: Elements of a General Theory of Narrative*, trans. Joel Golb (Berlin: De Gruyter, 2018).

11 See W. V. O. Quine, "Two Dogmas of Empiricism," *The Philosophical Review* 60 (1951), pp. 20–43. On the topic of post-empiricism and the theory of science, see James Bohman, *New Philosophy of Social Science: Problems of Indeterminacy* (Cambridge, MA: The MIT Press, 1991).

12 See Jorge Luis Borges, "On Exactitude in Science," in *Collected Fictions*, trans. Andrew Hurley (New York: Penguin, 1998), p. 325.

13 Nelson Goodman, *Ways of Worldmaking* (New York: Hackett, 1978).

14 This understanding of theory can also be seen in the context of the open and liberal spirit of American pragmatism and its experimental attitude. On neo-pragmatism, see the essays collected in Richard Rorty, *Consequences of Pragmatism* (Minneapolis: University of Minnesota Press, 2008).

15 See Hans-Jörg Rheinberger, *Experimentalsysteme und epistemische Dinge* (Göttingen: Wallstein, 2001). On the approach of experimentalism, see also Tanja Bogusz, *Experimentalismus und Soziologie: Von der Krisen- zur Erfahrungswissenschaft* (Frankfurt am Main: Campus, 2018).

16 The former model of the tree has been supplanted, so to speak, by that of the rhizome. See Gilles Deleuze and Félix Guattari, *A Thousand Plateaus: Capitalism and Schizophrenia*, trans. Brian Massumi (Minneapolis: University of Minnesota Press, 1987), pp. 3–25.

17 See, for instance, the contributions in *The Nexus of Practices: Connections, Constellations and Practitioners*, ed. Allison Hui et al. (London: Routledge, 2017).

18 In the history of theory, the idea of theory as a system and that of theory as a tool stand in opposition – sometimes tacitly – as two different understandings of theory. When dealing with theories, however, there is the possibility that one of the paradigms happens to be dominant on the part of the interpreter, regardless of the approach taken by the theorist in question. For the sake of didactic transparency and to encourage comparative analysis, for instance, university teachers will often be inclined to interpret "tool theories" as theoretical systems, thereby downplaying the former's experimental spirit. Max Weber's theory of modernity, for example, is often presented as a systematic design, even though Weber himself – who was ultimately a "tool theorist" – had never worked on such a system. I tend to favor the opposite strategy: theoretical systems, in my opinion, should be opened up and treated as tools. What sort of analytical tools can be borrowed from Marx or Luhmann? The crucial difference is that this might allow highly divergent vocabularies to be combined with one another in ways that clash with the intentions of those who developed them.

2. Practice Theory as Social Theory

1 See Pierre Bourdieu, *Outline of a Theory of Practice*, trans. Richard Nice (Cambridge University Press, 1977); Anthony Giddens, *The Constitution of Society: Outline of the Theory of Structuration* (Cambridge: Polity, 1984); Theodore R. Schatzki, *Social Practices: A Wittgensteinian Approach to Human Activity and the Social* (Cambridge University Press, 1996); Theodore R. Schatzki, *The Site of the Social: A Philosophical Account of the Constitution of Social Life and Change* (University Park: Pennsylvania State University Press, 2002). For general overviews of practice theory, see Andreas Reckwitz, "Toward a Theory of Social Practices: A Development in Culturalist Theorizing," *European Journal of Social Theory* 5 (2002), pp. 243–63; Theodore R. Schatzki et al., eds., *The Practice Turn in Contemporary Theory* (London: Routledge, 2001); Elizabeth Shove et al., *The Dynamics of Social Practice: Everyday Life and How It Changes* (London: SAGE, 2012); Hilmar Schäfer, ed., *Practicetheorie: Ein soziologisches Forschungsprogramm* (Bielefeld: Transcript, 2016); and Frank Hillebrandt, *Soziologische Practicetheorien: Eine Einführung* (Wiesbaden: Springer, 2014). A look back at the history of theory and philosophy will reveal a number of ideas that have influenced practice theory, not least Ludwig Wittgenstein's philosophy of the form of life (*Lebensform*).
2 See Viktor Vanberg, *Die zwei Soziologien: Individualismus und Kollektivismus in der Sozialtheorie* (Tübingen: Mohr, 1975).
3 In the field of cultural studies, the concept of the cultural technique has taken on a life of its own. See, for instance, Jörg Dünne et al., eds., *Cultural Techniques: Assembling Spaces, Texts, Collectives* (Berlin: De Gruyter, 2020).
4 This is an additional concept of culture that has played a part in the cultural turn. Below, I will introduce a narrower concept of culture that is based on ascriptions of value and is important for analyzing society.
5 For discussions of the difference between the micro and the macro, Jeffrey C. Alexander et al., eds., *The Micro–Macro-Link* (Berkeley: University of California Press, 1987).
6 Deleuze and Guattari, *A Thousand Plateaus*, pp. 314–15.
7 See Andreas Reckwitz, "Praktiken und Diskurse: Zur Logik von Practice-/Diskursformationen," in Reckwitz, *Kreativität und soziale Practice: Studien zur Sozial- und Gesellschaftstheorie* (Bielefeld: Transcript, 2016), pp. 49–67.
8 The modern educational system, for example, can be understood as just such a practice–discourse formation. Here, discourses about schools and education – in educational policy, the field of pedagogy, or media discourses, for instance – are tightly intertwined with non-discursive practices such as teaching itself, or administration.
9 See Andreas Reckwitz, "Practices and Their Affects," in *The Nexus of Practices*, ed. Hui et al., pp. 114–25; and Monique Scheer, "Are Emotions a Kind of Practice (and Is That What Makes Them Have a History)? A Bourdieuian Approach to Understanding Emotion," *History and Theory* 51/2 (2002), pp. 193–220.
10 See Andreas Reckwitz, *Subjekt*, 3rd edn. (Bielefeld: Transcript, 2021).
11 In this way, societies can be visualized praxeologically in terms of how closely or loosely they form a network of practices, and in terms of the particularly strong relations that exist between specific practices.
12 See Andreas Reckwitz, *Das hybride Subjekt: Eine Theorie der Subjektkulturen von der bürgerlichen Moderne zur Postmoderne* (Berlin: Suhrkamp, 2020), pp. 63–81.
13 The practice of going to the theatre, for instance, is part of both the middle-class form of life and the field of art. The practices of knowledge work belong to late modernity's educated middle class as well as to the field of cognitive capitalism.
14 This imperative, which stems from ethnomethodology, was formulated by Harold Garfinkel and Harvey Sacks. See Harvey Sacks, "On Doing 'Being Ordinary,'"

in *Structures of Social Action: Studies in Conversation Analysis*, ed. John M. Atkinson and John Heritage (Cambridge University Press, 1984), pp. 413–29.

3. The Practice of Modernity

1 Far from neglecting the ideas of early theorists, I aim to integrate several of their concepts, among them Weber's concept of formal rationalization, Simmel's notion of qualitative individualism, and Durkheim's distinction between the sacred and the profane.

2 Jean-François Lyotard, "Re-Writing Modernity," *Substance* 16/3 (1987), pp. 3–9.

3 See Claude Lévi-Strauss, *The Savage Mind* (London: Weidenfeld and Nicolson, 1966), pp. 233–4. One would, of course, have to point out that, historically, certain earlier advanced civilizations with state apparatuses and writing systems – such as the classical cultures of European, Chinese, and Indian antiquity – also developed a strong institutional awareness of contingency, but this awareness was nowhere near as radical as what one finds in modernity.

4 On the topic of contingency in the early-modern era and modernity, see Hans Blumenberg, "Phenomenological Aspects on Life-World and Technization," in *History, Metaphors, Fables: A Hans Blumenberg Reader*, ed. and trans. Hannes Bajohr et al. (Ithaca, NY: Cornell University Press, 2020), pp. 358–99; Niklas Luhmann, "Contingency as Modern Society's Defining Attribute," in *Observations on Modernity*, trans. William Whobrey (Stanford University Press, 1998), pp. 44–62; and Michael Makropoulos, *Modernität und Kontingenz* (Munich: Fink, 1997). On the discussion below, see also Reckwitz, *Das hybride Subjekt*, pp. 90–4.

5 See Peter Wagner, *A Sociology of Modernity: Liberty and Discipline* (London: Routledge, 1994).

6 See Ernesto Laclau and Chantal Mouffe, *Hegemony and Socialist Strategy: Towards a Radical Democratic Politics* (London: Verso, 1995).

7 See Reckwitz, *Das hybride Subjekt*.

8 This by no means excludes the possibility that certain developmental processes will be regarded as signs of progress by society itself. In fact, modern society cannot help but see itself in terms of progress. The theory of modernity, however, cannot simply accept the truth of society's self-perception without further ado.

9 On *posthistoire*, see Ludger Heidbrink, *Melancholie und Moderne: Zur Kritik der historischen Verzweiflung* (Munich: Fink, 1994), pp. 212–43.

10 See Niklas Luhmann, *Theory of Society*, 2 vols., trans. Rhodes Barrett (Stanford University Press, 2012–13); Bruno Latour, *An Inquiry into Modes of Existence: An Anthropology of the Moderns*, trans. Catherine Porter (Cambridge, MA: Harvard University Press, 2013); Luc Boltanski and Laurent Thévenot, *On Justification: Economies of Worth* (Princeton University Press, 2006).

11 For certain purposes of investigation, the analytic framework that I employ below can therefore be combined with those of Luhmann, Latour, or Boltanski and Thévenot. In my understanding of theory as a tool, there is no need to impose any restrictions in this respect.

12 For a more detailed discussion of this framework, see Andreas Reckwitz, *The Society of Singularities*, trans. Valentine A. Pakis (Cambridge: Polity, 2020), pp. 19–78.

13 See Max Weber, "Author's Introduction," in *The Protestant Ethic and the "Spirit" of Capitalism and Other Writings*, trans. Peter Baehr and Gordon C. Wells (New York: Penguin, 2002), pp. 13–31.

14 Different versions of generalization have also been in competition with one another. For instance, "doing generality" can tend to favor the norm of efficiency or the norm of social equality.

15 For a discussion of this conflict in the narrower context of the history of ideas, see Charles Taylor, *Sources of the Self: The Making of Modern Identity* (Cambridge, MA: Harvard University Press, 1989).
16 I therefore work throughout with two concepts of culture, one broader and one narrower. According to the broad concept of culture, "culture" designates the dimension of orders of knowledge and ascriptions of meaning (a dimension contained in every social practice). The narrower concept of culture, which I use when discussing culturalization, denotes a subset of these practices, namely those whose structure is not instrumentally rational but value-rational – practices, that is, in which value (in the strong sense of the term) is attributed to something.
17 See Max Weber, *Economy and Society: An Outline of Interpretive Sociology*, trans. Guenther Roth and Claus Wittich (Berkeley: University of California Press, 1978), p. 37; Émile Durkheim, *The Elementary Forms of the Religious Life*, trans. Joseph Ward Swain (London: G. Allen & Unwin, 1915), pp. 51–7.
18 In *The Society of Singularities*, I proceeded from the assumption that these sets of phenomena were necessarily coupled with one another, though there I referred to technological singularities as a special case. I have now developed this model in a more flexible direction, which has the advantage of making it possible to take into account, in a systematic manner, a fourth possible case: the culture of the general.
19 See ibid., pp. 49–50.
20 See Andreas Reckwitz, *The End of Illusions: Politics, Economy, and Culture in Late Modernity*, trans. Valentine A. Pakis (Cambridge: Polity, 2021), pp. 27–32. Approaches to combining the general with the valuable can also be found in monotheistic religions, for instance in Christianity. In the aesthetic realm, classicism and the modernist International Style provide further examples of such a combination.
21 For more detailed discussions of this phenomenon, see Andreas Reckwitz, "Jenseits der Innovationsgesellschaft: Das Kreativitätsdispositiv und die Transformation der sozialen Regime des Neuen," in *Kreativität und soziale Practice*, pp. 249–69; and Andreas Reckwitz, *The Invention of Creativity: Modern Society and the Culture of the New*, trans. Steven Black (Cambridge: Polity, 2017), pp. 27–46.
22 In rough terms, these three regimes of novelty correspond to the three historical forms of modernity: bourgeois modernity, industrial modernity, and late modernity.
23 See Andreas Reckwitz, "Auf dem Weg zu einer Soziologie des Verlusts," *Soziopolis* (May 6, 2021), https://www.soziopolis.de/auf-dem-weg-zu-einersoziologie-des-verlusts.html; and Peter Marris, *Loss and Change* (London: Routledge, 1974).
24 See Reckwitz, *Das hybride Subjekt*, pp. 94–103.
25 For a classic study of hybridization, see Homi K. Bhabha, *The Location of Culture* (London: Routledge, 1994).
26 On the tradition of modernization theories, see the critical assessment by Wolfgang Knöbl, *Spielräume der Modernisierung: Das Ende der Eindeutigkeit* (Weilerswist: Velbrück Wissenschaft, 2001).

4. The Theory of Society at Work

1 For a similar periodization of modernity into three phases, see Wagner, *A Sociology of Modernity*.
2 For a thorough discussion of this issue, see Bauman, *Modernity and Ambivalence*.
3 For a more detailed discussion of late modernity, see Reckwitz, *The Society of Singularities*.

4 I have chosen the term "recognition" (*Anerkennung*) because it is broad enough to encompass various symbolic as well as material or monetary forms of recognition. The problem of recognition thus crosses the distinction between the material and the cultural.

5 For more detailed discussions of this issue, see Reckwitz, *The Society of Singularities*, pp. 131–60; and Reckwitz, *The End of Illusions*, pp. 73–110.

6 For further discussion of this topic, see Reckwitz, *The End of Illusions*, pp. 111–30.

7 Alain Ehrenberg, *The Weariness of the Self: Diagnosing the History of Depression in the Modern Age*, trans. Enrico Caouette et al. (Montreal: McGill-Queen's University Press, 2010).

8 See Reckwitz, *The Society of Singularities*, pp. 161–95.

9 See ibid., pp. 267–309.

10 See Reckwitz, *The End of Illusions*, pp. 131–69.

11 See Reckwitz, *The Society of Singularities*, pp. 310–19. In the years 2020 and 2021, during which the present text was written, the COVID-19 pandemic held the global society firmly in its grip. In this regard, I do not want to endorse the (initially) quite common interpretation of this event, according to which the pandemic has created a rupture in society that will lead to a profound transformation. Nevertheless, one can say that, if only for a brief moment, the pandemic brought into public view all three of the aforementioned moments of crisis. The pandemic itself is not the crisis. Rather, it has drawn attention to preexisting moments of crisis and has thus amplified the critical discourse concerned with late modernity.

12 Of course, this raises the question of whether, on the global level, this issue will be perceived similarly outside of the West, or whether the orientation toward progress has simply been passed on to East Asia. On this topic, see Moritz Rudolph, *Der Weltgeist als Lachs* (Berlin: Matthes & Seitz, 2021).

13 This is also the thesis of Aleida Assmann's book *Ist die Zeit aus den Fugen? Aufstieg und Fall des Zeitregimes der Moderne* (Munich: Hanser, 2013).

5. Theory as Critical Analytics

1 See Max Horkheimer, *Critical Theory: Select Essays*, trans. Matthew J. O'Connell et al. (New York: Continuum, 2002); and Luc Boltanski, *On Critique: A Sociology of Emancipation*, trans. Gregory Elliott (Cambridge: Polity, 2011). For other recent discussions, see the contributions in Rahel Jaeggi and Tilo Wesche, eds., *Was ist Kritik?* (Frankfurt am Main: Suhrkamp, 2009). Regarding Luhmann's conflict with critical theory, see Jürgen Habermas and Niklas Luhmann, *Theorie der Gesellschaft oder Sozialtechnologie – Was leistet die Systemforschung?* (Frankfurt am Main: Suhrkamp, 1971).

2 On Foucault's understanding of critique, see Martin Saar, *Genealogie als Kritik: Geschichte und Theorie des Subjekts nach Nietzsche und Foucault* (Frankfurt am Main: Campus, 2007).

3 Without a doubt, such a normative critical theory is formulated most prominently in the works of Jürgen Habermas. Hartmut Rosa also situates himself within this tradition, and in his work he has focused on the concept of resonance as a central standard of evaluation. I would be reluctant, however, to group the entire so-called "Frankfurt School" (with all its heterogeneity) under the umbrella term of normative critical theory. Some of the theorists of its first generation, in particular, such as Theodor W. Adorno or Walter Benjamin, approximate critical analytics in their thinking.

4 I have borrowed this concept from Christoph Haker's book *Immanente Kritik soziologischer Theorie: Auf dem Weg in ein pluralistisches Paradigma* (Bielefeld:

Transcript, 2020). Such a critique also resembles Immanuel Kant's "critique of theoretical reason." It is an analysis of a phenomenon's conditions of possibility.

5 On the first three of these guidelines, see also Andreas Reckwitz, "Kritische Gesellschaftstheorie heute: Zum Verhältnis von Poststrukturalismus und Kritischer Theorie," in Reckwitz, *Unscharfe Grenzen: Perspektiven der Kultursoziologie* (Bielefeld: Transcript, 2010), pp. 283–300.

6 Here it is possible to integrate the program of the "sociology of critique."

7 At this point, it would be beneficial to recall Walter Benjamin's interest in unredeemed potential and in that which has been left unfulfilled or underutilized (*das Unabgegoltene*) in the process of history.

8 See Karl Marx, *Capital: Volume I*, trans. Ben Fowkes (New York: Vintage Books, 1977); Pierre Bourdieu, *Distinction: A Social Critique of the Judgement of Taste*, trans. Richard Nice (Cambridge, MA: Harvard University Press, 1984); and Michel Foucault, *The History of Sexuality*, Volume I: *An Introduction*, trans. Robert Hurley (New York: Pantheon Books, 1978).

9 In this respect, critical analytics shares similarities with the concept of critique developed by Ulrich Bröckling. See his book *Gute Hirten führen sanft: Über Menschenregierungskünste* (Berlin: Suhrkamp, 2017), pp. 365–82.

10 Here I follow the concept of the political (in contrast to that of politics), as developed by Laclau and Mouffe in their theory of hegemony. See Laclau and Mouffe, *Hegemony and Socialist Strategy*.

11 See Bruno Latour, "Why Has Critique Run Out of Steam? From Matters of Fact to Matters of Concern," *Critical Inquiry* 30 (2004), pp. 225–48.

12 Ibid., p. 246.

13 It was Paul Ricœur who coined the term "hermeneutics of suspicion." On this topic, see also Rita Felski, *The Limits of Critique* (University of Chicago Press, 2015), pp. 14–51.

14 See Reckwitz, *The End of Illusions*, pp. 158–63.

15 Ibid., pp. 127–30.

16 This should be kept in mind, in general, by anyone interested in the historical logic behind the critical movements in society. The strategy and the goals that were appropriate yesterday (and, for that historical context, also remain appropriate) can be inappropriate today; and tomorrow – in a new social constellation – it might be necessary yet again to formulate new strategies and forms of critique. In other words, we must assume that it is a historical necessity not only for critical analytics to change, but also for critical (political) movements to change. To return to my example above: "Today" it indeed seems appropriate and necessary to respond to the mechanisms of singularization with a politics of the general. "Yesterday," however – which is to say at a time when the social logic of the general was dominant in the welfare societies of the West – it was appropriate to pursue political strategies that promoted difference, uniqueness, dynamism, and the elimination of boundaries. Accordingly, strategies were implemented (compelled by countercultural forces and positive psychology) to counteract the society of industrial modernity, which was unemotional, inimical to pleasure, and skeptical of individuality. By now, however, it would be counterproductive to continue in this vein.

6. Coda: The Experimentalism of Theory

1 At least in part, this competition can be explained in field-theoretical terms with the help of Bourdieu's theory of academia; see Pierre Bourdieu, *Homo academicus*, trans. Peter Collier (Stanford University Press, 1988). However, the underlying attitude of theoretical "turf wars" also corresponds to a certain cultural habitus of modern masculinity. Interestingly, this habitus usually results

in the type of theory that I have called "theory-as-system." What one typically finds in this scenario is, on the one hand, a theorist who acts as a brilliant and charismatic leader and, on the other hand, the creation of a (theoretical) school of followers who willingly subordinate themselves to their famous leader.

2 Philipp Felsch, *The Summer of Theory: History of a Rebellion, 1960–1990*, trans. Tony Crawford (Cambridge: Polity, 2022).

3 In the realm of pure theory, this attitude is, rather, the exception. As a result, any theory that does not win over empirically minded readers, interdisciplinary readers, or readers from the general public – that is, any theory that remains ensconced within the realm of pure theory – will find itself in a precarious situation. The only people who might possibly be interested in it are the authors of competing theories. For theorists, this could be called (in Watzlawick's terms) "a pursuit of unhappiness."

4 With respect to the history of theory, such experimentalism can be related to John Dewey's pragmatism and his understanding of liberal democracy as a "community of inquiry." The experimental approach that I favor can also be applied to other cultural artifacts such as novels, films, or images.

5 Richard Rorty, *Contingency, Irony, and Solidarity* (Cambridge University Press, 1997).

Part II Rosa: *Best Account*

1. What Is a Theory of Society and What Can It Do?

1 See Charles Taylor, *A Secular Age* (Cambridge, MA: Belknap Press, 2007); Michael Warner et al., eds., *Varieties of Secularism in a Secular Age* (Cambridge, MA: Harvard University Press, 2010); and Craig Calhoun et al., eds., *Rethinking Secularism* (Oxford University Press, 2011).

2 See, for instance, Shmuel N. Eisenstadt, ed., *Kulturen der Achsenzeit: Ihre Ursprünge und ihre Vielfalt*, 3 vols. (Frankfurt am Main: Suhrkamp, 1987); Martin Fuchs et al., eds., *Religious Individualisation: Historical Dimensions and Comparative Perspectives*, Volume I (Berlin: De Gruyter, 2019).

3 See, for instance, Jürgen Kocka, *Capitalism: A Short History*, trans. Jeremiah Riemer (Princeton University Press, 2016).

4 See, for instance, Wolfgang Knöbl, *Die Kontingenz der Moderne: Wege in Europa, Asien und Amerika* (Frankfurt am Main: Campus, 2007).

5 See ibid.; and Hans Joas, ed., *Vielfalt der Moderne – Ansichten der Moderne* (Frankfurt am Main: Fischer, 2012), pp. 24–5.

6 See Ulrich Beck, *What Is Globalization?* trans. Patrick Camiller (Cambridge: Polity, 2000), pp. 64–8; and Wolfgang Luutz, "Vom 'Containerraum' zur 'entgrenzten Welt': Raumbilder als sozialwissenschaftliche Leitbilder," *Social Geography* 2 (2007), pp. 29–45.

7 See Göran Therborn, "Entangled Modernities," *European Journal of Social Theory* 6 (2003), pp. 293–305; and Dietrich Jung, *Muslim History and Social Theory: A Global History of Modernity* (London: Palgrave Macmillan, 2017), pp. 13–32.

8 See Bruno Latour, *We Have Never Been Modern*, trans. Catherine Porter (Cambridge, MA: Harvard University Press, 1993).

9 For an attempt to draw a systematic distinction between these different periods of modernity (based on the speed of social change in relation to the tempo of generational succession), see Hartmut Rosa, *Social Acceleration: A New Theory of Modernity*, trans. Jonathan Trejo-Mathys (New York: Columbia University Press, 2013), pp. 277–98.

10 See, for instance, Armin Nassehi, *Der soziologische Diskurs der Moderne* (Frankfurt am Main: Suhrkamp, 2006), pp. 407–12.

11 See Oliver Marchart, *Das unmögliche Objekt: Eine postfundamentalistische Theorie der Gesellschaft* (Berlin: Suhrkamp, 2013).
12 That the cost of renouncing the idea of a social formation is perhaps too high is clearly demonstrated by the fact that Latour, for instance, reintroduces it through the back door, so to speak, with his concepts of the assembly or the collective. The fact that these concepts also encompass non-social elements distinguishes them only at first glance from the concepts of culture and society, for the latter are always co-constituted by material elements. Factories and barracks, steel and coal, for example, are undoubtedly elements of industrial society (and working-class culture). In this respect, the German and French titles of Latour's most relevant book on this topic – *Eine neue Soziologie für eine neue Gesellschaft* and *Changer de société: Refaire de la sociologie* – are misleading, whereas the original English title of the book better reflects Latour's intentions: *Reassembling the Social: An Introduction to Actor–Network Theory* (Oxford University Press, 2005).
13 Both John Urry's book *Global Complexity* (Oxford University Press, 2003) and Latour's *Reassembling the Social* (and actor–network theory, in general) have indeed shown that innovative insights can be gained by doing exactly this.
14 For an instructive article on this topic, see Andreas Reckwitz, "Grundelemente einer Theorie sozialer Praktiken: Eine sozialtheoretische Perspektive," *Zeitschrift für Soziologie* 32 (2003), pp. 282–301.
15 See, for instance, Matthias Kaufmann and Richard Rottenburg, "Translation and Cultural Identity," *Civiltà del Mediterraneo* 12 (2003), pp. 229–348.
16 The most comprehensive attempt to do this can be found in Rahel Jaeggi's book *Critique of Forms of Life*, trans. Ciaran Cronin (Cambridge, MA: Harvard University Press, 2018). Here, following Lutz Wingert's formulation, she defines forms of life as "'ensembles of practices and orientations' and systems [*Ordnungen*] of social behavior" (p. 41). As enlightening as Jaeggi's considerations might be, such definitions do not solve the formation problem, but rather shift it on to the concepts of ensembles and orders. What makes a "cluster of practices" an ensemble? What defines an order? And when she writes that "forms of life are nexuses of practices and orientations and orders of social behavior" (p. 50), then the concept of the nexus, which here bears the formative burden, seems no less diffuse, as Jaeggi herself admits. With this critique, I by no means intend to discredit the concept of forms of life as such. As Jaeggi, Reckwitz, and many others have shown, it can be useful in many respects. It cannot, however, replace the concept of society.
17 See ibid., p. 51.
18 See Max Weber, "'Objectivity' in Social Science and Social Policy," in *Max Weber on the Methodology of the Social Sciences*, ed. and trans. Edward A. Shils and Henry A. Finch (Glencoe, IL: The Free Press, 1949), pp. 50–112, at pp. 80–1: "[A]n 'objective' analysis of cultural events, which proceeds according to the thesis that the ideal of science is the reduction of empirical reality of 'laws,' is meaningless. [...] It is meaningless [...] because knowledge of *cultural* events is inconceivable except on a basis of the *significance* which the concrete constellations of reality have for us in certain *individual* concrete situations. In *which* sense and in *which* situations this is the case is not revealed to us by any law; it is decided according to the *value-ideas* in the light of which we view 'culture' in each individual case. [...] The transcendental presupposition of every *cultural science* lies not in our finding a certain culture or any 'culture' in general to be *valuable* but rather in the fact that we are *cultural beings*, endowed with the capacity and the will to take a deliberate attitude towards the world and to lend it *significance*. Whatever this significance may be, it will lead us to judge certain phenomena of human existence in its light and to respond to them as being (positively or negatively) meaningful. Whatever may be the content of this

attitude – these phenomena have cultural significance for us and on this significance alone rests its scientific interest" (emphasis original).

19 See Charles Taylor, "Self-Interpreting Animals," in Taylor, *Human Agency and Language: Philosophical Papers 1* (Cambridge University Press, 1985), pp. 45–76; Charles Taylor, *Erklärung und Interpretation in den Wissenschaften vom Menschen: Aufsätze*, trans. Nils Lindquist (Frankfurt am Main: Suhrkamp, 1975); and Hartmut Rosa, *Identität und kulturelle Practice: Politische Philosophie nach Charles Taylor* (Frankfurt am Main: Campus, 1998).

20 See Theodor W. Adorno et al., *The Positivist Dispute in German Sociology*, trans. Glyn Adey and David Frisby (London: Heinemann, 1976).

21 Max Horkheimer, "The Present Situation of Social Philosophy and the Task of an Institute for Social Research," in Horkheimer, *Between Philosophy and Social Science: Selected Early Writings*, trans. G. Frederick Hunter et al. (Cambridge, MA: The MIT Press, 1993), pp. 1–14, at p. 9.

22 Charles Taylor, *Sources of the Self: The Making of Modern Identity* (Cambridge, MA: Harvard University Press, 1989), pp. 68–69 (my emphasis). See also Charles Taylor, "Theories of Meaning," in *Human Agency and Language*, pp. 248–9; and Hubert Dreyfus and Charles Taylor, *Retrieving Realism* (Cambridge, MA: Harvard University Press, 2015).

23 Of course, such sources of information (among many others) can and should be consulted!

24 On the concept of public sociology, which has been much discussed in recent years, see Michael Burawoy, *Public Sociology* (Cambridge: Polity, 2021).

25 Jürgen Habermas, *The Theory of Communicative Action*, Volume II, trans. Thomas McCarthy (Cambridge: Polity, 1987), p. 383. In this quotation, the term *Gesellschaftstheorie*, "theory of society," is rendered as "social theory."

26 See, for instance, Jörg Rössel and Gunnar Otte, eds., *Lebensstilforschung* (Wiesbaden: Verlag für Sozialwissenschaften, 2011).

27 See Dan Zahavi, *Subjectivity and Selfhood: Investigating the First-Person Perspective* (Cambridge, MA: The MIT Press, 2005).

28 See Anthony Giddens, *The Constitution of Society: Outline of the Theory of Structuration* (Cambridge: Polity, 1984).

29 Pierre Bourdieu, *Distinction: A Social Critique of the Judgement of Taste*, trans. Richard Nice (Cambridge, MA: Harvard University Press, 1984), p. 170.

30 Margaret Archer, *Realist Social Theory: The Morphogenetic Approach* (Cambridge University Press, 1995).

31 Ibid., pp. 93–134. It should also be mentioned that the approach of theoreti-
cally bracketing off one side of this dualism at a time, as Giddens suggests in *The Constitution of Society*, does not overcome this dilemma, because any interpretive proposal formed in this way ultimately leaves the two perspectives standing side by side without any mediation between them. In this regard, see Heide Gerstenberger, "Handeln und Wandeln: Anmerkungen zu Anthony Giddens' theoretischer 'Konstitution der Gesellschaft,'" *Prokla: Zeitschrift für kritische Sozialwissenschaften* 18 (1988), pp. 144–64.

32 See, for instance, Armin Nassehi, *Soziologie: Zehn einführende Vorlesungen* (Wiesbaden: Verlag für Sozialwissenschaften, 2011).

33 In their *Empire* trilogy, Michael Hardt and Antonio Negri borrow from Gilles Deleuze and formulate (though rather implicitly) a similar two-track or dualistic structure by drawing a contrast between empire, as a moribund structure of control, and the productive power and creative energy of the multitude. See their books *Empire* (Cambridge, MA: Harvard University Press, 2000); *Multitude: War and Democracy in the Age of Empire* (New York: Penguin Books, 2004); and *Commonwealth* (Cambridge, MA: Harvard University Press, 2009).

34 I have borrowed the term "perspectival dualism" from Nancy Fraser's article "Social Justice in the Age of Identity Politics: Redistribution, Recognition,

and Participation," in *Geographic Thought: A Practice Perspective*, ed. George Henderson and Marvin Waterstone (London: Routledge, 2009), pp. 72–90.

35 See Hartmut Rosa, Jörg Oberthür, et al., *Gesellschaftstheorie* (Munich: UTB, 2020).

36 See Weber, "'Objectivity' in Social Science and Social Policy," p. 112: "All research in the cultural sciences in an age of specialization, once it is oriented toward a given subject matter through particular settings of problems and has established its methodological principles, will consider the analysis of the data as an end in itself. [...] But there comes a moment when the atmosphere changes. [...] The light of the great cultural problems moves on. Then science too prepares to change its standpoint and its analytical apparatus and to view the streams of events from the heights of thought. It follows those stars which alone are able to give meaning and direction to its labor."

37 For an overview of Dewey's work, see Larry A. Hickman and Thomas M. Alexander, eds., *The Essential Dewey*, Volume I: *Pragmatism, Education, Democracy* (Bloomington: Indiana University Press, 1998).

38 See Michael Walzer, *Interpretation and Social Criticism* (Cambridge, MA: Harvard University Press, 1987); and Michael Walzer, *The Company of Critics: Social Criticism and Political Commitment in the Twentieth Century* (London: Peter Halban, 1989).

39 See, for instance, Luc Boltanski, *On Critique: A Sociology of Emancipation*, trans. Gregory Elliott (Cambridge: Polity, 2011).

40 For a radical critique of the idea that a critical theory should also formulate ways of measuring its own success, see Michael Brumlik, "Resonanz oder: Das Ende der kritischen Theorie: Rezension zu Hartmut Rosa, *Resonanz: Eine Soziologie der Weltbeziehung*," *Blätter für deutsche und internationale Politik* 5 (2016), pp. 120–3.

41 See Hinrich Fink-Eitel, "Innerweltliche Transzendenz," *Merkur* 47 (1993), pp. 237–45; and Axel Honneth, "The Social Dynamic of Disrespect: On the Location of Critical Theory Today," *Constellations* 1 (1994), pp. 255–69.

42 See Max Weber, "The Meaning of 'Ethical Neutrality' in Sociology and Economics," in *Max Weber on the Methodology of the Social Sciences*, ed. and trans. Shils and Finch, pp. 1–49. In this regard, see also Hans-Peter Müller, *Max Weber: Werk und Wirkung*, 2nd edn. (Cologne: Böhlau, 2020), pp. 174–84.

43 See Rosa, *Social Acceleration*, pp. 20–32, 122–30, 277–98.

44 See Reinhart Koselleck, *Futures Past: On the Semantics of Historical Time*, trans. Keith Tribe (New York: Columbia University Press, 2004).

45 For a comprehensive discussion of this topic, see Rosa, *Social Acceleration*, pp. 277–98.

2. Dynamic Stabilization and the Expansion of Our Share of the World

1 The concept of the moral map, which I have borrowed from Charles Taylor, is discussed in greater detail in my book *Identität und kulturelle Practice*, pp. 110–18. In this regard, "moral" is understood in a broad *cognitive-evaluative* sense.

2 On the concept of a subject's relationship to the world, see Hartmut Rosa, *Resonance: A Sociology of Our Relationship to the World*, trans. James C. Wagner (Cambridge: Polity, 2019), pp. 31–7.

3 I attempted to develop a comprehensive and complex model of such elastic combinations and the resulting pathologies in Hartmut Rosa, "Vier Ebenen der Selbstinterpretation: Entwurf einer hermeneutischen Sozialwissenschaft und Gesellschaftskritik," in *Weltbeziehungen im Zeitalter der Beschleunigung: Umrisse einer neuen Gesellschaftskritik* (Berlin: Suhrkamp, 2012), pp. 104–47.

4 Eleanor Rosch's work on this issue remains instructive; see, for instance, her article "Principles of Categorization," in *Cognition and Categorization*, ed. Eleanor Rosch et al. (Hillsdale: Lawrence Erlbaum, 1978), pp. 27–48.

5 Karen Barad, *Meeting the Universe Halfway: Quantum Physics and the Entanglement of Matter and Meaning* (Durham, NC: Duke University Press, 2007).

6 For further discussion of this phenomenon, see Hartmut Rosa, "Escalation: The Crisis of Dynamic Stabilization and the Prospect of Resonance," in Klaus Dörre, Stephan Lessenich, and Hartmut Rosa, *Sociology, Capitalism, Critique* (London: Verso, 2015), pp. 280–305; and Rosa, *Resonance*, pp. 404–20.

7 See Rosa, *Social Acceleration*, pp. 108–19.

8 See Claus Offe, *Strukturprobleme des kapitalistischen Staates: Aufsätze zur politischen Soziologie* (Frankfurt am Main: Campus, 2006).

9 See Jörg Blech, "So schmeckt die Zukunft," *SpiegelOnline* (March 17, 2017), https://www.spiegel.de/politik/so-schmeckt-die-zukunft-a-11dc193e-0002-0001 -0000-000150112489.

10 Max Weber, "Science as a Vocation," in *Max Weber: The Vocation Lectures*, trans. Rodney Livingstone (Indianapolis: Hackett, 2004), pp. 1–31, at p. 11.

11 See Boris Groys, *On the New*, trans. G. M. Goshgarian (London: Verso, 2014).

12 See Claus Offe, "The Utopia of the Zero-Option: Modernity and Modernization as Normative Political Criteria," *Practice International* 1 (1987), pp. 1–24.

13 Ian Morris, *The Measure of Civilization: How Social Development Decides the Fate of Nations* (Princeton University Press, 2013), pp. 61–6.

14 Claude Lévi-Strauss, *The Savage Mind* (London: Weidenfeld and Nicolson, 1966), pp. 217–44.

15 See Rosa, *Resonance*, pp. 110–24.

16 Strictly speaking, it would also be necessary to distinguish yet again between emotional–bodily and cognitive–evaluative aspects, because something can seem extremely desirable to me sensually (like the glass of schnapps in front of me), even though I regard it to be morally bad and know that it could trigger my alcoholism, so that, in cognitive–evaluative terms, it seems like evil itself. The inverse is, of course, just as possible. As a devout Catholic, Sunday mass may seem extraordinarily valuable and important to me, even though I utterly dislike it and would rather remain in bed (for a more detailed discussion of such relations, see ibid.). This matter is of little importance, however, to the present discussion.

17 Max Weber, *The Protestant Ethic and the "Spirit" of Capitalism and Other Writings*, trans. Peter Baehr and Gordon C. Wells (New York: Penguin, 2002).

18 See, for instance, Hans-Peter Hasenfratz, *Die toten Lebenden: Eine religion-sphänomenologische Studie zum sozialen Tod in archaischen Gesellschaften* (Leiden: Brill, 1982); and Rosa, *Resonance*, pp. 151–2.

19 On this argument, see Taylor, *Sources of the Self*, pp. 3–24; and Luc Boltanski and Ève Chiapello, *The New Spirit of Capitalism*, trans. Gregory Elliott (London: Verso, 2005), pp. 7–12.

20 In his large-scale attempt to develop and apply a trans-historical social development index, for example, Ian Morris at first provides a rather basic definition: "Social development, as I use the expression, is *a measure of communities' abilities to get things done in the world*" (Morris, *The Measure of Civilization*, p. 5 – emphasis original). He then goes on to define this index more precisely in terms of four parameters: energy capture, organization/urbanization, information technology, and war-making capacity. See ibid., pp. 39–40.

21 See, for instance, Martha Nussbaum and Amartya Sen, eds., *The Quality of Life: A Study Prepared for the World Institute for Development Economics Research (WIDER) of the United Nations University* (Oxford: Clarendon, 1993). The capabilities approach, which was developed by Sen in particular, is the basis of the United Nations' Human Development Index (HDI).

22 See Alasdair MacIntyre, "The Privatization of Good: An Inaugural Lecture," *The Review of Politics* 52/3 (1990), pp. 344–77.
23 See John Rawls, *A Theory of Justice* (Cambridge, MA: Belknap Press), p. 92: "Regardless of what an individual's rational plans are in detail, it is assumed that there are various things which he would prefer more of rather than less. With more of these goods men can generally be assured of greater success in carrying out their intentions and in advancing their ends, whatever these ends may be. The primary social goods, to give them in broad categories, are rights and liberties, opportunities and powers, income and wealth. (A very important primary good is a sense of one's own worth [...])."
24 Pierre Bourdieu, "The Forms of Capital," in *Handbook of Theory and Research for the Sociology of Education*, ed. John G. Richardson (Westport, CT: Greenwood Press, 1986), pp. 241–58.
25 For further discussion, see Rosa, *Resonance*, pp. 17–26.
26 Karl Marx and Friedrich Engels, "Manifesto of the Communist Party," in *The Marx–Engels Reader*, 2nd edn., ed. Robert C. Tucker (New York: W. W. Norton, 1978), pp. 469–500, at p. 477.

3. Desynchronization and Alienation

1 See Stephan Lessenich, *Living Well at Others' Expense: The Hidden Costs of Western Prosperity*, trans. Nick Somers (Cambridge: Polity, 2019).
2 See Herbert Marcuse, *Eros and Civilization: A Philosophical Inquiry into Freud* (Boston: Beacon Press, 1974), p. 110. Here, Marcuse is drawing on the work of Max Scheler.
3 See, for instance, Beate Schirwitz, "Wirtschaftswachstum und Beschäftigung: Die Beschäftigungsschwelle," *ifo Dresden berichtet* 12/3 (2005), pp. 34–7.
4 "Appropriation, Acceleration, Activation" is the title of a research initiative that was based in Jena from 2011 to 2020. The project, which was funded by the German Research Foundation, was directed by Klaus Dörre, Stephan Lessenich, and myself.
5 On the political consequences of these developments, see Stephan Lessenich, *Die Neuerfindung des Sozialen: Der Sozialstaat im flexiblen Kapitalismus* (Bielefeld: Transcript, 2008). Regarding economic and ecological appropriation, see Klaus Dörre, "Neue Landnahme? Der Kapitalismus in der ökologisch-ökonomischen Doppelkrise," *Vorgänge* 49/3 (2010), pp. 80–91. On the topic of excessive mental stress, see the articles collected in Vera King et al., eds., *Lost in Perfection: Zur Optimierung von Gesellschaft und Psyche* (Berlin: Suhrkamp, 2021); and in Thomas Fuchs et al., eds., *Das überforderte Subjekt: Zeitdiagnosen einer beschleunigten Gesellschaft* (Berlin: Suhrkamp, 2018).
6 Regarding the rising hostility of the political climate, see the ongoing research project titled "The Age of Hostility: Understanding the Nature, Dynamics, Determinants, and Consequences of Citizens' Electoral Hostility in 27 Democracies," which has been funded by the European Research Council and directed by the British political scientist Michael Bruter since 2018.
7 See, for instance, Ulf Bohmann et al., "Desynchronisation und Populismus: Ein zeitsoziologischer Versuch über die Demokratiekrise am Beispiel der Finanzmarktregulierung," *Kölner Zeitschrift für Soziologie und Sozialpsychologie* 58 (2018), pp. 195–226; Hartmut Rosa, "Airports Built on Shifting Grounds? Social Acceleration and the Temporal Dimension of Law," in *Temporal Boundaries of Law and Politics: Time Out of Joint*, ed. Luigi Corrias and Lyana Francot (London: Routledge, 2018), pp. 73–87; and Rosa, "Escalation," pp. 288–93.
8 See David Goodhart, *The Road to Somewhere: The Populist Revolt and the Future of Politics* (London: Hurst & Company, 2017).

9 See Hartmut Rosa, "Über die Verwechslung von Kauf und Konsum: Paradoxien der spätmodernen Konsumkultur," in *Die Verantwortung des Konsumenten: Über das Verhältnis von Markt, Moral und Konsum*, ed. Ludger Heidbrink et al. (Frankfurt am Main: Campus, 2011), pp. 115–32.

10 See, for instance, Alfons Maurer, "Das Resonanzkonzept und die Altenhilfe: Zum Einsatz digitaler Technik in der Pflege," in *Resonanz: Im interdisziplinären Gespräch mit Hartmut Rosa*, ed. Jean-Pierre Wils (Baden-Baden: Nomos, 2018), pp. 165–78.

11 A fundamental work on this topic is Jürgen Habermas's *The Structural Transformation of the Public Sphere: An Inquiry into a Category of Bourgeois Society*, trans. Thomas Burger and Frederick Lawrence (Cambridge: Polity, 1989). See also Hartmut Rosa, "Demokratischer Begegnungsraum oder lebensweltliche Filterblase? Resonanztheoretische Überlegungen zum Strukturwandel der Öffentlichkeit im 21. Jahrhundert," in *Ein neuer Strukturwandel der Öffentlichkeit?* ed. Martin Seeliger and Sebastian Sevignani (Baden-Baden: Nomos, 2021), pp. 255–77.

12 Regarding the theoretical foundations of this argument, see Rosa, *Social Acceleration*, pp. 259–76. For an empirical analysis of such desynchronization phenomena, see Bohmann et al., "Desynchronisation und Populismus."

13 See Niklas Luhmann, *Ecological Communication*, trans. John Bednarz (University of Chicago Press, 1989).

14 This is the topic of Bruno Latour's short but highly insightful book *We Have Never Been Modern*.

15 See Helga Nowotny, *Time: The Modern and Postmodern Experience*, trans. Neville Plaice (Cambridge: Polity, 1994).

16 See Richard Sennett, *The Corrosion of Character: The Personal Consequences of Work in the New Capitalism* (New York: W. W. Norton, 1998); and Hartmut Rosa, "Charakter," in *In Gesellschaft Richard Sennetts: Perspektiven auf ein Lebenswerk*, ed. Stephan Lorenz (Bielefeld: Transcript, 2021), pp. 39–53.

17 Thomas Fuchs, "Chronopathologie der Überforderung: Zeitstrukturen und psychische Krankheit," in *Das überforderte Subjekt*, pp. 52–79, here at p. 54.

18 See the contributions in Julian Savulescu and Nick Bostrom, eds., *Human Enhancement* (Oxford University Press, 2009); and in Robin Mackay and Armen Avanessian, eds., *Accelerate: The Accelerationist Reader* (Falmouth: Urbanomic, 2014).

19 See the contributions in King et al., eds., *Lost in Perfection*; and those in Fuchs et al., eds., *Das überforderte Subjekt*. A highly informative source on the development and prevalence of mental illness in the United States is the annually published "State of Mental Health" report. According to the report from 2020, for instance, the number of adolescents aged 12 to 17 who experienced a major depressive episode increased from 8.66 percent to 13.01 percent nationwide between the years 2017 and 2020. See https://imph.org/state-mental-health-america-2020.

20 Fuchs, "Chronopathologie der Überforderung," p. 54.

21 See ibid., pp. 52, 55.

22 Hans-Ulrich Wittchen and Frank Jacobi have estimated that between 5 and 6 million adults (between the ages of 18 and 65) in Germany, and more than 20 million in Europe as a whole, are affected by depression every year. See their article "Epidemiologie," in *Volkskrankheit Depression? Bestandsaufnahme und Perspektiven*, ed. Gabriela Stoppe et al. (Heidelberg: Springer, 2006), pp. 15–37.

23 See Tom Bschor et al., "Time Experience and Time Judgement in Major Depression, Mania and Healthy Subjects," *Acta Psychiatrica Scandinavica* 109 (2004), pp. 222–9.

24 Fuchs, "Chronopathologie der Überforderung," pp. 52–3.

25 See Alain Ehrenberg, *The Weariness of the Self: Diagnosing the History of Depression in the Contemporary Age*, trans. Enrico Caouette et al. (Montreal: McGill-Queen's University Press, 2010).

26 See Hartmut Rosa, *The Uncontrollability of the World*, trans. James C. Wagner (Cambridge: Polity, 2020), pp. 110–16; and Hartmut Rosa, "Spirituelle Abhängigkeitserklärung: Die Idee des Mediopassiv als Ausgangspunkt einer radikalen Transformation," in *Große Transformation? Zur Zukunft moderner Gesellschaften*, ed. Klaus Dörre et al. (Wiesbaden: Springer, 2019), pp. 35–55.

27 See the Basic Law for the Federal Republic of Germany: "All state authority is derived from the people. It shall be exercised by the people through elections and other votes and through specific legislative, executive and judicial bodies" (Article 20.2).

28 See the contributions collected in Hanna Ketterer and Karina Becker, eds., *Was stimmt nicht mit der Demokratie? Eine Debatte mit Klaus Dörre, Nancy Fraser, Stephan Lessenich und Hartmut Rosa* (Berlin: Suhrkamp, 2019).

29 The clinical term for this phenomenon – an unhealthy obsession with healthy eating – is *orthorexia*. See, for instance, Friederike Barthels et al., "Die Düsseldorfer Orthorexie-Skala – Konstruktion und Evaluation eines Fragebogens zur Erfassung orthorektischen Ernährungsverhaltens," *Klinische Psychologie und Psychotherapie* 44 (2015), pp. 97–105.

30 For further discussion, see Rosa, *The Uncontrollability of the World*, pp. 60–4.

31 Rahel Jaeggi, *Alienation*, trans. Frederick Neuhouser and Alan E. Smith (New York: Columbia University Press, 2014), pp. 3–50. See also Hartmut Rosa, *Alienation and Acceleration: Towards a Critical Theory of Late-Modern Temporality* (Aarhus University Press, 2010).

32 Rainald Grebe, *Global Fish* (Frankfurt am Main: Fischer, 2006), p. 13. The translation here is taken from Rosa, *Resonance*, pp. 468–9 (note 23).

33 My short book *The Uncontrollability of the World* is an exercise in working out this line of thinking, which brings the concept of uncontrollability close to that of non-identity, as Adorno understood the term. See Theodor W. Adorno, *Negative Dialectics*, trans. E. B. Ashton (New York: Continuum, 1973).

4. Adaptive Stabilization and Resonance

1 In my opinion, it was this passionate – and even despairing – concern that motivated the key works of the Frankfurt tradition: Horkheimer and Adorno's *Dialectic of Enlightenment*, Marcuse's *One-Dimensional Man*, and even Benjamin's *Arcades Project*.

2 According to Lévi-Strauss (*The Savage Mind*, pp. 233–4), a society oriented toward stopping historical change would be a "cold society." Anti-dynamic moments of this sort can also be identified in the medieval guild system. Regarding "hot societies," see ibid., and my discussion in section 3.1 above.

3 See Rosa, *Social Acceleration*, pp. 277–98.

4 Max Weber, *Economy and Society: An Outline of Interpretive Sociology*, trans. Guenther Roth and Claus Wittich (Berkeley: University of California Press, 1978); Weber, *The Protestant Ethic*; Karl Marx, *Capital: Volume I*, trans. Ben Fowkes (New York: Vintage Books, 1977); Émile Durkheim, *The Division of Labor in Society*, trans. W. D. Halls (New York: Free Press, 2014).

5 See Karl Polanyi, *The Great Transformation: The Political and Economic Origins of Our Time* (Boston: Beacon Press, 1957); and Nancy Fraser, "A Triple Movement? Parsing the Politics of Crisis after Polanyi," in *Beyond Neoliberalism: Social Analysis after 1989*, ed. Marian Burchardt and Gal Kirn (London: Palgrave Macmillan, 2017), pp. 29–42.

6 See Erik Olin Wright, *Envisioning Real Utopias* (London: Verso, 2010).

7 My own recommendations in this regard range from global debt forgiveness and a globally established inheritance tax to a fundamental cap on income disparities and capital accumulation, not to mention the nationalization of banks and

financial institutions and the establishment of firmer political control over the movement of capital.

8 Maurice Merleau-Ponty, *Phenomenology of Perception*, trans. Colin Smith (New York: Routledge, 2012).

9 See the article "Wie geht es nach der Krise weiter? Der Ökonom Clemens Fuest und der Soziologe Hartmut Rosa streiten über die Lehren aus Corona," *Stern* 32 (July 30, 2020), pp. 36–43, at pp. 40–41 and 43: "From an economic perspective, growth is ultimately an expression of individual decisions. It is people who generate the growth dynamic; their desires and decisions. Not one system or another. [...] Companies have to produce what people want."

10 Not coincidentally, such considerations lie at the core of the five types of alienation (from labor, from the products of labor, from nature, from others, and ultimately from ourselves) that Marx identified in his early economic and philosophical writings. See Karl Marx, *Economic and Philosophic Manuscripts of 1844*, trans. Martin Milligan (Mineaola, NY: Dover, 1988).

11 See MacIntyre, "The Privatization of Good."

12 I owe this insight to an intensive discussion with Henric Meinhardt, which we held over several days while hiking the Via Engiadina in the summer of 2020.

13 Charles Taylor, "Legitimation Crisis?" in Taylor, *Philosophy and the Human Sciences: Philosophical Papers 2* (Cambridge University Press, 1985), pp. 248–87, at p. 279.

14 This is, in fact, the starting point of Marx's *Capital*, the first sentence of which reads: "The wealth of societies in which the capitalist mode of production prevails appears as an 'immense collection of commodities'; the individual commodity appears as its elementary form" (Marx, *Capital: Volume I*, p. 125).

15 Charles Taylor, "Interpretation and the Sciences of Man," in Taylor, *Philosophy and the Human Sciences*, pp. 15–57, at p. 50.

16 See, for instance, Ellen Meiksins Wood, *Democracy against Capitalism: Renewing Historical Materialism* (Cambridge University Press, 1995).

17 See Herbert Marcuse, *One-Dimensional Man: Studies in the Ideology of Advanced Industrial Society* (Boston: Beacon Press, 1964), pp. 1–18.

18 The roots of this idea go back to Thomas More. In the twentieth century, its proponents included Erich Fromm; see his article "The Psychological Aspects of the Guaranteed Income," in *The Guaranteed Income: Next Step in Socioeconomic Evolution?* ed. Robert Theobald (New York: Doubleday, 1966), pp. 183–93. Numerous additional publications on this topic have appeared in recent years. See, for instance, Yannick Vanderborght and Philippe van Parijs, *Ein Grundeinkommen für alle? Geschichte und Zukunft eines radikalen Vorschlags* (Frankfurt am Main: Campus, 2005); and Sascha Liebermann, *Aus dem Geist der Demokratie: Bedingungsloses Grundeinkommen* (Frankfurt am Main: Humanities Online, 2015). Regarding the history of the idea, key texts have been collected in Philip Kovce and Birger Priddat, eds., *Bedingungsloses Grundeinkommen: Grundlagentexte* (Berlin: Suhrkamp, 2019).

19 This is not the place to enter the important discussion of how, exactly, such a basic income should be institutionally designed and financed. Countless national and international publications have already addressed this topic. I think, however, that the way in which such a system is implemented should not be theoretically predetermined. Instead, the matter needs to be subjected to democratic debate, and this debate should by no means come to an end as soon as such an institution is introduced. Rather, it would require and allow ongoing adjustments and corrections to be made according to the principle of trial and error.

20 Perhaps a guiding metaphor for the revolutionization of the present social formation can be found in Leonard Cohen's famous and inspiring song "Anthem" (Columbia Records, 1992): "There is a crack, a crack in everything, that's how the light gets in." Because human subjects, by virtue of being

subjects, are dependent on resonance, and because the contradiction between the capitalist pressure to escalate and the possibility of resonant connections is so apparent in our everyday lives, this crack or divide can be regarded as a decisive locus of resistance. After all, everyone knows or feels the tension in the situations that I have cited as examples here.

21 Weber, *The Protestant Ethic*, p. 121.

22 See Rosa, "Spirituelle Abhängigkeitserklärung."

23 For further discussion, see Rolf Elberfeld, *Sprache und Sprachen: Eine philosophische Grundorientierung* (Freiburg: K. Alber, 2011), pp. 228–59; and Béatrice Han-Pile, "Hope, Powerlessness, and Agency," *Midwest Studies in Philosophy* 41 (2017), pp. 175–201.

24 See Ruth C. Cohn and Alfred Farau, *Gelebte Geschichte der Psychotherapie: Zwei Perspektiven* (Stuttgart: Klett-Cotta, 2008), p. 359.

25 Matthias Fritsch of Concordia University in Montreal brought to my attention the remarkable fact that Jacques Derrida, in perhaps his most famous text ("La différance"), expressed this same idea with direct reference to the concept of resonance (!) and that he detected this same medio-passive meaning in the ending -*ance*: "In a conceptuality adhering to classical strictures '*différance*' would be said to designate constitutive, productive, and originary causality, the process of scission and division which would produce or constitute different things or differences. But because it brings us close to the infinitive and active kernel of *différer*, *différance* (with an *a*) neutralizes what the infinitive denotes as simply active, just as *mouvance* in our language does not simply mean the fact of moving, of moving oneself or of being moved. No more is resonance the act of resonating. We must consider that in the usage of our language the ending -*ance* remains undecided between the active and the passive. And we will see why that which lets itself be designated *différance* is neither simply active nor simply passive, announcing or rather recalling something like the middle voice, saying an operation that is not an operation, an operation that cannot be conceived either as passion or as the action of a subject on an object, or on the basis of the categories of agent or patient, neither on the basis of nor moving toward any of these terms. For the middle voice, a certain nontransitivity, may be what philosophy, at its outset, distributed into an active and a passive voice, thereby constituting itself by means of this repression." See Jacques Derrida, "Différance," in *Margins of Philosophy*, trans. Alan Bass (University of Chicago Press, 1982), pp. 1–27, at pp. 8–9.

26 Think of the famous last lines of William Butler Yeats's poem "Among School Children": "O body swayed to music, O brightening glance, / How can we know the dancer from the dance?"

27 See Martin Pfleiderer and Hartmut Rosa, "Musik als Resonanzsphäre," *Musik und Ästhetik* 24 (2020), pp. 5–36.

28 See, for instance, Bruno Latour, *An Inquiry into Modes of Existence: An Anthropology of the Moderns*, trans. Catherine Porter (Cambridge, MA: Harvard University Press, 2013), pp. 300–7; and Hartmut Rosa, "Einem Ruf antworten: Bruno Latours andere Soziologie der Weltbeziehung," *Soziologische Revue* 39/4 (2016), pp. 552–60.

29 This argument is based not least on the observation that a newborn's cry is a cry for nourishment *and* for resonance. The newborn experiences warmth, attention, nourishment, touch, closeness, and self-effectiveness (by generating a response to this crying) in a *single act*. From this perspective, to suffer hunger and to feel cold are elementary forms of alienation (the world is *not answering*). For this reason, it is categorically false to understand resonance as an aesthetic "luxury need." See Rosa, *Resonance*, pp. 17–43; and Hartmut Rosa, "Beethoven, The Sailor, the Boy and the Nazi," *Journal of Political Power* 13 (2020), pp. 1–18.

30 See Hannah Arendt, *The Human Condition* (University of Chicago Press, 1958).